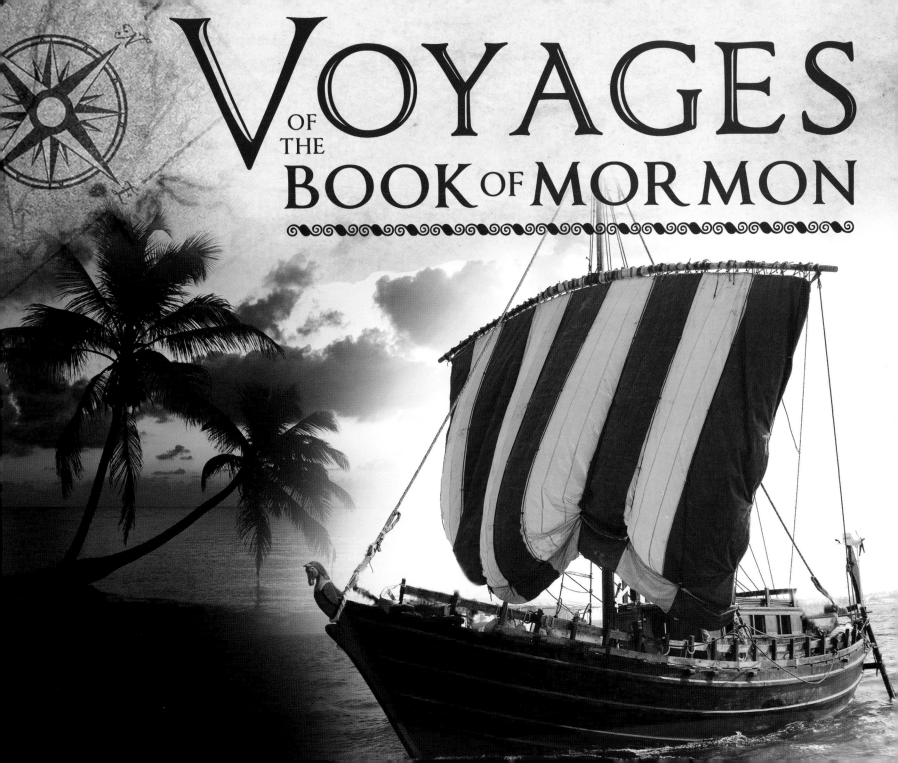

VOYAGES
OF THE
BOOK OF MOR MON

Cover collage includes a photo of the *Phoenicia*, a 21st Century replica of a
Phoenician/Mediterranean vessel circa 600 BC. See www.phoenicia.org.uk.

© 2011 George Potter, Frank Linehan, and Conrad Dickson

ISBN 13: 978-1-59955-946-9

Published by CFI, an imprint of Cedar Fort, Inc.
2373 W. 700 S., Springville, UT, 84663

Distributed by Cedar Fort, Inc., www.cedarfort.com

LIBRARY OF CONGRESS CATALOGING-IN-PUBLICATION DATA
    Potter, George, 1949- author.
    The voyages of the Book of Mormon / George Potter, Frank Linehan, Conrad
Dickson.
        p. cm.
    Summary: Covers in detail the art of ship building and the potential
routes that the Nephites in the Book of Mormon took to get to America.
    Includes bibliographical references.
    ISBN 978-1-59955-946-9
    1. Book of Mormon--Evidences, authority, etc. 2. Book of
Mormon--Geography. I. Linehan, Frank. II. Dickson, Conrad. III. Title.
    BX8627.P687 2011
    289.3'22--dc23
                        2011018417

Cover and book design by Angela D. Olsen
Edited by Melissa Caldwell
Cover design © 2011 by Lyle Mortimer

Printed on acid-free paper

Printed in China

10   9   8   7   6   5   4   3   2   1

VOYAGES
OF THE
BOOK OF MORMON

CFI, an imprint of Cedar Fort, Inc., Springville, Utah

GEORGE POTTER, FRANK LINEHAN, AND CONRAD DICKSON

Bow of Arab dhow.

THEY THAT GO DOWN TO THE SEA IN SHIPS, that do business in great waters; These see the works of the Lord, and his wonders in the deep. For he commandeth, and raiseth the stormy wind, which lifteth up the waves thereof.

They mount up to the heaven, they go down again to the depths: their soul is melted because of trouble.

They reel to and fro, and stagger like a drunken man, and are at their wits' end.

Then they cry unto the Lord in their trouble, and he bringeth them out of their distresses.

He maketh the storm a calm, so that the waves thereof are still.

Then they are glad because they be quiet; so he bringeth them unto their desired haven.

Oh that men would praise the Lord for his goodness, and for his wonderful works to the children of men!

Psalm 107:23–31

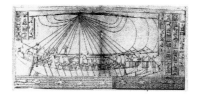

DEDICATED TO

The sailors of the Book of Mormon and

all the pioneers of the ancient seaways

for what they have passed on to us.

CONTENTS

In 2008–2010, the Phoenicia and crew in their replica ship successfully recreated a navigation around Africa, which Phoenician mariners first accomplished circa 600 BC.

ACKNOWLEDGMENTS

WE WISH TO THANK the following individuals who have invested time and effort into assisting the authors: Jay M. Todd for editing and refining our manuscript that was created by three sources, each contributor being more of an adventurer than an author. Jay's many contributions are of immeasurable value. Dennis Mead for his research assistance and Michael Dickson for his computer help. Melissa Caldwell for copyediting and Angela Olsen for design and layout, both of Cedar Fort, Inc. Robert Gehrsitz for permission to use Visual Passage Planner (VPP) for simulating passages, measuring distances, analyzing historical weather and current patterns, and plotting waypoints and routes. Permission to use this data in both print and web page display is greatly appreciated.

We highly recommend the use of VPP for any vessel making an offshore passage, which is available from Digital Wave, robertg@digwave.com, 8 Spring Court, Washington Crossing, PA 18977, www.digwave.com, (215-493-7463).

THE CREW OF UNUSUAL AUTHORS

THE WAYS OF THE LORD are many, including the variety of tools he uses to chisel the lives of his children into smooth statues of greatness. The Prophet Joseph Smith, Jr. declared: "I am a rough stone. The sound of the hammer and chisel was never heard on me until the Lord took me in hand."[1] From Peter's faltering walk on water to the Lord's calming of the stormy waters of Galilee, our Master has often used deep waters to transform the character of his people. Without the seas, what place in the order of prophets would Noah have had? What would Moses have parted to inspire the children of Israel for the ages?

When fully appreciated, the remarkable voyages of the Book of Mormon are as impressive as any exodus in the Holy Bible. Their acts of obedience served as final tests of the voyagers' faith before the Lord's chosen were given title to their promised lands. Perhaps even more important, the maritime feats recorded in the Book of Mormon provide each of us a gift of testimony. When we compare ancient voyages recorded on the golden plates to recent maritime archaeological discoveries, our added knowledge confirms once again that the Book of Mormon is a true historical account.

For those who succeeded in crossing the great deep, the Jaredites, the Lehites, the Mulekites, and the Hagoth colonies, we praise their acts of faith and courage. Brigham Young University scholar Hugh Nibley wrote of the challenge of one young Book of Mormon prophet: "Nephi was simply staggered when he was commanded to build a ship, and his brothers laughed their heads off at his presumption."[2] As we know, the always obedient Nephi was unmoved by the tottering of his siblings and achieved one of the most remarkable ocean passages ever recorded. To honor Nephi and the other maritime forefathers of our faith, we have decided that the mission of this book is to help readers appreciate the magnitude of what the Book of Mormon mariners accomplished as they put their very lives on the line to obey the will of the Lord. Even more than a work of archaeology and history, this book serves as a window to the world of the ancient mariners, a window that will help readers understand and appreciate our Book of Mormon pioneers.

Book of Mormon Explorer George Potter

The Voyages of the Book of Mormon marks the third book George Potter has authored or coauthored on the historical accuracy of the Book of Mormon. Preceded by *Lehi in the Wilderness* and *Nephi in the Promised Land*, this book completes George's trilogy about the sacred record that Nephi started nearly 2,600 years ago. Along with Timothy Sedor, he cofounded the Nephi Project, an independent research group (see www.nephiproject.com). He has edited the Nephi Project's newsletter for the last ten years. He has produced with Tim Sedor thirteen documentary films on the Book of Mormon and on Bible archaeology.

George has lived in Saudi Arabia for the past eighteen years. In 1995, he began his search in the Arabian Desert for evidences that the Book of Mormon contains a true history of a family crossing the Arabian peninsula in the sixth century BC. His journey of discovery has taken him deep into the most hellish desert in the world, the famous Empty Quarter, as well as having driven thousands of miles

Author George Potter in Inca temple above Lake Titicaca, Bolivia.

on sandy Bedouin trails. He has slept in Bedouin tents and dined on the ground in a Bedouin circle. He has climbed steep and slippery sandstone cliffs and weathered freezing nights and daily temperatures exceeding 120 degrees. His efforts have not been in vain. George has documented hundreds of new evidences in Arabia and South America that the Book

of Mormon is indeed a true history. His credits include finding compelling candidates for the Valley of Lemuel, the River Laman, Shazer, the "most fertile parts of the wilderness," the harbor where Nephi built his ship, the trail of the Jaredites, the land of the Jaredites in the promised land, the city of Nephi, and the new world Bountiful and Zarahemla.

George has a love for the sea. He was a Sea Explorer Scout in his youth. As an adult, he has sailed, fished, water skied, surfed, snorkeled, and canoed nearly every ocean in the world. He grew up within yards of the Pacific Ocean, falling to sleep at night to the rhythm of breaking surf. His experiences at sea caused George to ponder still another Book of Mormon question: *How did the people of this historical record cross the great oceans in ancient ships?*

Unfortunately, the Book of Mormon provides precious little information about the time the people of the Book of Mormon spent at sea. All the same, George will attempt to bring the scriptures alive by employing the latest in computer simulations, maritime archaeology, and most important, the experience and scholarship of two extraordinary Latter-day Saint sailors, Frank Linehan and Conrad Dickson. Totaling their sailing years, Frank and Conrad have sailed the world's seas for over one hundred years. There is not an ocean or a sea condition that these two old LDS salts have not challenged head-on and survived. From having seventy-five-foot storm waves crashing against their bridge room to skippering a small sailing boat through the horrific winds of a full-blown hurricane, Frank and Conrad have done it all.

Master Sailor and Chief Engineer Frank Linehan

When the other kids were playing baseball and basketball, Frank Linehan was always around boats and the sea. As a teenager in Long Beach, California, he spent a short while in the Sea Explorer Scouts, which led to his crewing offshore races for the late Percy Wood, the president of United Airlines. By the time Frank was a senior in high school, he knew he wanted to go to sea. In lieu of an appointment to Annapolis, the US Naval Academy, Frank accepted an invitation to the California Maritime Academy in the winter of his high school senior year. He graduated from the academy with a degree in marine engineering, a United States Coast Guard (USCG) license of 3rd Engineer, and a commission as ensign in the US Navy.

Frank's military commission sent him to Vietnam as a 3rd assistant engineer on an ammunition ship for the Military Sea Transportation Service (MSTS). After the war, he sailed for eleven years on vessels of all types and sizes in the United States Merchant Marines from 3rd engineer to chief engineer. Each ship or station upgrade required him to successfully complete a three- to four-day license examination. His transits at sea have covered over a million statute miles. For the next five years, he captained a small tanker in which he owned ten percent interest. When the vessel was sold, Frank became a consultant in the international marine industry. To spend more time with his family, Frank eventually went ashore and became a professional port engineer. In 1985, he was hired by the United States Maritime Administration. Overall, he has been in various facets of the maritime industry for over forty years. He has directed over twenty-five large vessel dry dockings and overseen a half dozen vessel reflaggings and has surveyed many ships for purchase. He has been a witness of fact for the Department of Justice and has repossessed ships for them. He has been involved in numerous sensitive projects involving ships and managed ship conversions for various branches of the United States Armed Services.

For the last thirteen years, Frank has managed the U.S. Defense Department's four Cape I Roll On-Roll Off vessels which belong to the Maritime Administration DOT. He is involved in all aspects of engineering, regulatory affairs, the hire of key personnel, and the budgeting of these massive vessels. During Frank's tenure, these four critical military ships have had a perfect operational record for safety and on-time deliveries of tanks, artillery, armored troop carriers, and other equipment for engagements such as Operation Iraqi Freedom.

Frank still has a current USCG issue chief engineer's license for diesel and gas turbine of Unlimited Horsepower, plus a 3rd Engineer's Steam with Unlimited Horsepower. He also held a GMDSS license, which is the equivalent of the modern radio operator's license. Over his career, he has held a chief engineer license for oil and mineral ships of Limited Horsepower, a chief engineer's license for uninspected vessels of Unlimited Horsepower, a first assistant engineer's license for ferry and towing vessels of Limited Horsepower, a second assistant engineer's license for Steam Unlimited Horsepower, and a California yacht and ship broker's license.

Having been a relief chief engineer on a coastwise tanker for five years, in addition to having cruised sections of the Pacific coast two separate times by yacht, Frank is an expert on the west coasts of South and Central America. Once, he sailed the coast on a seventy-foot schooner and once again on a sixty-five-foot custom

powerboat yacht for delivery to pianist Victor Borge. He has firsthand knowledge of where along the Pacific Ocean shoreline you can make a safe landfall and what size ship could be safely piloted into port without going aground. These areas are where scholars postulate as to where Nephi and company might have landed, where Hagoth departed, and where the Jaredites disembarked.

Frank has owned three sailboats in the course of time: a 36-foot Columbia sloop, a 41-foot Yankee Clipper ketch, and a 20-foot by 10-foot beam C-class catamaran. He also builds his own oceangoing kayaks and uses them to explore waters of the Pacific northwest.

From his genealogy, it appears that Frank has salt water in his DNA. He comes from a long seagoing lineage. He is related to both of the famous commodore Perrys, the one who was the commander at the Battle of Lake Erie of the War of 1812, and the other who opened Japan for trade.

Frank stands proudly before the ships he manages for the Navy.

4

His great-grandfather on his father's side, Captain Hines, owned a Gloucester fishing schooner and was lost in a northeaster. His father was a ship owner. His sister once was Miss Maritime in California and sailed as a social director and purser on a cruise ship. His cousin, on his mother's side, retired as a ship's chief engineer. His uncle sailed bos'n (unlicensed member of the crew) before, during, and after World War II, and his brother was in the US Coast Guard.

It was due to Frank's lifetime at sea, his interest in ancient ships, and his expertise in ship hulls, that George came to seek out his childhood friend. Frank provided George with valuable information during George's search for Nephi's harbor that was eventually published in the *Journal of Book of Mormon Studies* and in George's and Richard Wellington's book *Lehi in the Wilderness*. Timothy Sedor filmed Frank as a subject matter expert in the Nephi Project film *Discovering Nephi's Harbor*. When George asked Frank to tell in his own words a few of his sailing experiences at sea, he shared the following:

"My story begins in Long Beach, California, in 1958. That was the year I was first introduced to sailing in Alamitos Bay on a Sabot sailboat. I had a friend down the street whose father bought him a boat at twelve years old and who wanted someone to sail with him. At the time it seemed like a marvelous opportunity to learn sailing, even though I had no experience. It was a beautiful boat. It was a wood boat with multiple coats of varnish and bronze fittings. The first time out was memorable and not a bad experience at all. Nothing dramatic happened, like capsizing or running aground, and I had no sea sickness. It just felt natural. I could feel the wind, and the tiller seemed natural in its handling. This is where I first began learning the art and sport of dingy sailing.

"The boat handled well and it seemed as though the bay waters were not a challenge enough for us neophyte sailors. So, soon we were sailing out of the bay and through the jetties into the open sea. This is when I got 'hooked.' The motion of the sea, the sun, and the power of the wind made an imprint on me that would influence me for life. Sailing the little Sabot out to the Long Beach breakwater was a challenge at twelve to thirteen years of age and not without its dangers—too far to swim back in case of capsizing, not to mention the danger of sharks. My friend and I were probably in over our heads, but we had met the challenge of the sea and conquered the conditions of the day. Upon returning to Alamitios Bay that day, it was 'Victory at Sea' for two young boys.

"When I was sixteen, I moved with my family to the San Francisco Bay area to a town by the name of San Mateo. The desire to sail was still in my blood. So I looked into joining the Sea Scouts at Coyote Point, but they appeared to be more of a power boating troop than a sailing group. One day I was discussing this with my neighbor friend whose dad was vice president of United Airlines at that time. My friend's dad had a Holiday yawl, and he was into racing. My friend said, 'Hey, why don't you come racing with us next weekend as we are short a crew member.' I said, 'I don't have any big boat experience.' My friend replied, 'That's okay, we will teach you.' Okay then, I'll see you next weekend.' The next weekend saw me at Coyote Point Marina casting off lines on this beautiful wooden yawl that was finished immaculately with new sails.

"The race began, and my life took a change that would last for the next four or five years. Yacht racing for Percy Wood, who became president of United Airlines, would consume many weekends. Sailing

5

on San Francisco Bay was a challenge due to currents and strong winds and the cold water.

"Gradually I graduated to foredeck crew and eventually stood watch on the helm in the offshore races. The owner eventually bought a more competitive boat. It was a brand new Cal 36 with North Sails that were designed for racing in the 1960's. Boy, was it fast compared to the yawl. The boat was a Bill Tripp design in fiberglass, and in its day and class, it was unbeatable. This boat was set up for offshore racing. The owner had aspirations to take it on the Trans Pac race to Hawaii.

"Eventually, the boat was moved to St. Francis Yacht Club Marina where it was easier to make the major races. We practiced a full day before each race until as a crew we became a machine. Each man could do the other's job to some degree. Over time, we did not become intimidated by weather or night sailing. We learned to compete, whether we were wet or cold, without complaint. We sailed all the races relevant to the Bay Area. We became experts in the maneuvering required to be at the starting line at the gun. The boat was incredibly durable, as evidenced on a leg in the Raccoon Straits where we had

too large of a spinnaker sail up. One day a real strong gust knocked us down and the spinnaker filled with water, dragging the boat over to the point we were all standing on the fin keel wondering how we were going to right the boat. We were so full of adrenalin that we did even notice the cold water. We all had one thought, and that was to right the boat. Finally, one of us got in the water and was able to release the spinnaker from the winch. As soon as the sail was released, the boat righted and the cockpit drained. That was one of the wildest experiences I ever had on a sailboat in strong air.

"Another time we were sailing back from Drakes Bay and the swell picked up dramatically late in the afternoon. We knew we were going to be in for it when we hit the dangerous 'Potato Patch,' a hazardous stretch of the sea. Sure enough, the swells were mast high.

"Fortunately for us it was high tide and flooding, so the ocean wasn't breaking like it would be if it was ebbing or low tide. This was a wild ride in the evening, surfing down these huge swells under spinnaker. You couldn't see the boat ahead of you when it started surfing, other than the top of the mast would be visible. The

challenge was to keep the boat perpendicular to the swell while it drops down the wave and you have for a moment no control with the rudder. That is most unnerving because if you mess up, the boat will broach. Broaching occurs when the boat swings sideways to the wave, and worst-case, it pitch poles, which means 'game over.' Pitch poling is when the vessel literally goes 'head over heels.' This is very serious and often causes loss of boat and lives. Needless to say, we had an incredible evening of surfing with Percy's boat. The voyage is still vivid and memorable to this day. When we finally got back to the yacht club marina, there was a sigh of relief from all of us. But what a rush it was. The boat literally became a surfboard that evening. If we had made any mistakes on the helm that evening, I would not be spinning this yarn now.

"A serious boating experienced occurred after I had been a port engineer for five years and decided I needed to take a break and get back to the sea. So, with a minority partner, I bought a 41-foot Taiwan-built Yankee Clipper ketch in El Salvador and set sail down to Punta Arenas, Costa Rica, for the winter. This was a Garden design traditional ketch with teak decks, bow sprit, yellow house with teak trim, spruce spars, white hull with a black stripe, wheel steering, and a Perkins diesel with minimal electronics. I was smitten by the lines and even though it needed work, I wanted it.

"It was a nice short sail down to Costa Rica. Off the wind, the boat was easily handled with two men. However, some problems developed with the boat and I had to let her go. While there in Costa Rica, I met a fellow who was looking for somebody to help sail *Marmel*, his 58-foot, length on deck, hand-designed schooner. So I joined with a couple of other fellows and we cruised Central America. This schooner had won the Trans Pac race in the late forties, I believe. She had been converted from a gaff rig to a marconi rig, the latter being the conventional rig of today and the gaff being old style with the yard or gaff at the top of the sails on the main and mizzen. The *Marmel* had miles of running rigging tied off in the old way with belaying pins. In order to stand watch at night, you had to know where everything was in the dark. This was necessary in order to make sail adjustments in the dark. She was a lovely boat and sailed like a dream off the wind. When all sails were set and trimmed, she would sail herself like the proper lady she was. One could lock the wheel and walk around the boat and she would hold her course in anything but the very worst of conditions. She loved to run before the wind. In hard weather, she gave you nothing but confidence that she would handle it. Under sail she was just a delight to manage. The main sail was massive. It usually took two of us to raise it. The main was the driver. The vessel was very sea kindly. It didn't beat you up like many of the newer modern boats do.

"We took *Marmel* into open roadsteads and anchored her so that I could go surfing. The three of us knew the boat very well after being aboard her for a couple of months. So what a nice piece of irony it was that the owner decided since we had such a handle on the operation of the vessel he decided to go home for a few months and leave the vessel to us to use as we pleased. The only caveat was that in a few months time we had to deliver the vessel to Panama. Our only onus was that we had to take care of the vessel and not do any damage other than *force majeure* [acts of God]. We had a wonderful time sailing this seventy-foot length vessel all up and down Central America.

"I remember one time when it was my turn to navigate and we primarily did 'dead reckoning' with running fixes. We had Loran [a radio navigation system used to determine geographical position]; however, there were no stations in the area for it, and the RDF or the radio direction finder only worked if you were near a major city, so it was useless for the most part. This was all before the advent of GPS to the major public. What an absolute convenience it is to the modern yachtsman. We were coming down the coast from northern Costa Rica to Punta Arenas on the Pacific shoreline of Central Costa Rica at the start of the rainy season, yet thinking we were in for good weather. I had the mid-watch that night, and the seas were rolling with about ten to twelve knots of wind. My watch partner was a Costa Rican girl who knew how to sail and was traveling down with us. I had the rig balanced and trimmed nicely with the wheel locked. It appeared to me I could go below and take a quick nap, relying on my watch partner to call if anything happened because she convinced me that she knew how to keep the vessel on course with the compass. Needless to say, while I was asleep, the wind shifted about 270 degrees. But the rig was so well balanced that it just followed the wind around and thus didn't wake me up with the usual flap of sails as they luffed (high into the wind). However, if that boom had swung across the boat, it would have awakened everyone.

"By the way, sailors and seaman sleep differently than land types. They sleep with ongoing noise all night long, but their mind and ears are tuned to the unusual noises that generally mean something has happened that is different, hazardous, or even dangerous to the vessel and the lives it carries. They wake up automatically when something changes and go investigate. What woke me up was that the angle of heel changed in relation to the sea and the vessel from when I laid down for a nap.

"I came up to see what was going on. Fortunately, we were headed out to sea and not toward land or I might not be telling this story. I asked Margarite how long we had been on this course, and she didn't exactly know. I got the vessel back on course without knowing how far out in blue water we were. Here's where things got worse. The weather changed and began to rain, one of those tropical downpours. Now I was really lost. I drew a parallel 'DR' (Dead Reckoning) track to where I thought we might be and guesstimated when we might be at the entrance to the bay of Punta Arenas. I was hoping the rain would stop then and that I would get a visual fix. I had been in and out of that

Transom of traditional Arab dhow.

bay several times. But instead of a letup, it just kept raining. We are all standing in the cockpit—listening, watching, and tuning our senses to anything that might be land in our path. As hope might have it, the rain stopped and we were right in the entrance to the bay. Talk about luck or the power of prayer! I wouldn't want to be the one who had to tell the owner we ran

his gorgeous schooner aground outside of Punta Arenas.

"We were plagued with ill luck throughout this trip. We got into the bay of Punta Arenas. The wind came up, the sun came out, and we were sailing up the bay to the channel Punta Arenas. We turned outside the channel to drop our sails and motor in.

Lo and behold, we run aground. But fortunately on sand. We dropped our sails and carefully tried to back off using the diesel. We were really 'hard on.' So, we put the dingy over the side and take an anchor with some rope [anchor warp] from the transom [flat vertical end of the ship]. We put several wraps around one of the main sheet winches and, combined with the motor, try to winch ourselves off. No luck. Now we were starting to sweat it, and incidentally, it was getting a lot hotter also. Finally, we put heads together and came up with the idea of swinging the main sail boom out toward the channel. We hung an anchor off the boom and winched the vessel over in order to release the keel off the bottom. We then tried kedging the boat off the sand bar, using the winch with the stern anchor while backing up with the diesel. It was hard work, but finally it did the job. We were able to free ourselves and go into Punta Arenas more humble than we were a few hours earlier while blasting up the bay with all our sails up. I stayed a couple more months on that beautiful old schooner and then headed home to California.

"After a while, I decided to get another boat, but this time I concluded it would be a Catamaran, a fast one. I bought the hulls and rig. The hulls were filament-wound fiberglass. The sails were North Sails with a Tornado catamaran rig. I bought all of it in San Diego and drove it up to the Bay Area. This thing was 20-foot plus long and 10-foot wide of beam. It was going to be a rocket ship. With the help of a couple friends, we assembled the thing and installed various blocks, cam cleats, cleats, and lines. We lengthened the transom about six inches with mahogany. I had fabricated special transom plates with gudgeons, all of stainless steel. I changed out the fiberglass and foam extrusion for aluminum and welded on the mainsheet traveler to the aft extrusion. With the yellow hulls, it looked radical. We took it out in lighter airs the first couple of times to get used to its idiosyncrasies, which all boats have. It was quick.

"Then we had a day where it was blowing twenty-five knots. We took her off the trailer and put it in the water with a crane. We set up the rig and put on some wet suits. We were ready. We left Point Richmond and headed down to Berkeley doing an easy twenty-five knots across the wind window in front of the Golden Gate. She would fly off the waves and almost bury the leeward hull, but come right up and out of the water and scream off again downwind on a broad reach. It was intoxicating. My friend and I couldn't contain ourselves. We were just howling and hooting our lungs out. My creation just smoked by everything else in the Bay that day. It was success beyond my wildest dreams.

"Eventually, I took the boat up to Lake Tahoe where a sudden storm came up from the south and somehow blew her off her mooring, putting her on the beach where the waves broke apart one of the hulls and one of the extrusions. That was a sad, sad day for me. I felt like part of me was destroyed. There is a real feeling of accomplishment when you construct a vessel yourself and do your own personal design of the rig and boat. And it's an altogether different and unique feeling when you launch it and sail it. You know exactly what works and what doesn't work right. Your failures get right in your face, but if it all works well, it's a truly magnificent feeling and one I am sure Nephi experienced when they sea-trialed his vessel.

"I am presently building a seventeen-and-a-half-foot Pygmy Boats Queen Charlotte Kayak out of wood and fiberglass. It's a very time-consuming project that requires real patience and craftsmanship. It is something I couldn't have done years ago because I didn't have the knowledge and experience to build a vessel of this type. You have to love it in order to do it. This is why I believe Nephi had experienced craftsmen assist him and literally construct the vessel for him. Only simpleminded persons would think you could jump right in and construct a hundred-and-twenty-foot or greater vessel. An even greater challenge was to take that same vessel across two of the greatest oceans on the planet. The vessel would be in constant need of repair. This too would require skilled shipwrights in the crew. I am in awe of the undertaking and accomplishment that Nephi performed, no matter how he did it. It was a 'marvelous work and a wonder,' even with the Lord's help and guidance."

Master Sailor, Commercial Fisherman, and Marine Electrician Conrad Dickson

Conrad Dickson is a longtime friend, neighbor, and sailing companion of Frank Linehan. They both are members of the LDS Gig Harbor Washington Ward. Knowing Conrad's unique history, Frank invited Conrad to join George in studying the voyages of the Book of Mormon.

Conrad is a sailor's sailor. Viking kings of Finland, Sweden, Norway, and Denmark through the Normans of Normandy are Conrad's hereditary forebears. His early American family came from the Washington and Robert E. Lee families. The Dickson name comes from the Keith clan of Scotland, who were seafaring people. The grandmother side of the Dickson family came west in 1845 to what is now Oregon and Washington in the "Meek" wagon train. Grandfather Dickson arrived in the Pacific northwest from Texas in 1899. Conrad's father was a seaman in Alaska in the 1930s. His uncle also was a seaman in Alaska during the Great Depression and was a naval officer for over twenty-two years.

On his mother's side, Conrad's grandfather was a US Marshal in Alaska for twenty-five years during the time when it was still a rough and wild US territory. His great-grandfather Anderson on his mother's side left Ballard, Washington, in the early 1900s to fish halibut and never returned.

Conrad was born and raised in the Puget Sound area of western Washington. Loving the sea, his father named him after the famous maritime author Joseph Conrad. His family settled in Gig Harbor in 1950. The small community rests in the shadow of Mt. Rainer. The harbor was and still is home port for many fishing and pleasure vessels.

Being on or near the sea has been a major part of Conrad's life for the past fifty-nine years. He began fishing as a boy of ten with his school buddy and neighbor, Carl Colby. They helped support their family needs by catching sea run trout, salmon, and herring from Carl's leaky rowing skiff.

During high school, Conrad spent his summers in Alaska serving on fishing boats as crew and master's mate. These were dangerous summers for the young lad. On one occasion, his fishing vessel's net was struck by two whales. It took the better part of a week to repair the damage and return to fishing. He twice survived being washed overboard. While underwater, going down to sure death, during one of these events he was saved by being hooked under the arm with a lumberjack's pike pole. During one fishing season he contacted a serious case of fish blood poisoning in both hands and arms. A doctor told him he needed to be placed in the local hospital for care or he could lose his life. Rather than let his crew down and make them work shorthanded, he asked the doctor to pump his arms full of drugs and promised to return the next time they were in port. By the time he returned to land, the blood poisoning was gone and his swollen, grapefruit-size hands were normal. A few weeks later, he came close to death due to carbon monoxide poisoning from a leaky exhaust system while sleeping in the forepeak. A voice from the Spirit very loudly told him to get up and get out to fresh air. He managed to get to the main deck before he passed out for quite some time. He lay on deck, gray black in color, and most of the crew thought he was dead.

If fish blood poisoning and carbon monoxide couldn't kill Conrad, two hurricane force storms he weathered at sea couldn't kill him either. Making it home from Alaska during those years was sweet. There is an old Norse saying that says 'If you make it back alive, you have had a good trip.' Having come close to death so many times at sea, Conrad has developed a deep appreciation for life.

Conrad spent three years on active duty and another three on inactive duty in the US Navy as a missile technician. While in the Navy, he graduated from four missile schools and an abbreviated submarine school during the Cuban missile crisis. An appointment to the US Naval Academy and also to the US Naval Seal Buds School were offered him during his time of active duty. As a diver, he saved a diving buddy who had ruptured both eardrums while operating in deep, heavy seas. Twice he rescued other Navy divers while in heavy surf exercises. Due to the secret nature of his assignments, most of his naval record is sealed and cannot be disclosed. He served with honor and is proud of doing his part in being a volunteer for his country.

After leaving the Navy, Conrad returned to Alaska. Being the only diver west of Kodiak Island at the time, he spent many cold hours in 33-degree water repairing or clearing problems under vessels so that they could return to fishing. Once, while diving to salvage an old mail-boat engine, he survived an attack by a giant squid that nearly strangled him.

Working twenty-six years as a marine electrician for the federal government at Puget Sound Naval Ship Yard has given Conrad many insights into the world of the sea. While in government employment, he conducted pre-overhaul inspections,

Conrad Dickson (right) sailing the Puget Sound with Frank Linehan.

overhauls, and sea trials on almost every kind and class of ship the US Navy has, from submarines to aircraft carriers.

Conrad began sailing in earnest in the early 1970s while living at Horsehead Bay. He owned a Laser. Many nights after work were spent sailing in Henderson Bay around Deadman's Island until the wee hours of morning with his friend, Kris Overby. Saturdays were spent racing Lasers, International 14s, or sometimes San Juan 24s. In those days, Conrad had a lot of energy and managed to live on little sleep. Sailboat racing consumed his interest for years. To him, racing was like playing a three-level chess game with different vessels, different courses, and each with their own challenges.

While owning a charter sailboat business for four years, many qualities of being a vessel's captain were developed. Ownership of several sailing vessels and racing nationally and internationally in various classes for over thirty-four years has honed his seamanship skills to a fine edge. Throughout the Pacific Northwest sailing community, Conrad is known as a competent captain, navigator, helmsman, and sail tender. As a true sailor, his real joy has come from fishing and sailing waters from the Bering Sea to French Polynesia.

Conrad possessed a 100-ton Limited Merchant Marine Master's License with a steam, diesel, towing, and sailing ticket. A Master must know his vessel, his crew, the sea, and have an iron will. "No matter what, the vessel and crew must be safe and the voyage must be completed." Conrad's rise to Master is what is called a "Mustang" Limited Master, one who comes up through the ranks or up through the "hawspipe" without attending a merchant marine academy. However, one must still attend and graduate from a USCG approved merchant marine limited masters school. Passing four days of rigorous Coast Guard examinations is also a requirement. A very pointed oral examination had to be passed from a Licensed Unlimited Master. A final requirement was to be recommended in writing by four Masters and a chief engineer.

Conrad and his wife were married in 1964 and have a wonderful family. He became a convert to the LDS Church in 1976. The Dickson's present sailboat is a 51-foot cutter rig, Beneteau sloop called *Brigadoon*. They have owned her for fourteen years and have lived aboard for eleven. They enjoy spending summers cruising the Puget Sound, the San Juan Islands, the west coast of Canada, and the waters of southeast Alaska.

Using a Computer Simulator to Understand the Voyages of the Book of Mormon

Another amazing member of our authorship team is a computer simulator. This amazing software application uses data from centuries of accumulated maritime logs and navigators' input to predict the best course, estimate duration, and sea conditions of the voyages of ships at any particular time of the year. Using the maritime computer simulator Visual Passage Planner 2 by Digital Wave, Frank and Conrad have returned us to the oceans of the past, even to the times of our Book of Mormon heroes. Together, they will take us along the most likely routes traveled by Book of Mormon mariners and will describe some of the challenges the ancient voyagers would have experienced during each journey.

After we enter into the simulator our engineering specification estimates (vessel and speed profiles) for the vessels most likely used by each of our Book of Mormon sailing parties, the simulator estimates climatic, wind, current, and ocean condition patterns for each passage. Then, by using the "best passage scenario," the simulator estimates the length of each voyage. Using the simulator, each estimated Book of Mormon ocean transit was broken down into the "most favorable" route or course points, which are called "way points." The navigator and simulator functions of the software define the journey between each way point as a "leg." For each leg, the simulator calculates the distance in nautical miles, the elapsed time to complete the leg, average boat speed, boat speed made good, average wind speed along the leg, average direction from true north, average current drift, average current set, and the apparent wind angle information. The data predicted for each voyage is extensive, informative, and too excessive for the purposes of this book. For this reason, we have only provided summary information for each estimated passage. For the serious student, we have placed the complete Full Visual Passage Planner 2 simulation output data for the voyages of the Book of Mormon in this book on a CD available at the Nephi Project Discovery Store at www.nephiproject.com.

The thousands of navigation charts utilized by Visual Passage Planner 2 have

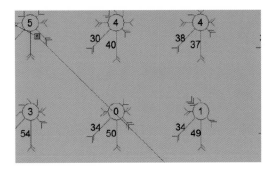

Example of quadrant roses.

their origins reaching far back into ancient times. Throughout the centuries, maritime nations gathered daily log readings from their vessels after they returned to home ports. Thousands of passages and master charts were continually refined to aid navigators. For trade and military advantage, each nation held their maritime charts in secret. Without accurate charts, a navy is ineffective, and without an effective navy, an empire could not expand across the seas. For this reason, when Scipio Africanus defeated Hannibal at Carthage, he killed the Carthaginian navy captains and burned the Carthaginian maritime charts. As a result, Carthage was never again capable of mounting an attack on Rome or its empire. Over time, sea depths were added to the charts as well as bottom-material information to aid seafarers while navigating in fog. This important process

of reading the sea continues. Indeed, as you read this book, maritime charts are being improved and computerized.

Modern maritime pilot charts plot average wind speed directions, current speed directions in percentages, and days of calm for each month of the year on what are called eight quadrant roses. Throughout the world, each main sea route has an eight-quadrant rose in one-degree increments. These roses are constantly updated each month. In other words, today's charts are the results of several hundred years of vessel log recordings, all combined into one document that is segmented monthly. Due to the physical size of the earth, individual pilot charts cover only portions of the seas. Pilot charts have been and are still a mainstay in planning the most favorable passage for commercial, military, and private vessels throughout the world.

Maritime charts are the basis for the computer simulation we used in writing this book. In fact, Frank and Conrad used these charts to plan and navigate their ocean passages before simulation became available. It would take a person weeks to do what the simulation program does in a matter of seconds. The program enables the operator to plug in different courses

Jody Lemmon aboard the Banyan.

and see the results at a particular time of the year in terms of wind speed, wind direction, current speed, current direction, water temperature, air temperature, swells (height and frequency), storms, and vessel profile in regard to the aforementioned.

Simulator charts are based on compilations of observations and calculations performed over the course of hundreds of years. Since there have been no dramatic changes in ocean sailing conditions in that 150-year period, we are confident we can extrapolate that data back 2,600 years and use the simulator as a basis for our assumptions and resulting hypothesis. In other words, because of the long-term stability of ocean cycles, the computer's simulated courses of yesterday (even circa 587 BC) are as sound today as they were then.

The Voyage of the Banyan

As we write this book, our friend Jody Lemmon and his friends are sailing from Long Beach, California, to the South Pacific in a 43-foot sloop. Jody has agreed to share with readers his modern sailing ship passage across the great Pacific to New Zealand. They sail in a technically advanced ship with powerful motors to aid their progress and with modern navigation and communication devices. The daily

Frank Linehan (left) with lifelong friend Bruce Lemmon, the owner of the sloop Banyan.

experiences of Jody and his crew will place us on the waters of the Pacific in a sailing ship and will illustrate to all of us some of the challenges the Book of Mormon sailors had to conquer. As we will see, the *Banyan*, Jody, and his experienced crew will appear to have been saved from the forces of the sea by a miracle.

By understanding the probable weather and sea conditions, the physical design and

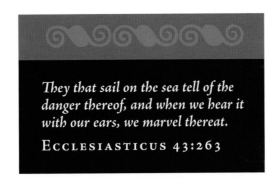

They that sail on the sea tell of the danger thereof, and when we hear it with our ears, we marvel thereat.

ECCLESIASTICUS 43:263

state of the ships of the Book of Mormon, and the emotional and physical challenges of their passengers, it is our hope that we will experience what it was like to have been aboard the ocean voyages described in the Book of Mormon. To bring alive again the challenges faced by our Book of Mormon heroes, our modern LDS sailors will describe what they believe the voyagers of the Book of Mormon would have experienced during their long and dangerous journeys. So read on and board in your mind's eye the ancient ships of the brother of Jared, Nephi, Mulek, and Hagoth.

Notes

1. *Teachings of the Prophet Joseph Smith*, sel. Joseph Fielding Smith (Salt Lake City: Deseret Book, 1977), 307.

2. Hugh Nibley, *Collected Works of Hugh Nibley, vol. 8: The Prophetic Book of Mormon* (Salt Lake City: Deseret Book, 1989), 277–78.

3. *Ecclesiasticus*, or the writing of the Jewish scribe Ben Sira of Jerusalem, also known as *Wisdom of Jesus son of Sirach*, the *Wisdom of Ben Sira*, is a work from the early second century BC, originally written in Hebrew.

> *Men go back to the mountains,*
> *as they go back to sailing ships at sea,*
> *because in the mountains and on the sea*
> *they must face up.*
> H ENRY D AVID T HOREAU

NEPHI'S HARBOR *

P UT YOURSELF in the sandals of a young lad from the land of ancient Jerusalem. He was born in a homeland nearly void of maritime skills. Generally, the only way the kings of his homeland could muster a navy was to hire the shipwrights, captains, and crews from seafaring neighbors. His own tribe was engaged in merchant trade, skilled in overland travel, cameleering, and the ways of the desert. However, they were alien to the ways of the sea and probably many did not even know how to swim. Born into a life of privilege, the lad's father suddenly called the family together to tell them they had to flee their comfortable life and dwell in tents in a desert wilderness. The teenager, now likely in his early to mid-twenties, took over the leadership of the family while they were in the desert (1 Nephi 16:38, Mosiah 10:13). The constant trials he faced in leading the family's desert exodus were extreme and must have

Harbor of Khor Rori, Oman.

* Based on article by Richard Wellington and George Potter, "From the Valley of Lemuel to Nephi's Harbor," *Journal of Book of Mormon Studies* 15, no. 2 (2006): 26–43.

seemed unbearable at times because of his older brothers constantly rebelling against him. On several occasions, his older brothers even tried to murder him. These lazy and violent brothers resisted obeying their younger brother, their father, and the Lord. By overcoming these and many other formidable obstacles during their long desert crossing, and by obeying each and every call from the Lord, the young adult eventually matured into a powerful king of great character.

Because of his faithfulness in his teens, he heard the voice of the Lord declare, "Blessed art thou, Nephi, because of thy faith, for thou hast sought me diligently, with lowliness of heart. And inasmuch as ye shall keep my commandments, ye shall prosper, and shall be led to a land of promise; yea, even a land which I have prepared for you; yea, a land which is choice above all other lands" (1 Nephi 2:19–20). However, the divine promise came with still another enormous test of the young man's faith. Before he left the Valley of Lemuel, Nephi realized that they would not walk to the choice land that he would rule; rather they would sail to the promised land across not one but many seas (1 Nephi 13:11–12). For the next eight years that Nephi was

in the wilderness of Arabia, he must have worried over and over again: *how could he possibly take his family across the vast oceans?* The very thought must have overwhelmed him. When the Liahona pointed toward southern Arabia, the land perhaps of the ancient world's greatest seafarers, Nephi must have realized that with each footstep he was drawing closer and closer to the hour of his greatest challenge—building a ship, convincing his family to board it, and sailing it across the many waters.

Let us approach Nephi's predicament in a more personal way. As you sleep in your bed tonight, suppose the voice of the Lord comes to you in a dream and directs you to build a wide-bodied jet airliner, convince your family to board it, and finally fly it to an unknown destination halfway around the world. Could you have slept the rest of the night? What would you do? Would you roll up your sleeves and get to work, or would you believe the Lord would simply do everything for you? Do you believe the Lord would provide you an already completely built wide-body jet with your name on it? Would an airport suddenly appear in your backyard? Do you think the Lord would send an angel to navigate for you? Do you believe that a commercial

pilot's license would suddenly appear in your wallet and somehow after breakfast it suddenly dons on you that you now know how to pilot a large aircraft? The Lord generally does not work that way in our lives. Why? Because the Lord wants us to learn and grow through challenges.

From his Book of Mormon account, we note that Nephi had to walk or ride a camel every step of the 2,100 miles from Jerusalem to Oman where we believe he built his ship. He was not handed a magic carpet. Yet that is how a number of writers about Nephi's ship have presented the events surrounding his voyage. We refer to their approach as a bedtime story. The story line goes something like this: Nephi and his family arrived at a place in Oman in southern Arabia. They called it Bountiful. No one lived anywhere near their shoreline camp. Thus, there was absolutely no one to assist them in any way. There were no farmers, yet their wilderness campsite abounded with fruit trees. Despite the Doctrine and Covenants telling us that Nephi converted persons in the wilderness (33:7–9), this story line seems to imply that prophets like Lehi avoided people at all cost. Although no known timber has ever grown in Oman from which a large

Sycamore Fig, typical of trees in Oman—unsuitable for shipbuilding.

ship could be built, this story line suggests that the Lord somehow provided Nephi in his wilderness camp a huge load of straight hardwood timber.

The story line doesn't end there. Undoubtedly, Nephi knew nothing or next to nothing about shipbuilding when he arrived at Bountiful. Likely never having built even a dingy, this son of a wealthy father and without training was somehow transformed into a remarkable craftsman, having learned apparently without an instructor hundreds of unique shipwright skills that each sometimes requires years of practice to master. We must acknowledge that Nephi's ship was no small fishing boat; rather, it was a huge vessel that held a large party and all their provisions. As the story line goes, Nephi apparently built his ship on a beach with breaking surf and without a shipyard ramp to move his ship into the

water. The story line doesn't explain where Nephi found the cotton for his ship's sails, fiber for the ropes needed for his ship's riggings, or the antifouling coating compound he needed to protect the hull of his ship so it would not be eaten through in a few weeks by sea worms. To persons who have actually sailed a large ship, however, the greatest of all these many unrecorded marvels would be Nephi's sudden ability to cast off an anchor and successfully command a ship across two massive oceans.

So, how did Nephi accomplish such a feat? We believe he did it probably not too removed from the same way other oceangoing ships were being built at his time—except that Nephi needed the Lord's instructions on how to find the skilled persons and unique resources he needed to build such a ship, and he very much needed divine instructions on how to modify the ship to give it the strength it needed to reach the New World (1 Nephi 17:8). If this approach is correct, then the question begs to be answered: "How were oceangoing ships built at 600 BC in the ancient world?" A recent discovery at the Egyptian Red Sea port of Wadi Gawasis in 2010 provides a window into the ancient maritime arts.

Among other artifacts uncovered by the USA-led Bard-Fattovich excavation team, the archaeologists found parts of the oldest oceangoing ship yet discovered. The ship was built over a thousand years before Nephi set sail for the promised land. It was built so that Pharaohs could trade with the port of Punt, which some scholars believe was the ancient frankincense harbor of Khor Rori[1] in southern Arabia, the very place George Potter and Richard Wellington surveyed in 1999 and concluded the deep lagoon was the best candidate for where Nephi built his ship.[2] The ancient Egyptian vessel and its port provide a clear picture on *where* and *how* ancient ships were built. As reported in the Boston Globe:

> Boston University archeologist Kathryn Bard and her colleagues are uncovering the oldest remnants of seagoing ships and other relics linked to exotic trade with a mysterious Red Sea realm called Punt.
>
> "They [the ancient ships] were the space launches of their time," Bard said of the epic missions to procure wondrous wares.
>
> Then the team led by Bard and an Italian archeologist, Rodolfo Fattovich, started uncovering maritime storerooms in 2004, putting hard timber and rugged rigging to the notion of pharaonic deepwater prowess.
>
> The remote desert site at the sea's edge was established solely to satisfy the craving of Egypt's rulers for the luxury goods of faraway Punt: ebony, ivory, obsidian, frankincense, precious metals, slaves, and strange

CHAPTER ONE

Omani historian Ali Al-Shahri in front of frankincense tree.

beasts, such as dog-faced baboons and giraffes.

Starting in the middle of the last decade, the Bard-Fattovich team grabbed the attention of nautical archeologists with the unearthing of ship timbers, limestone anchors, steering oars, and hanks of marine rope. The precisely beveled deck beams, hull planks, and copper fittings belong to the oldest deep sea vessels ever found, dating back at least 3,800 years.

The craft appear to have been up to 70 feet long, powered by rowers and sail and capable of navigating deep seas.

. . . So, using timber hewn from the mountains of Lebanon, Egyptian shipwrights built big vessels on the banks of the Nile, near modern Qift, according to archaeology-based theory.

"These were then disassembled and transported, with all other supplies, over the desert by donkey, a journey of 10 days" to reach Wadi Gawasis, Bard said. The site adjoined a lagoon, in which a port was built. The ship parts were marked and rebuilt by number or color code. The lagoon has long since been swallowed by sand, but satellite images hint at the remains of a shipway or dock.

Here were ships' timbers. Here were sea

George purchasing frankincense in a Saudi Arabian incense store.

anchors. Here were bundles of intact nautical rope.

Here was a tantalizing tale of ancient seafaring. "The rope was neatly stored, coiled, and knotted, exactly as some sailor left it," Bard said. It was a moment perfectly frozen in time for 3,800 years."[3]

As we start our analysis of where and how Nephi built his ship, keep in mind what ancient Egyptian shipbuilders required:

hard timbers (when not present they had to be **imported** from distant lands), **precisely beveled beams and planks** (something a novice shipbuilder could not achieve without proper tools and years of experience), and a source of materials for **sails** and **coils of rugged rigging**. Finally, the ancients built their ships on land above the calm waters of a **lagoon** (inlet) and then lowered their heavy ships into the

21

water using gravity via ramps or **shipways**.

From Jerusalem to Nephi's Harbor

In their book, *Lehi in the Wilderness*, George Potter and Richard Wellington documented eighty-one evidences that the Book of Mormon is a true history. They made their discoveries by retracing the route of the ancient frankincense trail that led from Palestine to what is today Oman. It was the only trail down western Arabia in Lehi's time, and thus the only route where Lehi would have found food and water. Since a desert changes slowly, it was not hard to trace the ancient trail. What George and Richard found was precisely what was recorded by Nephi.

When Lehi left Jerusalem to start his journey, the Arabian Peninsula had been inhabited for a great many generations. According to the Bible, southern Arabia was populated shortly after the flood by the thirteen sons of Joktan, just generations removed from Noah's descendant (Genesis 10:26–30).[4] The limited number of wells that existed in Arabia were well known by Lehi's time and all were under ownership of tribes who guarded them closely. Travel to and from these wells could not be undertaken without permission of the Arab tribes who owned the lands and who profited from selling water and access rights. In other words, we think Lehi had no other choice but to take an existing trail down western Arabia. The trail allowed the family access to water, the right to cross tribal lands, and to receive protection from bandits. The trail led down Arabia in a south-southeast direction to southern Arabia (1 Nephi 16:13–14).[5] The trail was maintained to transport frankincense, the highly prized sap of the tree Boswelia sacra from the trees that grew in the more fertile areas of southern Arabia and that then was transported to Egypt, Mesopotamia, Syria, and Israel to the north. Thus, the Potter-Wellington model for Lehi's trail departs from previous ideas that Lehi traveled down the shoreline of the Red Sea.[6] This would have been impossible since there was no trail along the coast and thus no organized string of wells along the Red Sea shoreline until the ninth century AD.[7] As Lynn and Hope Hilton succinctly summarized, "Lehi could not have carved out a route for himself without water, and for a city dweller to discover a line of water holes of which desert dwellers were ignorant is an unlikely prospect."[8] "The family, therefore, must have traveled and survived in the same area as other travelers of their day did, going from public waterhole to public waterhole."[9] Besides, as the Roman historian Pliny pointed out, those who left the official trail were summarily executed by the Arab-ruling hegemonies.[10]

Since one could not wander far from the sometimes miles-wide trail without being executed, we can assume that wherever it ended was the locale the Lord desired the family to reach. Having promised Nephi a choice land across the many waters, we should not be surprised to learn that the trail ended at Khor Rori, the ancient frankincense harbor. But Khor Rori was no common port. It was the home port of ancient shipbuilders and sailors who appear to have possessed the highest level of seafaring knowledge of their time. Nephi was bound for the promised land with a perfect faith "that the Lord giveth no commandments unto the children of men, save he shall prepare a way for them that they may accomplish the thing which he commandeth them" (1 Nephi 3:7). In a very real sense, Khor Rori would have provided Nephi a "prepared way" to reach the promised land.

Bountiful—Where Nephi Built His Ship

Various LDS authors have suggested

Harbor of Khor Rori with ruins of ways (ancient ramps) on left.

Though the two sites—al-Balīd and Wadi Sayq—possess unessential features that could connect them with Bountiful, in our opinion Khor Rori (and Khor Rori only) offers dimensions that the other two sites do not. These dimensions are the three maritime resources that Nephi needed to reach the promised land: materials to build an ocean-going ship; a protected harbor for building; and shipwright and seamanship knowledge necessary to build and master an oceangoing ship. There is a growing body of evidence that says that the ancient frankincense port of Khor Rori possessed in Nephi's day these unique maritime resources, as well as all the other attributes mentioned in Nephi's record.[14]

Khor Rori is a large and calm waterway extending over 1½ miles inland. The

locations for Bountiful. The Hiltons focused on the inlet bay at Salalah, the ancient al-Balīd.[11] Warren and Michaela Aston settled on Wadi Sayq (Khor Kharfot).[12] If Lehi and his family had taken the route eastward from Yemen to Dhofar in modern Oman, the area generally considered to be where Bountiful was situated,[13] they would have followed that trail until it ended on the Salalah plain where the harbor at Khor Rori formed one of the largest ancient ports in southern Arabia. George Potter and Richard Wellington were the first to suggest that Khor Rori was the logical place to start the search for the place Nephi called Bountiful, the place where the family lived and where Nephi and others built and launched his ship.

23

The natural harbor of Khor Rori, the ancient port of the frankincense trade.

Khor has several natural places where ships could moor, making it the likely reason that Khor Rori and the nearby town of Taqah were called Merbat (the moorings) anciently. Today, there is a sandbank across the Khor, closing it off from the sea. This sandbank was not always present, however. Dr. Eduard G. Rheinhardt believes that a drop in sea levels around the fourteenth and fifteenth centuries AD caused the closure of the harbor's mouth. Radiocarbon dating establishes that there was a stable and final closure occurring around AD 1640–1690.[15] Huge cliffs line the sea entrance to Khor Rori, forming natural breakwaters that allowed ancient ships to sail out 400–450 yards into the Indian Ocean with protection from the surf.[16] This was the great strength

Giant cliffs at Khor Rori that provide a natural breakwater.

of Khor Rori as a port; the natural break-water provided protection from both the summer southwest monsoon and the winter northeast monsoon winds. Thus, the port could be used all year long for shipping and shipbuilding.

Khor Rori was the premier port of the Dhofar region of Oman and was involved in seafaring as early as the fifth-fourth millennia BC.[17] Both Khor Rori and the adjacent town of Taqah were settled long before Lehi's arrival in southern Arabia. Archaeologist Juris Zarins found evidence that a large scale Bronze Age presence was there,[18] as well as evidence of an Iron Age settlement.[19] Ceramic typology suggests that Taqah's human occupation dates to the late phase of the Bronze Age, and this is supported by C^{14} dates averaging 1800 BC.[20] Zarins concludes: "All the evidence placed together then suggests Moscha [the port's name known to the Greeks] was Sumhuram/Khor Rori. The last suggestion is that Khor Rori/Sumhuram was Ptolemy's Abissa town (Van Wissmann 1977: 32–33, Groom 1994: 207), based on the natural falls upstream at Wadi Darbat."[21]

About 150 years after Lehi's time, an impressive fortress settlement called

Ruins of Sumhuram at Khor Rori.

Sumhuram was built on the edge of the inlet by the Hadramautis, who invaded Khor Rori to take control of the frankincense harbor. Four phases of construction of buildings at Sumhuram have been identified, the earliest dating to between the late fourth, early third, and mid-second century BC.[22] It should be remembered that Khor Rori was inhabited prior to the construction of Sumhurum.[23] The remains of stone fences constructed for irrigation at the Khor, together with pollen samples from inside the buildings at Khor Rori, indicate that the people at the inlet cultivated fields and gardens of wheat (*Triticum* group), barley (*Hordeum* group), and date palms (*Phoenix dactilifera*),[24] raised sheep and goats,[25] and ate seafood extensively.

Examination of the area around Khor Rori

25

shows that the fundamental element that gave "Bountiful" its name—fruit—would have been present at the shoreline exactly as Nephi described it. The shoreline of Dhofar is mainly rocky and there are few places where ancient cultivation is found at the shoreline. Yet, Nephi mentioned that when they arrived at Bountiful they camped on the seashore and called the place Bountiful because of its much fruit (1 Nephi 17:5–6). In fact, any cultivated plants would have been classified by Joseph Smith as "fruit" since Noah Webster's 1828 American usages dictionary defines "fruit" as:

1) "In a general sense, whatever the earth produces for the nourishment of animals or for clothing or profit. Among the fruits of the earth are included not only corn of all kinds, but grasses, cotton, flax, grapes and *all cultivated plants*. In this comprehensive sense the word is generally used in the plural.

2) "In the more limited sense, the production of a tree or plant; the last production for the propagation of plants, or *the part that contains the seeds; as wheat, rye, oats, apples, quinces, pears, cherries,*

acorns, melons, etc. (italics added)."[26]

Sorghum (*Sorghum bi color*), millets (*Eleusine sp.*, *Pennisetum sp.*), cotton (*Gossypium sp.*), and indigo (*Indigofera sp.*) were cultivated in Dhofar possibly as early as 4000 BC.[27] It should be noted that in 1 Nephi 17:5 where Nephi informs us that the honey in Bountiful was wild, he specifically avoids saying what the fruit was.

Jim Anderson at Salalah fruit stand near Khor Rori.

Fruit plantations 3 miles west of Khor Rori harbor.

While today Khor Rori and the surrounding coastal plain appear barren, the arid condition is a recent phenomenon due to changing rainfall levels. Local historian Ali Al-Shahri writes: "It was the most important agricultural area until 40 years ago, growing corn, millet, and lots of other grains. A long time ago, this plain was watered by many streams, which flowed into the sea. Even up to 30 years ago many of them were still flowing. . . . This area was covered with forest and grass perennially." *The Periplus of the Erythraean Sea*, written in the early Christian centuries and perhaps as late as the fourth century, mentions the presence of trees and rivers on the coastal plain.[28] During his youth, Al-Shahri watched his father's livestock in the valley just above Khor Rori. Just 2.5 miles from the harbor, Al-Shahri showed us where a man came to collect wild honey in the caves.[29]

Indeed, there is significant evidence that all the other peripheral elements of Bountiful existed at Khor Rori in Nephi's time: wild honey, a tall mountain (slopes of the highest peak in southern Oman are only two miles to the north), a Neolithic flint quarry (4.5 miles to the east[30]; just a mile east of the flint deposit BYU researchers discovered iron ore[31]; see 1 Nephi 17:11), and a

Jim Anderson finds flint nodes at ancient flint quarry near Khor Rori.

iron smelting slag discovered among the ruins at Khor Rori[32] (1 Nephi 17:9–10). Of special interest to students of the Book of Mormon is that a bronze plate was found in the temple at Khor Rori depicting a man dressed in robes and standing with his arms in a formal manner, as well as a bronze plate with words embossed on it.[33] The discovery of these bronze plates

Ancient brass plate discovered at Khor Rori.

27

at Khor Rori provides a possible idea as to how Nephi learned to form metal plates for the recording of his people's history.

Further, Khor Rori is due east of the current candidates for Nahom,[34] the place where Ishmael died. Nephi indicated that from Nahom (thought to be near 16 degrees N) his family traveled "nearly eastward" to reach Bountiful (see 1 Nephi 16:34, 17:1; Khor Rori is located at 17 degrees N). In addition, the Khor Rori area has domesticated animals and wild beasts for hides and meat[35] (1 Nephi 17:11, 18:6). Finally, the Khor has towering cliffs that are directly above deep water (1 Nephi 17:48).

Three Maritime Requirements for Bountiful

For any candidate to be considered a possible site for Bountiful, it is absolutely critical that it meet three essential criteria. It must be possible that in Nephi's time it had the resources necessary for Nephi to 1) build, 2) launch, and 3) sail a large ship. We believe that Khor Rori is the only place in southern Arabia that could have met these criteria, plus it possessed the other attributes Nephi attributed to the land Bountiful.

How Large Was Nephi's Ship?

The largest Arab freighters of Nephi's time were probably over fifty feet long, pointed at both ends with a small or perhaps no decks. They used a quarter rudder, square sails, and were sewn together with coconut rope instead of being fastened by nails. There are several reasons to believe that Nephi's ship was quite a bit larger than the regular Arab merchant ships of his day.

1. The Number of People Aboard

His ship's hull, perhaps with a partial or full deck, had to be large enough to carry the entire family group and their provisions to the New World and still allow for an open area where they could dance (1 Nephi 18:9). Ship size was a direct function of the number of people on board and the provisions carried. The size of the ship would in turn have determined the dimensions of the port Nephi would have needed. To establish if a port existed in Dhofar (Salalah) that could have accommodated Nephi's ship, we needed to make a rough census of how many people would have been in the party. Lynn and Hope Hilton estimated that there were seventy-three on board Nephi's ship.[36] John Tvedtnes estimates that there could have been up to sixty-eight persons.[37]

What would be realistic numbers for persons aboard? The Book of Mormon does not mention sixty or seventy people. If, for example, we assume that the text of 1 Nephi 18:6, "Wherefore, we did all go down into the ship, with our wives and our children," means possibly two children between each of the married couples, there would have been a minimum of twenty-one people (seventeen adults and four children) on board. However, the text in the Book of Mormon gives many clues that tell us there were far more in the ship than this. Let us analyze the issue.

Lehi and Sariah had two children while traveling in the wilderness (1 Nephi 18:7). We might expect the younger couples to have had at least as many children as their parents did over that same time period.

Nephi's sisters are not mentioned until the family reaches the New World (2 Nephi 5:6), but we know they were married to Ishmael's sons.[38] Nephi went back to get Ishmael's family, and thus we assume his sisters were already married to Ishmael's sons before they left Jerusalem. Since these couples (at least two) had been married for over eight years at sailing time, they most likely had more than four children each. Nephi states that his "children" traveled

on the ship (1 Nephi 18:19). Thus, the youngest of the four sons of Lehi born in the land of Jerusalem already had "children" aboard the ship.

Nephi's three older brothers, married during the same period he did, each presumably would have had multiple offspring before entering the ship. Laman and Lemuel infer that each couple had a number of children (1 Nephi 17:20). In the land of promise we are told that Lehi blessed the sons and daughters of Laman and the sons and daughters of Lemuel: thus, each had at least four children (2 Nephi 4:3, 8). We also know that this blessing took place shortly after they arrived in the New World, since Joseph, who was born in the wilderness, appears to have been a small child at the time (2 Nephi 3:25). The implication is that shortly after arriving in the promised land, Laman and Lemuel already had at least four children and probably more. Most of them, if not all, were aboard Nephi's ship.

Other members of the group. When referring to the number of people who would board the ship, the Lord spoke of Nephi's "people" and not his "family" (1 Nephi 17:8). It would have been the norm for a wealthy man of Lehi's social stature to

have had household servants. It is hard to imagine Lehi fleeing into the wilderness with only his immediate family members and, in essence, cruelly deserting at least some of his faithful servants in a city that was about to be destroyed. It is a real likelihood that Lehi took with him a somewhat larger party than we think, at least larger than basic family members. This thinking also provides a plausible explanation for how the Lamanite and Nephite nations became a large multitude so rapidly in the New World.

If Lehi had taken some servants with him to the land of promise, why didn't Nephi mention them? Zoram was a servant, so why were not possible other servants mentioned? The answer is as straightforward as the patriarchal society they all came from. Such servants were not yet free, thus they were not part of Lehi's family. Zoram had been set free, thus he was made a freeman. In those days, he would have been given the choice to be an official member of the family and as such even given the rights to marry into the tribe (1 Nephi 4:33–34; 16:7). Had it not been for this adoption, Zoram's name most likely would not have been mentioned on the plates.

Unfortunately, the omission of menial tribal

members from official records has a long tradition, both in the East and the West. Up until the last two centuries of our own millennium, the names of women, children, and servants were seldom mentioned in literature. A review of ancient scriptures reveals only a handful of names of women or servants. Nephi was a prophet, but he was also a product of his time. It does not appear to have crossed his mind to record the names of his sisters (1 Nephi 5:6), the daughters of Ishmael (including the name of his own wife), (1 Nephi 16:7), let alone any possible servants.

Michael Crichton placed the manuscripts of Ahmad Ibn Fadlan's report to the Caliph of Baghdad in a novel format. In AD 922, Ibn Fadlan had been sent as an ambassador to the king of the Bulgars. Crichton writes, "Ibn Fadlan never states that his party is greater than a few individuals, when in fact it probably numbered a hundred people or more. . . . Ibn Fadlan does not count literally slaves, servants, and lesser members of the caravan."[39]

One cannot rule out the possibility that, in addition to possible servants, some local persons from Dhofar joined the family. The Omanis have a great tradition of seafaring. When building the ship, the family

29

Nephi's ship was large enough to dance on the deck.

Omani sailors as the core members of his crew. More on this later. We now have a party of seventy-five—thirty children and forty-five adults. This estimate is very much in line with Hilton's thinking.

So, how large was Nephi's ship? As we consider its necessary capacities, keep in mind that Columbus's *Niña* is estimated to have had an "overall length (between perpendiculars) about 70 feet, length of keel about 50 feet, beam about 23 feet, depth of hold amidships about 9 feet."[40] She carried a crew of about only 24 men![41]

2. FOOD AND WATER FOR A PACIFIC CROSSING

Once past India, there were not many ports, perhaps none, where Nephi could have restocked his ship en route to Chile (see Potter's *Nephi in the Promised Land* for a compelling case for the Lehites' arrival in Chile in South America). Presumably, they fished and collected rainwater when possible, but we imagine they stopped along the way to search for water and food. Depending on winds, the voyage to the New World doubtless took many months. Still, it is certain Nephi needed to have taken on board large stores of food and water. New Zealand historian Harry

likely had help from the locals. Perhaps some local men would doubtless have been drawn to the adventure and romance of a far journey, and their already experienced seafaring skills would have been vital for the ship's crew.

Perhaps the estimate of the number on board must now be increased. Seven couples could have had at least four children each, a total of at least twenty-eight children. One servant per adult adds seventeen servants in all, plus one nursemaid per family with children adds seven maids. In addition, some Omani men may have helped form the ship's crew. Let's suggest that Nephi likely used four experienced

Morton notes, "In the Pacific, especially, it is necessary to plan well. An accurate estimate of time was . . . important in planning for provisions or equipment for the voyage. . . . Almost any Pacific voyage was a long one."[42]

When marine archaeologist Tim Severin sailed his replica Arab ship to China, he covered a distance less than half Nephi's voyage, and he carried a crew of only twenty men. Severin describes loading his eighty-foot ship, the *Sohar*, with provisions:

> There was not enough room to store all the provisions for the entire journey. I calculated that we would carry a basic store of rations, and supplement our supplies with purchases made at countries along the route. . . . We had boxes of nuts and dried fruit, hundreds of eggs preserved in grease and wrapped in sawdust, sacks of onions, dried peas, rice and packets of spice. For variety there was a selection of tinned foods and sauces. Our cooking would be done on deck over a simple charcoal fire burning in a tray of sand. . . . I watched a ton of dates being manhandled aboard *Sohar* in sacks. . . . The list of necessities was unending. Half a ton of charcoal for the cook box . . .[43]

Nephi's use of the phrases we "prepared all things," taking "much fruits and meat," "honey in abundance," "provision according to that which the Lord had commanded," "all our loadings and our seeds," and "whatsoever thing we had brought with us" suggest that the ship carried several tons of provisions (1 Nephi 18:6). Further, without refrigeration, it was common for ships in former eras to take onboard live animals for milk and fresh meat. It is easy to picture a few caged goats on the deck of Nephi's ship, including bundles of fodder to keep them alive until their meat was needed.

Severin's replica ship was eighty feet long and carried only twenty men, yet he wrote: "With a crew of twenty hard-working, hungry men there was not enough room to store all the provisions for the entire journey."[44] Severin made

Display of a ship's cooking box. Bahrain National Museum.

Drawing of the Sohar. Illustration by Jose Flores.

several stops to purchase food and other consumables en route to China. There are no presently known ports-of-call beyond India and once out in the Pacific on Nephi's passage there were few if any islands to explore for food while crossing the Pacific.

Furthermore, Nephi's ship had to carry in its hull enough fresh water for perhaps seventy-five people who would have been exposed to hot tropical conditions. For his entire twenty-man crew, Severin rationed only twenty-five gallons of water a day for drinking and cooking. All washing was done in sea water, while cooking water was diluted, half and half, with sea water. His ship carried a month-and-a-half supply of water, roughly eleven hundred gallons.[45] It is reasonable to assume that Nephi's ship required a water reserve at least twice that amount. One of Severin's greatest fears was that the ship would be trapped in doldrums for weeks on end without being able to move forward. In fact, Severin's ship experienced such doldrums. He recalls, "After three weeks at sea we had consumed half our fresh water supply, yet we were no nearer Sumatra than the day we had left Galle. Effectively, therefore, there was no way we could get back to

Lower deck of this traditional style 74-foot-long Arab dhow is only 6½ feet tall.

replenish our fresh water."[46] Fortunately, Nephi's ship carried enough water for them to have survived the "great calm" that seems to have entrapped the ship between the time of the tempest and the time when there was once again enough wind to sail (1 Nephi 18:21–22).

Water would be the biggest problem in a voyage of this length. Nephi would have wanted to carry at least a hundred days supply for 70 people. If you allowed a gallon per person, that is 70 gallons per day or 7000 gallons for 100 days. This would have been doable because Nephi's people

32

were desert people and used to water rationing. At 42 gallons per barrel (marine measure), that would be 166 barrels of water alone. The weight of the water alone would equal about 56,000 pounds or 28 tons, which does not include the weight of the barrels. All this had to be loaded and stored below, so perhaps Nephi carried a minimum of 30 days or only the equivalent of 55 barrels due to space requirements. All of it would have to be accessible as well as secured so that it wouldn't shift in the heaviest of weather.

3. Ship's Repairs and Tools

Without ports-of-call, Nephi probably had thoughts similar to those of German philosopher Otto Neurath who wrote, "We are like sailors who must rebuild their ship on the open sea, never able to dismantle it in dry-dock and to reconstruct it there out of the best materials." A wooden ship is in constant need of maintenance, an endless effort that once is stopped dooms the ship. Nephi had to maintain his ship while en route to the land of promise. It is also probable that during the great storm in which his ship nearly sank, the vessel was damaged (1 Nephi 18:13–15). It would be almost certain or expected that Nephi beached his vessel once or twice for repairs; but as for shipbuilding yards, there were none. Thus, he needed to carry with him all the tools and supplies necessary to maintain the ship, its riggings, and its sails.

En route to China, Severin purchased many supplies along the way. Still, he took aboard many maintenance supplies, enough to maintain an early medieval ship at sea for eight months. He writes:

> The ship rapidly began to fill up with hundreds of items necessary for a sea voyage that would last seven or eight months. The forepeak was stuffed with bosun's stores—coil upon coil of rope of every size, from bundles of light lashing twine to 8-inch-thick halyards. There were dozens of extra blocks, each one lovingly carved out of a single chunk of wood and with their wooden wheels revolving on wooden pins. . . . There were spare sacks of lime for the day when we careened the ship in a foreign port and smeared on a new coat of the traditional antifouling. There were tins of mutton fat, rank and nauseating, to mix with the lime or to grease the running ropes and tackle. There were marlin spikes and mallets, chest of carpenter's tools, odd lengths of spare timber, bolts of spare sailcloth, . . . spare ox hide, and the needle thread to sew chafing patches.[47]

There would have had to have been enough extra cordage to rerig the running rigging and the fixed rigging two times over to be self sustaining for 180 days. This would also include two additional sets of sails or the equivalent in canvas.

The fact that Nephi's ship was new does not mitigate the need for repairs and maintenance. Severin's ship had only sailed for a few weeks, yet it needed repairs before it reached its first stop on the west coast of India.[48] Severin describes what happens to new wooden ships, "If *Sohar* had been a new car, she was now due for her all-important 1000-mile servicing."[49] Included in these repairs was a new coat of antifouling compound, which if not maintained would allow the destructive teredo worms to eat through the hull.[50] To maintain Columbus's fleet of three ships, the famous admiral had three full-time specialists aboard his ships, a carpenter, a cooper, and a caulker, as well as all the materials the craftsmen needed to maintain the ships.[51]

The pounding pressures of the sea constantly wear at even a modern sailing vessel. Place yourself in the middle of a vast ocean, knowing that your ship is slowly weakening and falling apart. Two reports we received from Jody Lemmon aboard the

Banyan en route from California to New Zealand explains why it is important even today to have the skills and parts to repair a ship during its voyage. Nephi, of course, didn't have the luxury of shipyards where he could shop, purchase parts, and acquire skilled repairmen. All of Jody's reports are as he wrote them—casual and informal in style and in punctuation and so forth.

Sohar under sail.

May 27, 2009

Hey Mom and Dad,

It is rough out here. Today the entire rail of the boat was under water practically all day. Twice it was so bad that water poured over the decks and of course my cabin window was open. Whole buckets of water came pouring onto my bed. It is a really novel experience to be thrown violently against your bedroom wall and then looking up to see, as if in slow motion, a wall of cold Pacific blue come streaming down on you like a waterfall. I changed my bed sheets once and then closed all but one little hatch. Just now, as darkness was falling it happened again, but much worse, the whole cockpit filled with water and again poured into my small hatch—drowning myself and my bed once again. I am now into my spare sheets, which have been kept safe and dry in a plastic bag. It's amazing how nice clean sheets can be. I must guard these with a vigilance I have never before practiced and form a complete and stubborn resolve to keep them safe from the creeping fingers of the sea. For, if I get these wet I will be in a most desperate situation for sure.

Besides that we almost lost the starboard surfboards today. They ripped off when the rail became submerged. We barely caught them and after dragging them back on board we lashed them securely to the deck. The waves are now a bit bigger than they have been, 3 ft or so. They look quite menacing as they race down upon us. A huge pod of small dolphins were about a 1/4 of a mile off the bow today, apparently hunting, as they paid no attention to our rag tag approach. Besides that we haven't seen any wildlife, except of course the multitude of flying fish and squid that we are constantly attempting to fling back in to the sea before they expire on our decks. The Southern Cross can be plainly seen now at night and it is a nice thing to wonder at.

Yesterday during my deck checking I noticed a washer lying on the upper decks. That was not a nice thing to find. Upon an investigation I found the source. The gooseneck bolt holding the main boom to the mast had come undone—a very scary situation. I was able to find the nut, luckily, and as night was falling we located our wrenches and put the assembly back together. It's amazing how the noticing of small things like a bolt coming loose can prevent a very unfortunate chain of events. "It's in the details, my dear Watson."

love, Jody

180 miles at 7.1 mph in 25.5 hours
SPOT Check OK. Banyan checking in.
ESN:0-7458317
Latitude:-6.1421
Longitude:-108.929
Nearest Location: not known
Distance: not known
Time:05/27/2009 09:25:21 (US/Pacific)

Oct.13, 2009—Sheered-off bolt

Hey, guys. We are in a little harbor on Savaii (Samoa). I'm afraid I have more drama for everyone. Last evening, after we looked at the charts and our guidebook, we decided to move into a little bay on Savaii. We even saw a sailboat anchored deep inside so we assumed that if all three pieces of info said it was okay to go in we should go in—right? As we pulled in to the channel leading into the lagoon the water started to get shallow—very quickly! We hit bottom. We were stuck solid on a shallow sand bar with rock and reef strewn all about. The boat immediately started lurching back and fourth. I thought for sure we would be another shipwreck, just like a trawler that was high and dry on the reef 500 yards away. We all basically freaked out and began yelling at each other. That didn't work so we launched the dingy with all the anchor chain and anchor, and Matt got into position about 100 feet out to throw the anchor overboard. Our plan was to use the anchor as a winch and drag ourselves off the sand bar. The bottom of the boat was now grinding herself on the reef and the incoming tide and winds were pushing us into shallower and shallower water. I tried to put the boat in forward and all we did was grind more.

We basically gave up hope at this point, Matt was not making much headway due to the drag of the anchor chain and he was vainly trying to motor the dingy back out into deeper water. After about 20 minutes of this we got a break—big time. The current somehow pushed us into a slightly deeper spot so I cranked the wheel and we were able to motor out with about 1 inch of water under the keel. We motored and grinded our way back out and

somehow made it to deeper water. We were almost there when the anchor chain caught on a coral head. We were then jerked backwards and began to be sucked back into the shallows again. We all yelled at Matt to pull up the anchor chain as fast as he could. Mike meanwhile was on the bow pulling in the chain with the anchor windless and looking out for coral heads. Somehow Matt used super human strength and was able to unlodge the chain. We then motored out of the death trap with Matt in the dingy with 300 feet of rusty chain.

By this time it was nearly dark. We were worried about the hull, but after inspection we realized she wasn't taking on water so we set our sails and simply sailed away from land. We spent the night in 20-knot winds and tacked out 25 miles until 4 am. The night wore on and on and our frazzled nerves didn't help. As the winds came up at around midnight we had to douse our salvaged and delicate head sail for our cutter sail, which dropped our speed to 3 knots.

Other cruisers we had spoken to said the charts were off for this place. They are all based on 100-year-old German surveys done when they controlled this area. We spent the whole morning trying to figure out where a good anchorage was. After motoring back and fourth along a 5-mile stretch and looking at tourist maps with pictures of hotels on the beach we finally figure it out.

Once we dropped the anchor it was time to see what kind of damage was done. I quickly realized that the same problem that had happened to our rudder in the Marqueses had happed again. The bolt that replaced our bent chuck key snapped and the rudder was

no longer aligned. The steering quadrant was out of place and needed to be taken apart. The keel and rudder sustained minor scrapes and dings but nothing major.

After we got out of the water it was time to go into our tiny, hot, little death hole where we access the rudder and steering quadrant. We dismantled the apparatus and realized that yes the bolt was sheered off. I was able to push the bolt through with the broken piece once we had separated the quadrant apart. Then we needed to find another bolt. This took some time and we finally found one, our last one on the boat. The threads matched but the bolt was only threaded half way; the other half was smooth metal. The smooth metal part was slightly bigger than the threads, so when I tried to tighten down the bolt it wouldn't go in far enough to reach the shaft. I realized I had to use the grinder to make the smooth part smaller, meanwhile being extremely careful not to drop the bolt into the ocean. Well, after going back and forth for a while we were able to get it all back together. The new system is actually not bad, because the bolt breaks first and actually acts like a sacrificial piece that snaps before something else more important breaks. The only issue now is that we are down to our last bolt!

The good news is that we are back in action and in a nice harbor. We will take a break here and wait for a weather window to head to Tonga.

Hey dad when you get a chance could you give us a forecast between Samoa and Tonga. We are all okay, just slightly shaken up!

Love, Jody

4. EXTRA SAILS AND RIGGING

We can be assured that Nephi's ship needed several sets of sails, and so she needed a large space to hold the extra sails. Sailing ships carried one suit of sails for night and bad weather and others for day and fair weather. The wrong sail in the wrong wind conditions can lead to a ship being capsized. The main sail on Severin's medieval ship required three thousand square feet of canvas.[52] During one stormy day in the China Sea, his ship had five sails "ripped to shreds."[53]

5. TENTS

Nephi's family took tents with them to the land of promise (1 Nephi 18:23). Traditional Middle Eastern goat and camel hair tents are heavy and consume a large space when folded up. Nephi's ship carried at least eight married couples. A folded 10′ x 10′ goat hair tent measures 3′ x 3′ x 6.5′ or 58.5 cubic feet. Multiply that by eight families and the tents form a stack 13 feet long, 6 feet wide and 6 feet tall, not counting floor rugs, bedding, and a least a ton of tent poles and stakes.

6. ANCHORS, WEAPONS, PLATES, AND OTHER ITEMS

Resting the ship required heavy anchors. Ancient anchors were made from stone, and ships carried many anchors, usually at least five, which could be of considerable size; this was so even on small ships.[54] Fragments of stone anchors have been found in two pottery scatters at Sumhurum.[55] The heaviest anchor recovered in Omani waters was found during the 1997 Expedition and it was nearly 3 meters (10 feet) long and weighed 1.3 tons (2,860 lbs).[56] Severin's ship carried four anchors.

What other items did the ship need? We suspect that they would have taken one sword for each man in the party. To this day, pirates plague the waters off the Malacca Strait. We know that at least one sword was on board; that of Laban. We assume that Nephi took his bow and arrow and some form of tackle or netting for catching fish. A sand pit for cooking, pots, and other kitchen items seem part of the story, along

Stone anchors at Maritime Museum Salalah, Oman.

with a large store of charcoal or firewood, as well as flint. Finally, we know the ship carried the brass plates.

7. Large Enough to Survive Large Storms

Another reason Nephi's ship likely was quite large is that it had to withstand great storms. If Nephi traveled east toward the Pacific, the winds that carried his ship in that direction are strong. Alan Villiers sailed in large wooden sailing ships off Oman. His research was based on first-hand experience. He wrote of the summer monsoon, "The weather is unusually so bad that the exposed ports on the Indian coast are closed and the smaller trading vessels take shelter."[57]

Severin noted that four of his eight Omani crew members had been shipwrecked during their careers at sea.[58] Nephi reported his ship being out of control and driven back four days in a "terrible tempest" that became "exceedingly sore" (1 Nephi 18:13–15).

Nephi's Ship

The idea that a small ship or overcrowded large raft made from local softwoods and carrying tons of provisions could stay

George aboard a 74-foot Arab dhow, shipyard in Bahrain.

afloat during the four-day storm that Nephi described is naïve in the extreme. The question remains, how large of a ship did Nephi require to make the passage to the New World? To answer this question, we turned to Chief Engineer Frank Linehan, our hull expert. He calculates that it would be a stout vessel of at least 100 to 120 feet in the length, but could have been as small as 80 feet with a wide beam, high freeboard or bulwarks, and light tonnage of no less than 300 tons. The

length of Nephi's voyage required that his vessel be a type of cargo ship. Indeed, his ship was a significant ship and required a long list of resources to build and sail. A possible design of Nephi's ship will be discussed in detail in the next chapter.

1. Materials needed to build an ocean-going ship

The building of Nephi's ship was an enormous undertaking that likely spanned years and required massive quantities of very

37

specific natural resources. Nephi's voyage to the New World would have taken many months and any feasible route would have covered over 15,000 miles of the roughest water on earth. About 150 years before Nephi built his ship, King Jehoshaphat, King of Judah, built a fleet of ships designed to sail to Tharshish in the Indian Ocean, "ships of Tharshish to go to Ophir for gold" (1 Kings 22:48). According to Princeton University historian Raphael Patai, these ships never sailed from the port they were constructed in but "were broken" apart at Ezion-geber (see 2 Chronicles 20:36–37). Patai suggests that this was "either due to a storm or simply because they were inexpertly constructed."[59] Nephi's ship had to endure at least one major storm that lasted for four days (1 Nephi 18:13–15). Clearly, Nephi's ship must have been crafted as well as any of its day and certainly it must have been constructed to a higher standard and from better materials than the fleet that Jehoshaphat's shipwrights built for it to have survived such a journey.

Ore

After the Lord told Nephi "Get thee into the mountain" (1 Nephi 17:7), Nephi noted that he needed a source of ore from which to make tools for constructing the ship

George finds ore deposits in wash near Khor Rori.

(1 Nephi 17:9). Subsequently, the Lord showed him where to find ore. Researchers from BYU have discovered small quantities of iron ore in Dhofar, their "most exciting and significant discovery" being found only six miles east of Khor Rori at the foot of Jabal Samhan, the largest mountain in

Dhofar, known in the Old Testament as mount Sephar (Genesis 10:30).[60] Though small, these local deposits were obviously of sufficient size to produce enough ore for metal production because iron and copper slag have been found from remains of a smelting furnace that once operated in the ruins of Sumhuram at Khor Rori.[61] Nephi noted that once in the New World, he "did teach my people to build buildings, and to work in all manner of wood, and of iron, and of copper, and of brass, and of steel, and of gold, and of silver, and of precious ores" (2 Nephi 5:15). William R. Phillips of Brigham Young University has suggested that Nephi's skills in metallurgy "may have been learned from the local smiths of Dhofar or from the Indian traders that passed through nearby trading ports."[62] Recently excavated artifacts at the Khor Rori Sumhuram ruins include iron axes, iron nails, an iron knife, an iron razor, and iron smelting slag, as well as bronze nails, a bronze bell, and a small bronze plaque.[63] We were informed by local Dhofar historian Ali Al-Shahri that during the first excavation of Sumhuram in the early 1950s, the American archaeologist Wendell Phillips discovered seven bronze plates engraved with text. Four of the metal plates had thamudic script etched on them, while the three remaining plates were written in the yet-to-be-deciphered south Arabian "Shahri"[64] language.[65]

Frank Linehan considers the discovery of iron nails at Khor Rori significant because the Lord directed Nephi to build a ship not after the manner that men were building in his day, but declared, *Thou shalt construct a ship, after the manner which I shall show thee, that I may carry thy people across these waters* (1 Nephi 17:8). Linehan points out that ships being constructed in Oman in the sixth century BC lacked the structural strength to cross the Pacific. The hulls of Omani ships of that day were tied together with rope, thus the name "sewn ships." Over time, the pounding of the waves would weaken the ropes and the ships literally fell apart. After enduring a four-day "terrible tempest" that nearly sank Nephi's ship (1 Nephi 18:13–15), we know his ship was still strong enough to successfully cross the mighty and powerful Pacific. Linehan is convinced the Lord intervened and instructed Nephi to use nails or wooden pegs or both to strengthen his ship. Otherwise, the family would have been doomed. In fact, Frank believes the scriptures hint that Nephi used nails to increase the ship's structural strength and that this was one of the features that the Lord showed Nephi that would make his ship different from the way other men were building ships at Khor Rori. The Lord said, "That I may carry thy people across these waters." Furthermore, as soon as the Lord showed Nephi how to build the ship, Nephi immediately asked the Lord, "Whither shall I go that I may find ore to molten, that I may make tools [nails] to construct the ship after the manner which thou hast shown unto me?" (1 Nephi 17:9).

In today's American English usage we seldom refer to "nails" as "tools." However, in Noah Webster's 1828 *American Dictionary of the English Language* a "tool" is defined as any "instrument," and says of a nail: "to be driven into a board or other piece of timber, and serving to fasten it to other timbers. The larger kinds [as would be required in ship-building] of 'instruments' of this sort are called *spikes*."[66]

Timber

Nephi needed hardwood to build a ship strong enough to survive an ocean crossing. The assumption is usually made that Nephi used trees that grew in Bountiful to build his ship. This overlooks one major problem—nearly all of the woods native to Dhofar in southern Oman are permeable softwoods and could not be used for shipbuilding.[67] The hardwoods that are found in Oman are short, gnarly, and unsuitable for the fabrication of the massive structural components of a large sailing vessel

Ships hulls need to be braced and enforced by long straight hardwoods. Illustration by Jose Flores.

39

Reinforced 6" x 17" cross beams illustrate the type of timbers needed to build a sailing ship.

as Nephi needed. Historically, hardwoods had to be imported into Arabia for shipbuilding. The first records of timber being imported into the Persian Gulf region from foreign lands date to an inscription of Ur-Nanshe, King of Lagash in Sumer in about 2500 BC.[68] Hardwood, or an impermeable softwood, was an absolute requirement for the building of a seaworthy ship. Indian archaeologist Ratnagar points out that "In the historic period, most Indian boats were made of teak. Even Arab craft were made on the west coast of India, due to the availability of wood."[69] Regarding the source of wood for ships built in Oman, Tom Vosmer, Director of the Traditional Boats of Oman Project, noted, "Most, if not all, planking timber had to be imported; teak (*Tectona grandis*), venteak (*Lythracea lanceolata*), mango (*Mangifera indica*), as did spar timber."[70] Famed maritime archaeologist Tim Severin noted, "The timber for building Omani ships is brought nearly 1300 miles from the Malabar coast of India. It is a trade which goes as far back as the earliest records, because Oman lacks trees large enough to provide first-class boat timber."[71]

The softwoods that grow in Dhofar never would have been strong enough to survive long at sea. Hardwoods are used not only for their strength but also for their longevity. The wood used for a boat is subject to many dangers, particularly marine borers that attack the boat and decompose it very rapidly. Some species of tropical shipworms

10" x 9" log forms keel and bow timbers of an Arab dhow.

grow to six feet in length and attain the thickness of a man's arm.[72] If the reader has not sailed in the open seas aboard a wooden ship, it is hard to understand the relentless pressures the waves displace upon the planks and the absolute necessity to have a strong hull. Conrad Dickson recalls that one summer while fishing as a master's mate off the Washington coast, his fishing boat experienced a series of summer storms, one of which came very close to sinking the vessel as result of sprung planks causing a tremendous amount of sea water to flood the inner hull and engine room. As the boat was literally falling apart, Conrad steered the vessel behind the rocks at Cape Elisabeth near a very dangerous lee shore into calmer water, enabling the crew to use all the pumps to get ahead of the leakage. After the storm abated, the vessel limped into La Push for hauling to make repairs. Prior to landing, Conrad had not been sure the boat would make it back in harbor, for many times while entering West Port or La Push harbor to off-load fish, this vessel would literally surf like a surfboard upon the breaking waves.

In order to carry all of the provisions needed for a long trans-oceanic journey, Nephi would have needed a ship that was large by the standards of the day. Let us recall that maritime archaeologist Tim Severin built an eighty-foot long replica wooden medieval Omani ship, the *Sohar*, that he sailed from Oman to China. Granted that his ship was a medieval replica, still, his basic needs would have been similar to Nephi's because wooden ships changed little in design until the sixteenth century.[73] While Severin's vessel was probably not identical in size to Nephi's, the list of materials Severin needed to build his ship is

Ideal trees for shipbuilding, teak trees in India.

Straight timbers used to support ribs of the hull. Ribs are 5 inches thick.

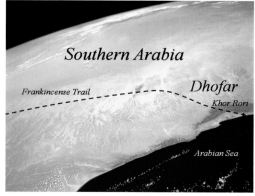

Map of Southern Arabia, Empty Quarter above Frankincense Trail.

useful because it gives us a general idea of the magnitude of the amount of materials Nephi would have needed to construct his ship.

Severin had to find a tree suitable for the eighty-one-foot main spar and a sixty-five-foot log that was to be tapered into the mast.[74] He wrote that a ship's keel "is long, straight and massive; it is the very backbone of the vessel . . . the piece to my replica needed to be 52 feet long, 12 inches by 15 inches in cross section, and dead straight."[75] Severin imported the timber for his Arab ship from India because Oman historically lacked "suitable timber for large boat building."[76]

If good shipbuilding timber never grew in Oman, then Nephi must have used, like the Arab shipwrights, imported materials from India and the islands thereabout. The Omani Ministry of National Heritage and Culture notes this of Omani shipbuilding: "Teak and coconut wood were used exclusively for building hulls. Teak had to be imported from India. . . . Indeed, the virtues of the wood would have been known in the Gulf from the earliest sea voyages to the Indus in the third millennium BC." The Omani Ministry adds, "Coconut wood also had to be imported—mainly from the Maldives and Laccadive Islands from where it is possible that the coconut tree spread to Dhofar in the Middle Ages."[77] Recent discoveries in Egypt confirm that

Indian teak wood was used for construction of ancient ships that sailed the Indian Ocean.[78]

But would this timber imported from India have been available to Nephi at Khor Rori in the sixth century BC? The Omani Ministry of National Heritage and Culture says that Dhofar "grew from obscure beginnings before 1,000 BC . . . Its growth was the major stimulus to the reopening and expansion of Indian Ocean maritime routes."[79] German maritime archaeologist Dr. Norbert Weismann, who specializes in Oman, writes of Dhofar, "Certainly it was involved in the traffic to India in Greco-Roman times, but there was trade with white India much earlier."[80] Nephi's text alludes to the fact that the timber they were working had already been cut somewhere else. He wrote, "We did work timbers of curious workmanship" (1 Nephi 18:1). How could the timbers have been curious to Nephi and his workers if they had logged and cut the lumber themselves? Apparently, some of the timbers Nephi used to construct his ship were precut in an unfamiliar manner or a manner that he would modify. We suggest this because we know that hardwoods were being imported into the Arabian Gulf since the third millennium BC and that a

few centuries after the time of Christ their export from India in the form of precut beams and rafters was a common practice.[81]

Solomon had a navy of Tarshish (see "Tarshish" in the LDS Bible Dictionary: "the name came to . . . denote ships of the largest size, suitable for long voyages") bringing gold, and silver, ivory, and apes and peacocks from Ophir (1 Kings 10:11, 22). It is often suggested that Tarshish was

a port on the Indian Ocean and it has been put forward that Ophir is synonymous with modern Dhofar.[82] Local historian Ali Al-Shahri is a member of the Shahri tribe and can trace his genealogical records to the man Ophir! His family owns the land surrounding the harbor of Khor Rori and claims that Khor Rori is the Biblical port of Ophir.[83] The three-year-long voyage of Solomon's ships of Tarshish returned with peacocks, which are found in India (but not Africa).[84] These ships must have

Riggings on traditional Arab dhow. Illustration by Jose Flores.

been to India or traded with merchants from India who would have been found at Indian Ocean ports like Khor Rori. The ships of Tarshish also returned carrying Almug wood, a hardwood that was used in the construction of the temple and was presumably not native to Dhofar but imported from India.[85] It should be noted that "Almug" appears in the plural form, which Biblical scholars have taken to mean that the wood was delivered in planks.[86]

Rope (Lines)

Of course, Nephi needed much more than just timbers to build his ship. A quotation attributed to Rabbi Shim'on ben Laqish, a second century AD Palestinian sage, said, "A flesh and blood (i.e. mortal man), if he wants to build a ship, first he brings beams, then he brings ropes, then he brings anchors, then he places in it seamen."[87] The importance of ropes cannot be overemphasized. According to Raphael Patai, the Biblical name for a ship's captain was *rabh hahobhel* or "master roper" (Jon. 1:6).[88] Historically, the planks of ships built in Oman were sewn together with rope. It took 50,000 coconuts to make the 400 miles of lines Severin needed to build his sewn ship, the *Sohar*.[89] Even if Nephi had used nails, he still required rope for riggings and anchor lines. Coconuts are not native to Dhofar, and if Nephi made ropes from coconut, these also had to be imported. Otherwise, he needed a port where he could have purchased rope made from imported coconuts.

This still leaves another question to be answered. Without people, like those in Dhofar who possessed the skill of making lines from coconuts, how would Nephi have known how to make rope from the husk of the coconut? The processes of making this cordage required at least six steps:

"1) Husk mature dry coconuts and break into 8–10 sections, then remove the shorter fibers next to the outer shell of the husk and discard. 2) Soak sections for 2 weeks, or until they are easy to work. Soaking fibers in running water helps in the process. . . . 3) Remove sections—work sections by twisting or use table edge and press sections over the edge and discard outer skin. 4) Beat each section with a wooden mallet. Use a piece of hardwood or a flat stone for an anvil. 5) Start beating. Beat sections starting from the center and working to the edge. Turn sections around and start process to remove extraneous matter. 6) Rinse to separate "chaff" from fibers. Shaking the bundle helps to remove the "chaff." Tools like a strong comb help you remove extraneous material. Wash the rope to clean away the loose fibers. Tie each section around the middle."[90]

Those are the steps required just to make the cordage. Nephi still would have needed someone to show him how to make it into strong rope.

Fabric for Sails

As noted earlier, oceangoing sailing ships require several sets of sails. Night sailing require different sails, while storms require smaller sails than for light winds. Besides being smaller, storm sails are constructed dramatically stronger so they do not blow out in heavy airs. Sails made from traditional materials also stretch and need to be replaced. Severin had to replace the sails on the *Sohar*.[91] His replacement sails required two and a half tons of canvas. One sail alone measured three thousand square feet.[92] Traditionally, the sails on Arab ships were woven from coconut or palm leaves, or made from cotton cloth.[93] Cotton would have been available either as a locally grown product or imported from India or Egypt: "Fine linen with broidered work from Egypt was that which thou spreadest forth to be thy sail" (Ezekiel 27:7). According to the *Periplus of the Erythraean Sea*,[94] cloth was one of the products the inhabitants of Dhofar imported in return for their frankincense.[95] Ibn al-Mujawir wrote in AD 1221 that caravans bought fabrics from Baghdad to Dhofar.[96] As noted earlier, cotton was introduced in southern Arabia in antiquity, possibly as early as 4000 BC.[97]

Shipwrights

The Book of Mormon makes two things quite clear about the construction of Nephi's ship. First, when Nephi arrived in Bountiful, he did not know how to build a ship (1 Nephi 17:18–19). Second, the Lord instructed Nephi from time to time in the construction of the ship (1 Nephi 17:51). What is unclear for us is what the Lord told Nephi. Was it in how to modify a ship to make it strong enough to reach the New World (1 Nephi 17:8; 18:2)? Or did the Lord provide specific instructions on how to make a ship, including where to find skilled shipbuilding master craftsmen who could help Nephi? Certainly, one man could not have constructed by himself a ship of the size Nephi needed. The timbers required are far too heavy to lift or hold in place during construction by just one man. At the same time, the Book of Mormon

hints that Nephi's brothers may not have continually helped him. While he wrote that his brothers repented and helped him work timbers (1 Nephi 18:1), Nephi did not give them credit for actually building the ship ("neither did I [not we] build the ship after the manner of men" (1 Nephi 18:2). Further, he wrote that "after I had finished the ship . . . my brethren beheld that it was good, and that the workmanship thereof was exceedingly fine" (1 Nephi 18:4). This passage may suggest that Nephi constructed much of his ship away from the sight of his brothers, and only when they finally beheld the finished ship did they see that it was of excellent workmanship.

If his brothers were not always helping Nephi create a ship of such fine workmanship, then who was assisting him? Even if his brothers did periodically assist, the skills needed to do all the work surely exceeded what Nephi's untrained brothers could offer. Who, then, could be of

Becoming a master shipbuilder takes many years.

skilled assistance? The logical conclusion is that Nephi had the assistance of shipwrights at the frankincense harbor of Khor Rori. If so, why didn't Nephi mention that he received help in constructing the ship? First, we don't know what was written in Lehi's record that Joseph Smith put aside after the loss of the 116 pages. Second, as noted earlier, the literary form of Nephi's day was to only write about the principal men in the story. Thus, Nephi's account would not have mentioned hired laborers, servants, or women.

Though desolate today, in antiquity Khor Rori was a principal market place. In 2000,

Rock art copied near Khor Rori by Ali Al-Shahri.

the World Heritage Committee of the United Nations Educational, Scientific and Cultural Organization (UNESCO) designated Khor Rori as a World Heritage site, noting its trade in frankincense as "one of the most important trading activities of the ancient and medieval world."[98] Shipwrights of Magan, in northern Oman, are mentioned in a text from the Sumerian city of Lagash of about 2000 BC.[99] Dhofar also would appear to have its own tradition of shipbuilding. Several kinds of ancient ships are depicted in rock art drawings found in caves in sight of Khor Rori (just two and a half miles from the harbor).[100] The stick figure representations

of humans in the Dhofar ships give the drawings a rough dating of 1000 BC.[101] According to Muhammed Abdul Nayeem, professor of archeology and muselogy at King Saud University, the rock art drawings of ships in Dhofar "are different from the presentations in northern Oman."[102] The implication is that the unique style of ships depicted on the rocks near Khor Rori means that the ancients who lived there built ships and did so in their own style. The rock art seems to confirm that Khor Rori had active shipbuilders long before Nephi's arrival. The Omani Ministry of National Heritage and Culture states that shipbuilding at Dhofar may go back into great antiquity.[103]

Severin had great respect for the shipwrights who built his replica of Sindbad's ship. His commendations also point out the advanced carpentering skills required to build a sailing ship, talents one would not expect Nephi, the son of a wealthy land owner, to have known without a master shipbuilder instructing him. Severin writes:

> Their tools were hammer and chisel. Whether cutting a foot-thick lump of timber to size, or shaping the finest sliver of wood for a delicate joint, 90 percent of

the green shirts' [his shipwrights] work was done with hammer and chisel; only very reluctantly did they pick up a saw or a plane. The soft iron chisel was their tool, and with it they could work wonders. They could carve a plank into delicate curves, or they could shape the 60-foot spar into a taper as if it had been turned on a giant lathe. They were craftsmen whose original caste in India had been carpenters. Their fathers, grandfathers

Traditional shipwright applying caulking to hull of wooden dhow in Bahrain.

46

Traditional shipwright in Bahrain uses chisel and hammer to seal planks with oil-soaked cotton line.

and great-great grandfathers, and untold generations before that, had been carpenters. There had never been any question as children but that they would also become carpenters; and they had begun work as soon as they were big enough to pick up a mallet. Now, as grown men, they performed like well-oiled machines. . . .

The accuracy expected of the carpenters was extraordinary. . . . So the hull of the new ship had to be made a perfect shell before it was ever put into the water. This meant placing planks edge to edge, without even a hairline crack, along a length of as much as 80 feet. It was an achievement which some European engineers who came to visit the worksite considered virtually impossible, and which would have been prohibitively expensive in a European boatyard because it required the most minute attention to detail. . . . A visiting engineer calculated that this work demanded an accuracy of better then 1/64 inch along the full length of the plank.[104]

If Nephi did not learn how to build a ship from experienced shipwrights, how would he have known how to protect his workmanship once it sat in the ocean or how to recoat the ship with more antifouling compound during its journey to the promised land? The hull of Severin's new ship needed a fresh coat of antifouling compound after its short passage to India.

Workers applying antifouling compound.

He writes: "The muck came off easily, because the old lime and fat coat peeled away and took the fouling with it. The timber underneath seemed sound. But the panels of unprotected wood, which we had attached to the hull as an experiment, were honeycombed with wormholes as thick as a large knitting needle, for they had been ravaged by worms in the two months since they had been up in place. The worse panels, slabs of wood 2½ inches thick, could be snapped with one's bare hands like wafers. It was a sharp lesson in the importance of protecting *Sohar's* hull from teredo [worms]."[105] In other words, if no one taught Nephi how to make an antifouling compound or how to apply it or when to reapply it or how to dry dock his ship on poles or careen it in order to reapply the compound during the voyage, his ship would have fallen apart at sea.

Adze, ancient tool still used to shape timbers in Omani shipyards.

47

Dhow at low tide in Bahrain harbor.

George and friends examine remains of 1 of the 8 ancient shipbuilding "ways" at Khor Rori.

When Severin recoated the *Sohar*, his crew careened her by unloading all the provisions and ballast and then tipped her to one side and then to the other as the tides changed. He writes: "*Sohar* was now light enough to be careened. Leaving a guard on the pile of stores on the quayside, we towed her across to a sandbar on the opposite bank of the river. At high tide we put her ashore, rigged block and tackled to her masthead, and on the falling tide laid over on one side so we could clean the hull."[106]

While we suggest that the things Nephi needed to build his ship were available at the time at Khor Rori, one could ask how Nephi could have afforded the imported goods. Actually, there would have been a number of funding options: selling their camels, exchanging Lehi's services as a scribe and merchant, or perhaps even arranging to have Lehi's property sold in Jerusalem.

2. A protected harbor for building, launching, and mooring a large ship

It is likely that Nephi's ship would have been of such a size and weight that it could only have been built in a crib on "ways" (wooden rollers) above the tide line and then rolled down into the water. Once moored in sheltered waters, the construction could continue, adding the weight of outfitting, riggings, and tons of ballast and provision. The picture above shows George and friends inspecting remains of ancient shipbuilding "ways" at Khor Rori.

From time immemorial, large hulls have been launched from harbors, and Nephi's text implies that his ship was no exception. The coastline of Dhofar is known for its heavy surf and is made up of rocky cliffs alternating with sandy beaches. Launching a hull weighing at least 200 tons and which has no means of power or control from a shallow beach into breaking surf with strong currents is physically impossible and would only result in shipwreck. S. B. Miles commented that, "Owing to

Huge surf common along shoreline of Dhofar, southern Arabia.

Ship under repair on "way" in Bahrain bay.

the violent surf which breaks on the coast for a great part of the year, vessels touching at Dhofar are in great need of shelter and security, but protection could be well provided in the creeks near Thaka [Taqah two miles from Khor Rori] at that time before the bars were formed."[107] Yet Nephi's text implies a calm, orderly, and seemingly routine embarkation where party members all boarded the ship before they "did put forth into the sea" (1 Nephi 18:8). There is only one way that everyone could be on board ship and then "put forth into the sea"—they had to be moored in a deep, calm harbor.

When Nephi's wooden ship set forth into the sea, it could not have been the first time the ship was in the water. The reason for this is that a ship must be placed in water earlier in order for the hull to be tightened. Patai noted that both Hebrew and Egyptian shipbuilders used this technique: "Under the influence of the water the planks of the ship's hull swelled at the seams, and every seam, split, or crack became tightly closed."[108] After Nephi was sure the hull was watertight, he could then load the tons of ballast into the ship and perform sea trials to make sure the ballast was of the correct weight and position for the sails. Only when all these things

were done could he load the provisions on board and set forth into the ocean. Nephi not only needed a harbor, he needed a large one where the preliminary trials could take place. Khor Rori is essentially the only harbor in Dhofar that is large enough and deep enough to allow this.[109]

While there is no written archaeological evidence dating the use of the port to 600 BC, there is evidence that the port was in use during the Iron Age, the time when Nephi was there. Dr. Jana Owen of UCLA, director of "The Transarabia Coastal Survey" that in 1995 made a study of the ancient ports of Dhofar, wrote, "We know about the Hadrami invasion but I believe that it [Khor Rori] would have been used previous to that

One ship on "way," another moored in water.

invasion. Again, around the settlement we have surveyed a good deal of Iron Age lithics, this is prior to the work that is now being done by the Italians from Pisa.[110] We also did a dive survey of the lagoon and there is evidence of modification on the northeastern edge of the lagoon and obviously the size is indicative of large ship docking. Doesn't it make sense that they didn't wait until the turn of the Common Era to figure this out?"[111] Peter Vine is also of the opinion that the port of Sumhuram was in use prior to the time of the Hadramauti expansion, which took place about the time of Christ: "It is clear that a substantial settlement existed at the site long before King Iliazzyalit instructed the builders to construct a city there."[112] Saeed Al-Mashori, the Omani Supervisor of Excavations at Khor Rori, showed us eight clearly defined "way-ramps" where large ships were launched into and retrieved from Khor Rori. The ramps are located just south of the Sumhuram fortress and included moorings where large ships were finished and loaded.[113]

Are there any other nearby inlets that Nephi could have used to build his ship? There are a number of other inlets in Dhofar, all of which are much smaller than Khor Rori. We studied each of these inlets to determine if they were year-round protected harbors in Nephi's day, if they were large enough to accommodate ocean-going ships, and if these inlets would have had the resources Nephi needed to build a ship in the beginning of the sixth century BC. In all, we visited nine inlets besides Khor Rori.[114] Most of the inlets were too small for large ships to enter. There is only evidence that three of them were used in the past.

The most westerly of these is Raysut, situated some six miles west of the modern town of Salalah. Jana Owen wrote of Raysut, "We believe from surface collection and the obvious suitability of the area that there would have been an ancient docking area there." The harbor at Raysut

Protected waters of Khor Rori.

faces east and provided protection from the southwest monsoon, which blows in summer, but provided no protection from the winter northeast monsoon. While Raysut provides anchorage, it would not have provided year-round protection for the vessel that Nephi was building.

The second site is Khor al Balid in the modern town of Salalah that the Hiltons suggested as the place Nephi called Bountiful.[115] A sandbar now closes off the Khor. It was the only other inlet to provide year-round protection (necessary for the building of the ship that would have taken longer than the period between the monsoon seasons) and be wide and deep enough to build and launch a large vessel. But there is no evidence that this harbor was used in Nephi's time. The Khor was associated with a city of the same name that was built around the tenth century AD by Persian conquerors who moved the capital to al Balid from Khor Rori, some fifteen miles (25 km) to the east.[116] Ibn Batuta mentioned that the port was thriving in AD 1329. It would appear that the harbor was in use only much later than Lehi's time. Owens says, "We believe that this harbor functioned around the turn of the Common Era.

This is based on lithics and a small amount of ceramics.[117]

The third inlet is Khor Suli which was judged to have been an "Adite port, close to their city of Ain Humran"[118] but it is very narrow and has barely the width to allow a ship to turn around on its axis, let alone allow any sea trials.

Khor Kharfot (Wadi Sayq) also has been suggested as the location of Nephi's harbor,[119] and for that reason we note it here. It is an isolated inlet sixty-six miles west of Salalah, forty miles from the nearest known ore deposits, and a seventy-mile journey over mountains from the ancient port where Nephi would have found ship-building timber, cotton, rope fiber, and other necessary resources. Nephi would have needed to haul all of these heavy imported goods to Khor Kharfot in order to build his ship. Khor Kharfot is presently closed off by a sandbar. There is no documented evidence that the Khor was open to the sea in Nephi's time, but if it were, it is very narrow and the floor is strewn with huge boulders that would have posed considerable risk to anything other than small, shallow draft vessels attempting to use it. For these and other reasons, we do not consider it a candidate for Bountiful.

3. Seamanship skills needed to sail a large ship

The last element Rabbi Shim'on ben Laqish listed for the building of a ship was the "seamen." Nephi needed a crew, and he needed to acquire the skills to train them. It takes years to learn and practice skills needed to control a sailing vessel at sea. A large Omani sailing dhow (ship) required a crew of between 25–40 trained seamen.[120] Frank, an experienced transoceanic sailboat skipper, notes, "Even with the inspiration of the Lord, it was simply impossible for Nephi to have sailed to the New World without training."[121] Historian Maurizio Tosi writes of the ancient Arabian captains: "For the first navigators it was like venturing into outer space, and only a body of accumulated experience, strengthened by tradition, would have ensured their survival at sea."[122] For Nephi, the same learning experience had to take place. Nephi could not have merely guessed how to sail the Pacific Ocean or have succeeded unless both he and his crew knew what they were doing.

The *Periplus of the Erythraean Sea* mentions that Khor Rori was a safe haven for ships held up in the winter: "The place goes by the name of Moscha—where ships from

Cana (*Yemen*) are customarily sent; ships come from Dimyrike (*southern India*) and Barygaza (*modern day Broach in India*) which cruise nearby, spend the winter there due to the lateness of the season."[123] Undoubtedly the later Greek captains learned from the Arabs before them the advantages of mooring in the protected waters of Khor Rori during the winter northeast monsoons. During the winter at Khor Rori were experienced captains who knew how to sail a large ship across the open seas of the Indian Ocean from whom Nephi could learn and who had idle time to spend.

Yet, however well trained Nephi might have been at commanding a ship, no one person could sail an ancient ship. Without modern pulleys, gears, blocks, and light-weight sails and riggings, it would have taken every adult member of Lehi's family to sail the ship. That meant both men and at times women of Lehi's family had to tackle the demands of the sea and the wind. The work not only required strength, it subjected every person on deck to injury; and once seriously and physically impaired and without modern medicine, the sailor's odds of making it ashore alive were low. It goes without saying that unless Nephi had a trained crew aboard the ship, the large

Without pulleys, ancient sails had to be raised solely by muscle power.

and slow-to-respond sailing ship would not have made it out of the harbor, let alone across two mighty oceans. Severin describes what the crew of his replica ship had to do when the wind changed direction:

> Sometimes the wind changed direction with the passage of a squall so that *Sohar* began to run in dangerously toward the

coast. Then I rang the brass bell which summoned all hands on deck. Up they came, rubbing the sleep from their eyes, and stumbling to their regular positions. "Khai-or! Wear ship!" The maneuver of wearing ship meant shifting the mainsail with its huge mainspar from one side of the mast to the other by swinging the whole mass of sail and timber, more than a ton of it, around the foreside of the mast. If the ropes and canvas got in a tangle which checked the smooth swing of the mainspar, the sail would be ripped to shreds, or we could snap the mainspar. It was a difficult and dangerous operation by day, and at night it required real care. Every man had his allotted position on deck so that he knew exactly where to lay his hands on the right rope in the dark, and when to dodge safely out of the way of the lethal sweep of the butt of the mainspar as it swung across the ship. When everyone was in their right place, the helmsman turned *Sohar* to run downwind. The foredeck crew dragged in the lower end of the diagonal mainspar so that its peak rose vertical, and it hung above the deck like an enormous lance, dangling from the masthead sheaves, the tip fully 80 feet above the deck.

Next, Saleh's madcap figure scrambled around the outside of the ship, skipping along the top of the rail, round the

foredeck, and back down the opposite side of the vessel. He carried the heavy rope which controlled the mainsail, and which had to be transferred from one side of the ship to the other. As soon as this rope was in position and made secure, the helmsman began to swing *Sohar* on her new course. A quick, probing flash of a powerful torch beam aloft checked that the ropes and rigging were not tangled, and the maindeck crew cautiously began to ease out the ropes controlling the angle of the mainspar so that it began to tilt back to a diagonal, this time on the opposite side of the mainmast. When the spar had reached its correct angle, half the crew quickly laid hold of the main-sheet and hauled in so that the sail set correctly. The remainder moved about the deck, resetting the rigging, tightening up and making fast ropes, wearing round the smaller mizzen sail, rehoisting the jib, and finally the job was done. It usually took half an hour of hard work before the off–duty watch could turn in below to catch up on their sleep . . . until the next time that the fickle wind changed direction, and the anxious voice of the watch-leader called softly to me . . . "Captain . . . wear ship?"[124]

At times, the crew on Nephi's ship would have light duty, but on innumerable occasions, everyone would have had to act

quickly and without fault. Otherwise, the ship would have been doomed to capsize, run aground, or left with torn sails to founder in the ocean until they died of thirst or starvation. At such critical times, everyone had to know what his or her role was and to do it just the right way, at just the right time, each and every time. Such sequences of events happened during the first days of Nephi's voyage. They set sail in calm weather, but soon some took time to dance and to make merry with much rude-ness (1 Nephi 18:9). But after the mutiny of the older brothers, the lame brothers steered the ship into a "great and terrible tempest" (1 Nephi 18:13). Although the ship came close to sinking, the fact that it survived meant the crew had the skills necessary to keep the ship afloat. In 1834, Richard Henry Dana Jr. joined the crew of the *Pilgrim*, a small brig of 180 tons burden and 86 feet in length, a ship of compa-rable size to the one Nephi's crew would have sailed. Leaving Boston for California, Dana recalls:

> However as much I was affected by the beauty of the sea, the bright stars, and the clouds driven swiftly over them, I could not but remember that I was separating myself from all the social and intellec-tual enjoyments of life. Yet, strange as it

may seem, I did then and afterwards take pleasure in these reflections, hoping by them to prevent my becoming insensible to the value of what I was leaving.

But all my dreams were soon put to flight by an order from the officer to trim the yards, as the wind was getting ahead; and I could plainly see by the looks the sail-ors occasionally cast to windward, and by the dark clouds that were fast coming up, that we had bad weather to prepare for, and had heard the captain say that he expected to be in the Gulf Stream by twelve o'clock. In a few minutes eight bells were struck, the watch called, and we went below. I now began to feel the first discomforts of a sailor's life. The steerage in which I lived was filled with coils of riggings, spare sails, old junk and ship stores, which had not been stowed away. Moreover, there had been no berths built for us to sleep in, and we were not allowed to drive nails to hang our clothes upon. The sea, too, had risen, the vessel was rolling heavily, and everything was pitched about in grand confusion. There was a complete "hurrah's nest," as the sail-ors say, "everything on top and nothing at hand." A large hawser had been coiled away upon my chest, my hats, boots, mattress and blankets had all fetched away and gone over to leeward, and were jammed and broken under the boxes and

55

coils of rigging. To crown all, we were allowed no light to find anything with, and I was just beginning to feel strong symptoms of sea-sickness, and that listlessness and inactivity which accompany it. Giving up all attempts to collect my things together, I lay down upon the sails, expecting every moment to hear the cry of "all hands ahoy," which the approaching storm would soon make necessary. I shortly heard the rain-drops falling on deck, thick and fast, and the watch evidently had their hands full of work, for I could hear the loud and repeated orders of the mate, the trampling of feet, the creaking of blocks, and all the accompaniments of a coming storm. In a few minutes the slide of the hatch was thrown back, which let down the noise and tumult of the deck still louder, the loud cry of "All hands, ahoy! Tumble up here and take in sail," saluted our ears, and the hatch was quickly shut again. When I got upon deck, a new scene and a new experience was before me. The little brig was close hauled upon the wind, and lying over, as it then seemed to me, nearly upon her beam ends. The heavy head sea was beating against her bows with the noise and force almost of a sledge hammer, and flying over the deck, drenching us completely through. The topsail halyards had been let go, and the great sails were filling out and backing against the masts with a noise like thunder. The wind was whistling through the rigging, loose ropes flying about; loud, and, to me, unintelligible orders constantly given and rapidly executed, and the sailors "singing out" at the ropes in their hoarse and peculiar strains. In addition to all this, I had not got my "sea legs on," was dreadfully sick, with hardly strength enough to hold on to anything, and it was "pitch dark." This was my state when I was ordered aloft, for the first time, to reef topsails.

How I got along, I cannot now remember. I "laid out" on the yards and held on with all my strength. I could not have been of much service, for I remember having been sick several times before I left the topsail yard. Soon all was snug aloft, and we were again allowed to go below. This I did not consider much of a favor, for the confusion of everything below, and that inexpressible sickening smell, caused by the shaking up of the bilge-water in the hold, made the steerage but an indifferent refuge from the cold, wet decks. I had often read of the nautical experiences of others, but I felt as though there could be none worse than mine; for in addition to every other evil, I could not but remember that this was only the first night of a two-year voyage.[125]

That was Dana's first night aboard a ship with a seasoned crew and in a storm certainly of lesser magnitude than the one Nephi's crew had to handle. Stormy seas can make skilled sailors, but only if they are already skilled at the craft. Otherwise, stormy seas will take the unwary, and the crew and ship are lost. Further, a ship and its crew's ability to survive a bitter tempest or hurricane reveals a treasure of information about the skill of the shipwrights who built the ship, as well as the expertise of the crew that sailed her. For this reason, the authors will return again and again to this "moment of truth" in the sea for Nephi, his crew, and his ship of fine workmanship. Surprisingly, when the tempest the Lehites endured is viewed from different perspectives, it is amazingly rich in yielding new insights and information. To have survived the storm, Nephi's crew members could not have been a group of organized neophytes who had never set foot on a ship before setting sail into the open seas. Any crew that has a chance of making it across an ocean must have been trained by a team of experienced sailors and practiced over and over the required moves to set the sails and riggings for various seas and under different weather conditions. Even in a modern sailing vessel, an untrained crew

is generally doomed. Consider this report we received from Jody Lemmon aboard the Banyan after he and his experienced crew fought to save the ship.

The *Banyan* experienced the above difficulties in the waters off Tahiti. For Nephi, the closer he sailed to the more southerly waters, the more difficult the conditions would be. Jody reported:

August 4, 2009

Aboard the Banyan

Good-bye, Tahiti! This morning we loaded the boat with food, diesel, gasoline, and water. As we waved good-bye to our friends, on the various boats scattered about the anchorage, we made ready for the 6-day passage to the Cook Islands 850 miles away. The reef pass appeared to be uncharacteristically calm with small waves and light winds marking our passage.

We raised the main and let out the jib making our course to just off the tip of the small island of Moorea some 15 miles away. The watch schedule was figured out and Matt was to take first duty. Mike and I went below to get some rest until we were called for the mandatory 4-hour watch.

After about 2 hours I awoke to spray coming over the bow and the boat heaving. "Batten the hatches," was heard from above. Soon I was on deck to see what was going on. The wind had come up to 20 knots and we

were bashing into a ten-foot swell. The decision was made to reef in the sails. The ocean was quickly changing for the worse. A light rain began to fall and a glance to the sky told us that much worse was in store.

By the time we had the sails under control, with just a small sliver of main and a 1/3 jib, we were quickly approaching Moorea. The winds increased and were soon blowing over 30 knots during gusts. We decided to completely furl in the jib. At this time we were going straight downwind and this is not the best position to attempt to furl a headsail, as we were soon to find out. Suddenly a gust hit us at 40 knots and the headsail furler became jammed. The top 1/3 of the sail had actually twisted backwards on itself. Our headsail was twisted one way at the lower half and the opposite way at the top half. This created a real mess. Meanwhile the winds had kicked up and we were now regularly experiencing 40-knot gusts. The headsail was flapping like crazy and was in danger of being blown to bits. I was at the wheel and yelled for the boys to go up to the foredeck and spin the sail in by hand. This worked a bit, but as soon as a gust would hit, the top portion of sail which was furled the wrong way would become unfurled and act like a small parachute. This was horrible, as it caused the entire headsail to shake and vibrate with so much fury that the entire boat would shudder and tremble. I steered the boat off the wind, hit the autopilot and went up to try and help. Matt and I spent the next 10 minutes attempting to furl in the sail with no success. I could see that the sail was already ripping in a number of places, especially where the repairs had just been made.

I was aware that we could attempt to let the jib go and then pull it down by hand. The problem was that it was so twisted I was afraid it

would not unfurl and we would then be stuck with a larger portion of the sail unfurled and thus have an even greater problem. The winds were getting worse and we were now getting too close to the reef off of Moorea. I finally decided to get a knife and chop the jib sheets free. At this point a 40-knot gust hit us and the whole entire headsail became free and was now flapping with a vengeance. We then let the halyard go and pulled the sail down onto the deck. At last we were safe!

The protected side of the island was only about 15 minutes away. We headed that direction surfing down 10-foot seas at speeds of up to 9 knots just on our main. Once around the point the winds dropped to 20 knots and we made our way in to the protective anchorage. The winds were still gusting up to 30 knots but the seas were calm enough now for us call it pleasant. Just as the sun was setting we dropped anchor among fifteen or so other sailboats in 15 feet of water and climbed below. Everything was in chaos. We spent a few minutes cleaning up, ate some hot soup and bread, and climbed into our bunks. It was only 6:30pm. We slept the whole night and didn't wake up until this morning.

This morning (the 5th) we are going to evaluate the damage to our headsail. It is torn in a number of places for sure, but hopefully it is only the sunshade cover and not the actual sail. If the damage isn't too bad we will continue on to the Cooks or possibly to Rangiroa where good boat repair facilities are located. Also, we have a friend of ours who has a sewing machine in Rangiroa. If the damage is too bad we will have to go back to Tahiti.

Jody

Sep. 3, 2009

Arrival at Palmerston from Papeete

We made it! The longest 48 hours of my life. We left Rarotonga exactly 2 days ago and proceeded through absolute hell. The boat's motion was the most unpleasant that we have experienced thus far. The rolling was so extreme that Matt, Mike, and myself all lost our lunches into the sea multiple times. During the last 24 hours Mike and I couldn't even hold water in our stomachs . . .

The worst part of the adventure began last night. I had been suffering from a headache for 30 hours straight and needed air badly. I opened one small porthole to allow some airflow below and of course, that was a really bad idea. At exactly 3 am, a rogue wave hit us broadside sending the boat into a wild fish-tail. The wave broke over the cockpit where Mike was holding on amidst the 35-knot gale. The wave entered my porthole and proceeded to pour, what must have been, close to 10 gallons of Pacific blue directly on top of our heads. We were swimming in bed! The mid-ship hatch was also cracked, so water poured in and got the settee wet as well, but not nearly as wet as my bed. We had to move into the salon and make due with a wet bed that had no lee cloths. So, every time the boat fishtailed we would be thrown on top of Mike sleeping on the floor. From 3 am until dawn was one of the most trying times of this leg of our journey. Then, as dawn arrived and I came on deck to relieve Matt, we found that my starboard board bag was gone . . . Mike's brand new [surf] board and my two favorite boards were gone, lost into the sea! Another casualty to try and forget . . .

We pulled into the lee of Palmerston Atoll at around 1 pm today. A panga met us about a mile out and Simon showed us the way to his mooring ball next to two other cruising boats. The winds were blowing 25–30 knots and tying up to a mooring ball in those conditions proved to be trying. When we finally secured ourselves it was time to dry out everything. Soon laundry and mattresses were strung from every corner of the boat. At about that time the authorities showed up to procseed with the check-in formalities. After that was taken care of our host, Simon asked, "You guys ready to head to shore then?" Matt was below cooking up our first real meal in the last 30 hours, so we had to postpone our land arrival until the next day.

At about this time we realized that our toilet was again acting up. I took apart the system and found a spring that was not placed correctly. One problem fixed. Then, we attempted to discharge our full tank overboard. No luck. Mike and I gloved up and began the process of elimination to find the clog. After pumping air through various lengths of pipe with the dinghy air pump we finally realized where the clog was. The tube that came out of the tank was clogged at the actual tank fitting. Mike proceeded to take off the hose clamps and disconnected the last hose connecting to the tank. Nothing came out. I, then, handed him a metal coat hanger, which he used to jam into the tube. After some serious pokes with the hanger he finally managed to burst through the clog and suddenly the dam was released! Success! However, it was at the cost of sewage spewing out all over the place.

After the clean up we were free to put the boat back together and go for a swim in the crystal clear, blue water. The island looks incredibly beautiful. It has every character-istic that a small tropical atoll should have in one's imagination. We are all really excited to be picked up in the morning by Simon and shown the "ropes." We all wonder what type of work we will be doing and what activities the islanders have in store for us.

The wind is still howling. The wind generator is actually charging at 10 amps!!!! Amazing. I can't wait to climb into my bed tonight and get a good night sleep. I hope that my mattress has dried out. It's dark now so, I should prob-ably go and bring it in . . . Ciao from the middle of nowhere . . .

Love, Jody

One of the numerous fruit stands at Salalah near Khor Rori.

Jody's examples of sailing in unfavorable sea conditions should illustrate without doubt that the core of the crew aboard Nephi's ship had to have been experienced sailors. They had to have been a well-trained team who responded immediately and took the right actions every time or the ship could have been lost at sea. For this reason, we consider only Khor Rori as a possible candidate for where Nephi built his ship. Moored in the natural harbor, Nephi's crew could have taken their ship on numerous training exercises under the mentorship of experienced Omani sailors. It is even more likely that Nephi took several seasoned Omani sailors as the core of his crew.

In summary, the specific essential items Nephi needed to build his ship would have been available to him only if he were at an established port. The strength of Khor Rori over other locations proposed for Bountiful, which is where Nephi built his ship, is that it is the only established large port in Dhofar in Nephi's time. Khor Rori provides a model for Bountiful where one does not need to rely on a long list of incredible miracles in order to make the location fit the necessary requirements essential for building, launching, and sailing a large ship. No location other than Khor Rori has yet been able to meet these criteria.

Based on their research, in 1999 George Potter and Richard Wellington proposed that there finally existed a strong candidate for the place where Nephi built his ship and that Khor Rori could stand up to the scrutiny of thorough investigation. Every resource Nephi needed to build, launch, and sail a ship toward the promised land can be identified at Khor Rori. Furthermore, there is significant evidence that all the other peripheral elements of Bountiful existed at the Khor in Nephi's time: fruit orchards on a beach, wild honey, a tall mountain, flint, evidence of smelting, being located east from the current candidates for Nahom,[126] beasts for hides and meat, and tall cliffs directly above deep water.[127] In addition, the harbor is located

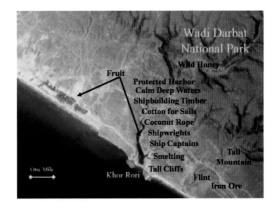

All the attributes of Nephi's Bountiful are found within six miles of Khor Rori.

at the end of the Frankincense Trail along the course where qualified candidates exist for the Valley of Lemuel, the River of Laman, Shazer, the "more fertile parts," the "most fertile parts," Nahom, the trail east, the land Bountiful (Dhofar), and the place Bountiful (where much fruit occurs at the seashore). It is of more than passing interest that modern scholarship from non-LDS researchers is helping to show that this element of the Book of Mormon narrative is in perfect harmony with the historical setting of mid-first millennium BC Arabia. It took George and Richard six years, thousands of hours of research, and reference to many hundreds of books, articles, and maps, and thirty-five thousand miles of personal travel to verify that what Nephi wrote in his account stands up against modern research as an accurate historical portrayal of a journey along the only known trail that led from Jerusalem to Dhofar in 600 BC. It is remarkable that the poorly educated nineteenth-century farm boy, Joseph Smith Jr. who had never left the eastern United States and had access to none of these resources, dictated the Book of Mormon pages that covered this journey in just over one day![128]

Notes

1. Hussein Shehadeh, "Vibrant Civilization Uncovered in Oman," March 28, 2009, http://sci.tech-archive.net/Archive/sci.archaeology/2009-03/msg00380.html.

2. George Potter and Richard Wellington, *Lehi in the Promised Land* (Springville, Utah: Cedar Fort, 2003), 139–62.

3. Colin Nickerson, "Sailing into Antiquity," *Boston Globe*, January 11, 2010, http://www.boston.com/business/articles/2010/01/11/boston_university_archeologists_digs_uncover_clues_to_egyptian_mariners/.

4. S. B. Miles, *The Countries and Tribes of the Persian Gulf*, 2nd ed. (London: Frank Cass and Co, 1966), 2.

5. In medieval times, a second route came into being that ran along the Arabian coast. This was built at great expense to provide protection from Bedouin raiders who were attacking Muslim pilgrims traveling along the old Frankincense Trail on their way to perform Haj and Umra in the Muslim holy cities of Mecca and Medina. This route came into being approximately 1,400 years after Lehi traveled through Arabia. Abdulla Al-Wohaibi, *The Northern Hijaz, In the Writings of the Arab Geographers [AD] 800–1500* (Beirut: Al-Risalah, 1973), 324, 325, and map in back of book.

The Lord on high is mightier than the noise of many waters, yea, than the mighty waves of the sea.

PSALM 93:4

60

Tim Sedor stands above 100-foot-tall cliffs at Khor Rori (where Nephi could have been thrown into the depths of the sea—depth approximately 30 feet at base of cliff).

6. Thus we agree with Hugh Nibley's proposal that the route Lehi took was inland, east of the Hijaz mountains. Hugh W. Nibley, *The Collected Works of Hugh Nibley*, vol. 5: *Lehi in the Desert; The World of the Jaredites; There Were Jaredites*, eds. John W. Welch, Gary P. Gillum, and Don E. Norton (Salt Lake City: Deseret Book; Provo, Utah: FARMS, 1986), 112. See also Lynn Hilton and Hope Hilton, *Discovering Lehi* (Springville, Utah: Cedar Fort: 1996), map on p. 34. Lynn M. and Hope A. Hilton drove down the west coast of Arabia and suggested this was the route Lehi took and a map of this route was placed on FARMS website for many years. This map was removed a few years ago and S. Kent Brown produced a map. See S. Kent Brown, *Echoes and Evidences of the Book of Mormon*, ed. by Parry, Peterson, and Welch (Provo: FARMS, Brigham Young University; 2002) 58. This map essentially mirrors the route we proposed to FARMS in 1998.

7. Al-Wohaibi, *The Northern Hijaz*, 325.

8. Lynn and Hope Hilton, *In Search of Lehi's Trail* (Salt Lake City: Deseret Book, 1976), 44.

9. Ibid., 41.

10. Andrew Taylor, *Traveling the Sands* (Dubai: Motivate, 1995), 12.

11. Hilton, *In Search of Lehi's Trail*, 105–7.

12. Warren P. Aston, "The Arabian Bountiful Discovered?" *Journal of Book of Mormon Studies*, 7/1 (1998): 4–11.

13. Hugh Nibley, *Collected Works*, vol. 5, 110–13; Lynn M. and Hope A. Hilton, *Discovering Lehi* (Springville, Utah: CFI, 1996), 150.

14. Abundant and a wide variety of fruits (1 Nephi 17:5; 18:6); wild honey (1 Nephi 17:5); a mountain nearby (1 Nephi 17:7); ore available locally (1 Nephi 17:9; see Wm. Revell Phillips, "Metals of the Book of Mormon," *Journal of Book of Mormon Studies*, 9/2 (2000): 38).

15. Dr. Eduard G. Rheinhardt, assistant professor, School of Geography and Geology, McMaster University, Hamilton, Ontario. Personal communication with the authors, 12 April 2001.

16. Measured by Doug Esplin, using Google Earth software tools.

17. Juris Zarins, *The Land of Incense, Archaeology and Cultural Heritage Series*, vol. 1, Archaeological Work in the Governorate of Dhofar, Sultanate of Oman 1990–1995. The Project of the National Committee for the supervision of Archaeological Survey in the Sultanate, Ministry of Information (Sultanate of Oman: Sultan Qaboos Unversity Publications Al Nahda Printing Press, 2001), 64, 76, 154.

18. Ibid., 74, 88.

19. Ibid.

20. Ibid., 72, 88.

21. Ibid., 139.

22. Professor Alessandra Avanzini (Dipartimento del Scienze Storiche di Mondo Antico, Università degli studi di Pisa, Italy) and Professor Dr Alexander V. Sedov (Institute of Oriental Studies Russian Academy of Sciences, Moscow, Russia) "Stratigraphy of Sumhuram: New Evidence," Abstract. The 2004 Seminar for Arabian Studies, Thursday 22 July–Saturday 24 July, 2004, British Museum, London, U.K.

23. Archeological research undertaken in early 2006 by the University of Pisa group concluded, "The possibility that the foundation of Sumhuram interacted with a pre-existing indigenous culture (cfr. Zarins, 2001 and Morandi Bonacossi, 2002) is not excluded by the results of the intensive survey." Mauro Cremaschi and Alessandro Perego, "Land Use and Settlement Pattern in the Archaeological Sumhuram: An intensive survey at Khor Rori," Sumhuram Preliminary Report (Pisa: University of Pisa, 2006), 28. Bonacossi D. Morandi, "Excavation at Khor Rori, the 1997 and 1998 Campaigns," in *Archaeological Studies: Khor Rori Report 1*, ed. Avanzini (Pisa: Edizioni Plus, Pisa, 2002), 29, 52. Juris Zarins, "The Land of Incense," Archaeology and Cultural Heritage Series, vol. 1, Archaeological Work in the Governorate of Dhofar, Sultanate of Oman 1990–1995. The Project of the National Committee for the supervision of Archaeological Survey in the Sultanate, Ministry of Information (Sultanate of Oman: Sultan Qaboos University Publications Al Nahda Printing Press, 2001), 60.

24. Ibid., 23 and 27 making reference to M. Mariotti Lippi, "Indagini palinologiche nel sito archeologico di Sumhuram (Khor Rori) in Dhophar (Oman)," Primi risultati, Egitto e Vicino Oriente (2002), 25, 145, 149. M. Mariotti Lippi, R. Becattini, and T. Gonnelli, "Archeopalinology at Sumhuram (Dhofar, Sultanate of Oman)" in *Archaeological Studies: Khor Rori Report 1*, ed. Avanzini (Pisa: Edizioni Plus, Pisa, 2002).

25. Ibid., 23.

26. Noah Webster, *An American Dictionary of the English Language*, vol. 1; a facsimile of: Noah Webster's Original 1828 Edition (New York: Johnson Reprint, 1970), no page numbers, see "Fruit."

27. Zarins, *The Land of Incense*, 60.

28. Ali Ahmad Al-Shahri, *The Language of Aad* (Dhofar Salalah: self-published, 2000), 21.

29. Ali Al-Shahri showed George Potter and fourteen other LDS members the cave where wild

honey was collected on 22 September 2006.

30. Zarins, 37. Site TA 95:227 is on the west side of Wadi Sinur (see fig. 28 "Archaeological sites located on the Salalah Plain (1992-1995)." The distance to Khor Rori is four miles.

31. Wm. Revell Phillips, "Metals of the Book of Mormon," *Journal of Book of Mormon Studies* 9, no. 2 (2000): 38.

32. Jeffrey M Bradshaw, PhD (senior research scientist, Institute for Human and Machine Cognition, Pensacola, Florida), email correspondence with authors, including photographs of copper and iron smelting slag found at the ruins of Sumhuram as well as the remains of a smelting furnace inside the city dating to the Sumhuram 1 period. Dr. Bradshaw was shown the copper and iron smelting slag and furnace by Saeed Al-Mashori, supervisor of the Khor Rori excavation for the Al-Bilad Archaeological Park, Salalah, Oman on 30 May 2006.

33. Author observed both bronze plates on exhibit at the Heritage Museum, Frankincense Museum Hall of History, 28 November 2008.

34. Wadi Nahom is 16 degrees north; Khor Rori is 17 degrees north (to the nearest degree).

35. Both wild and domesticated animals were present in Dhofar.

36. Hilton and Hilton, *In Search of Lehi's Trail*, 143.

37. John Tvedtnes, review of *Multiply Exceedingly*, 24.

38. Sidney B. Sperry, "Did Father Lehi Have Daughters Who Married the Sons of Ishmael?," *Journal of Book of Mormon Studies* 4, no. 1 (1995): 235.

39. Crichton, *Eaters of the Dead* (New York: Ballantine Publishing, 1992), 12.

40. Samuel Eliot Morison, *Admiral of the Ocean Sea: a Life of Christopher Columbus* (New York: MJF Books, 1970), 115.

41. Ibid., 148.

42. Harry Morton, *The Wind Commands: Sailors and Sailing Ships in the Pacific* (Middletown CT: Wesleyan University Press 1975), 164, 197.

43. Tim Severin, *The Sindbad Voyage* (New York: G. P. Putnam's Sons, 1983), 81, 82.

44. Ibid., 81.

45. Ibid., 162.

46. Ibid., 163.

47. Ibid., 80, 81.

48. Ibid., 132.

49. Ibid., 127.

50. Ibid., 132.

51. Morison, *Admiral of the Ocean Sea*, 147.

52. Severin, *Sindbad Voyage*, 133.

53. Severin, *Sindbad Voyage*, photos.

54. J. S. Illsley, "History and Archaeology of the Ship, Anchors", http://cma.soton.ac.uk/HistShip/shlect34.htm.

55. Cremaschi and Perego, "Land Use," 25.

56. Tom Vosmer, Patrick Baker, Jon Carpenter, "Field Report, Oman Expedition 1997, Western Australia Maritime Museum Report No. 130," (Fremantle, Australia: Western Australia Maritime Museum, Department of Maritime Archaeology, Department of Materials Conservation, 1997), 18.

57. Lionel Casson, *The Periplus Maris Erythraei* (Princeton, N.J.: Princeton University Press, 1989), 283.

58. Severin, *Sindbad Voyage*, 66.

59. Raphael Patai, *The Children of Noah: Jewish Seafaring in Ancient Time* (New Jersey: Princeton University Press, 1998), 13.

60. Al-Shahri, *The Language of Aad*, 31–34.

61. Personal communication to the authors from Jeffrey M. Bradshaw, 23 June 2006. Dr. Bradshaw was shown the iron and copper slag and the smelting furnace at Khor Rori by Saeed Al-Mashori, Supervisor of the Khor Rori Excavation for the museum at Salalah, the "Al-Balid Archaeological Park" on 30 May 2006.

62. William R. Phillips, "Metals of the Book of Mormon," 36–43.

63. "Excavations and Restoration of the Complex of Khor Rori, Interim Report" (October 2000–April 2001), (Pisa: Universita di Pisa, 2001), 4, 12–15.

64. In 1991 Ali Ahmed bin Mahash Al-Shahri reported his discovery of an inscription in an unknown language on the wall of a remote cave in Dhofar ("Recent Epigraphic Discoveries in Dhofar," *Proceeedings of the Seminar for Arabian Studies,* 21). He would appear to have given the language of the inscription this name, although it is elsewhere referred to as one of the Dhofar dipinti and may possibly be part of the group known as the non-Sayhadic languages (M.C.A. MacDonald, "Reflections on the Linguistic Map of Pre-Islamic Arabia," *Arabian Archaeology and Epigraphy* (2000):11, 30, 32.)

65. Ali Al-Shahri, Khor Rori historian, conversation with George Potter on 23 September 2006.

66. Webster, *American Dictionary of the English Language,* see "Nail" and "Tool."

67. Softwoods and hardwoods can be differentiated by the material that fills their cells. The cellular structure of softwoods, with few exceptions, is

63

filled with water. Hardwoods, on the other hand, have solid material inside the cells. Therefore, softwoods make poor building materials when exposed to the weather because water passes easily through the cell wall. The solid material in the cells of hardwoods provides a resistance to the transfer of water through the material. The exceptions to this rule are cedar, cypress, and California Redwood that have cells filled with a resinous material which provides the same type of resistance to water transfer as do the hardwoods. For further reference, see Bruce Haodley, *Understanding Wood* (Bethel, CN: Bethel Books, 1997).

68. Gerd Weisgerber, "Dilmun—A Trading Entrepot" in *Bahrain through the Ages, the Archeology* (London: KPI Ltd., 1986), 137.

69. Sherren Ratnagar, *Encounters: The Westerly Trade of the Harappa Civilization* (New Delhi: Oxford University Press, 1981), 164–65.

70. Email to the authors from Tom Vosmer, 25 May 2000.

71. Severin, *Sindbad Voyage*, 31.

72. Morton, *The Winds Commands*, 207.

73. John Illsley, "History and Archaeology of the Ship, Lecture Notes, Nautical Archaeology" (Bangor University, May 5, 2000), lecture 2, p.1. http://www.cma.soton.ac.uk/HistShip /shlect02.htm.

74. Severin, *Sindbad Voyage*, 43.

75. Ibid., 37, 38.

76. Tim Severin, "Construction of the Omani Boom Sohar," *The Sewn Plank Boats*, ed. Sean McGrail and Eric Kentley (Oxford: B.A.R., 1985), 279–80.

77. Omani Ministry of National Heritage and Culture (MNHC), *Oman, a Seafaring Nation,*

2nd ed. (Sultan of Oman: Oriental Printing Press, 1991), 107.

78. John Noble Wilford, "Under Centuries of Sand, a Trading Hub" July 9, 2002, http://www.nytimes. com/2002/07/09/science/09SILK.html?ex=1 027207913andei=1anden=ed0f8dbf96a1968a.

79. Omani Ministry of National Heritage and Culture, *Oman, a Seafaring Nation*, 20, 22.

80. Norbert Weismann, email correspondence with authors, Kamen, Germany, 17 May 2000.

81. Omani Ministry of National Heritage and Culture, *Oman, a Seafaring Nation*, 107–8.

82. Bertram Thomas, *The Arabs* (London: Thornton Butterworth, 1937), 262. Nigel Groom notes the similarity between the names of *Zufar* (Dhofar) and *Ophir*: "Zufar is sometimes proposed as a likely word etymologically close to Ophir, while the nineteenth-century traveler Vod Wrede observed that the Mahra of south Arabia, who lived adjacent to Zufar and whose language has very ancient origins, used the word 'ofir' to mean 'red' and called themselves the tribe of 'Ofir', meaning the 'red country.'" Nigel Groom, *Frankincense and Myrrh, A Study of the Arabian Incense Trade* (London: Longman, 1981), 49–50.

83. Al-Shahri, *The Language of Aad*, 30–35.

84. See "peafowl," *The New Shorter Oxford English Dictionary*, vol. 2, ed. Lesley Brown (Oxford: Clarendon Press, 1993), 2132.

85. Almug (1 Kings 10:11, 12) = algum (2 Chronicles 2:8; 9:10–11), in the Hebrew occurring only in the plural almuggim (indicating that the wood was brought in planks); the name of a wood brought from Ophir to be used in the building of the temple and for other purposes. Some suppose it to have been the white sandalwood of India, the Santalum album of botanists,

a native of the mountainous parts of the Malabar coasts. It is a fragrant wood and is used in China for incense in idol worship. Others, with some probability, think that it was the Indian red sandal-wood, the pterocarpus santalinus, a heavy, fine-grained wood, the Sanscrit name of which is valguka. It is found on the Coromandel coast and in Ceylon. See M.G. Easton, 1897 Bible Dictionary, World Wide Web Version, http:// www.ccel.org/e/easton/ebd/ebd/T0000100. html#T0000182.

86. M.G. Easton, 1897 Bible Dictionary, World Wide Web Version http://www.ccel.org/e/ easton/ebd/ebd/T0000100.html#T0000182.

87. Gen. Rab. 12:12, Theodor-Albeck 1:110–11, as recorded in Patai, *The Children of Noah*, 37.

88. Patai, *The Children of Noah*, 47.

89. Severin, *Sindbad Voyage*, 41.

90. Chad Baybayan, Rowena Keaka, Melissa Kim, Beatrice Krauss, and Mollie Sperry, "Plants Used for Building Canoes," Polynesian Voyaging Society (Hawaii), 2.

91. Ibid., 132.

92. Ibid., 133.

93. Omani Ministry of National Heritage and Culture, *Oman, a Seafaring Nation*, 113.

94. *The Periplus of the Erythraean Sea*, literally meaning "roundtrip," is an account of a trading journey between Egypt and India made by an unknown merchant or ship's master. The date of authorship is not known and may be somewhere between AD 40 and the early 3rd century.

95. *The Periplus of the Erythraean Sea, by an Unknown Author: With Some Extracts from Agatharkhides "on the Erythraean Sea,"* translated and edited by G. W. B. Huntingford (London: The Hakluyt Society, c/o the British Library, 1980), chapter 32.

96. Zarins, *The Land of Incense*, 20.

97. Ibid., 60.

98. "Report of the World Heritage Committee of the United Nations, Educational, Scientific and Cultural Organization," Convention concerning the Protection of the World Cultural and Natural Heritage, Cairns, Australia, 27 November to 2 December 2000. See http://whc.unesco.org/en/news/184.

99. Omani Ministry of National Heritage and Culture, *Oman, a Seafaring Nation*, 16.

100. Ali Al-Shahri took George Potter and fourteen other LDS members to the caves on 22 September 2006.

101. Muhammed Abdul Nayeem, *The Rock Art of Arabia* (India: Hyderabad Publishers, 2000), 447.

102. Ibid., 445.

103. Omani Ministry of National Heritage and Culture, *Oman, a Seafaring Nation*, 146.

104. Severin, *Sindbad Voyage*, 58–59.

105. Ibid., 132.

106. Ibid.

107. Miles, *The Countries and Tribes of the Persian Gulf*, 517.

108. Patai, *The Children of Noah*, 37–38.

109. There are a number of Khors (inlets) in Dhofar. Khor Salalah is the third largest after Khor Rori and Khor al Baleed. Khor Salalah is a modern bird sanctuary. It is a large Khor and appears quite deep but it has, in common with all of the Khors that open directly onto the beach, a relatively narrow opening, which would have made it difficult to guide a large ship into and out of, not to mention the breakers. Dr. Jana Owen of UCLA was not able to dive in Khor Salalah because it is a protected area. Regarding its suitability as a port in Lehi's time, she noted in a personal communication to the authors, "Possible, but is very small and we cannot be sure about the depth in antiquity."

110. The Italian Mission to Oman (IMTO) headed by Prof. Alessandra Avanzini (Dipartimento del Scienze Storiche di Mondo Antico, Università degli studi di Pisa, Italy).

111. Dr. Jana Owen, UCLA. Personal communication with the authors, 14 August 2000.

112. Peter Vine, *The Heritage of Oman* (London: Immel Publishing, 1995), 50.

113. Saeed Al-Mashori, supervisor for excavations at Khor Rori for the Al-Balid Archaeological Park, Salalah Oman, showed George Potter and fourteen other LDS members the ramp-moorings at Khor Rori on 23 September 2006.

114. The Khors or inlet bays include Kharfot, Reysut, Quran al Kabeer, Awqad, al Baleed, Dhahariz, Suli, Taqah, Rori, and Mirbat.

115. Hilton and Hilton, *Discovering Lehi*, 166.

116. The town flourished from the early twelfth to the sixteenth century. It was about 1 mile (1.6 km) long by about 1/3 mile (0.5km) wide. In 1285 Marco Polo described it as "a great and noble and fine city. It stands upon the sea and has a very good haven, so that there is a great traffic of shipping between here and India, and the merchants take hence a great number of Arab horses to that market, making great profit thereby. Much white incense is produced here." As quoted from Miles, *The Countries and Tribes of the Persian Gulf*, 507.

117. Jana Owen, UCLA. Personal communication with the authors, 14 August 2000.

118. Nicholas Clapp, *The Road to Ubar* (Boston: Houghton Mifflin Co., 1998), 278.

119. Aston, "The Arabian Bountiful Discovered?" 5–11.

120. Omani Ministry of National Heritage and Culture, Oman, *Oman, a Seafaring Nation*, 96.

121. Frank Linehan, Personal communications with the authors, June 1999.

122. Maurizio Tosi, "Early Maritime Cultures of the Arabian Gulf and the Indian Ocean," in *Bahrain through the Ages, the Archeology*, 94.

123. *Periplus of the Erythraean Sea*, as quoted in Omani Ministry of National Heritage and Culture, Oman, *Oman, a Seafaring Nation*, 26.

124. Severin, *Sindbad Voyage*, 142–43.

125. Dana, *Two Years Before the Mast*, 44–46.

126. Khor Rori is 7 degrees east of Wadi Harib Nahom.

127. Potter and Wellington, *Lehi in the Wilderness*, 121–36.

128. It is generally accepted that Joseph Smith translated the Book of Mormon in 63 days, or about 8½ pages per day. In 1 Nephi 2 and 16–19, it covers the information about the journey in less than 11 pages in total. See Richard L. Bushman, "The Recovery of the Book of Mormon," in *Book of Mormon Authorship Revisited* (Provo, UT: FARMS, 1997), 23.

NEPHI'S SHIP AND HER CREW

CHAPTER TWO

SINCE NEPHI'S SHIP survived a "great and terrible tempest" that lasted four days (1 Nephi 18:13–15) in the Indian Ocean and then endured the strong winds and ever pounding swells of a long Pacific passage, the vessel had to have been extraordinarily constructed for its time. The young prophet's ship had to be built to standards so that the seams would not open in a storm and the hull and superstructure remain strong enough to hold together during a transit of more than 14,800 nautical miles. Even with the Lord's assistance, constructing the ship required a great deal of vessel knowledge and experience in ship construction in order to build a vessel to meet those parameters. For this reason, to us it seems that the Lord led Nephi to the shipyards and ways of Khor Rori to fulfill his purposes—"That I [the Lord] may carry thy people across these waters" (1 Nephi 17:8).

It is doubtful that the best ships built in ancient Oman could reach the Pacific Ocean, let alone cross the largest body of water on earth. The Lord realized that Nephi would need to modify the design and strength of his ship beyond the process by which ships were being built at that time at Khor Rori. For example, Tim Severin's replica of a medieval Omani ship barely held together during its maiden voyage to China. Though Severin's ship traveled only one-third the distance of Nephi's voyage and had the advantage of being repaired at ports along the route, Severin's *Sohar* was leaking badly, taking on a foot of water per day as it entered the China Sea. After reaching China, the *Sohar* never sailed again. A Pacific crossing would have been out of the question.

Hull of Nephi's ship. Illustration by Jose Flores.

For this reason, it is obvious the Lord needed to transfer to Nephi some ship design technologies that were far ahead of their time. Thus, the instructions from the Lord that Nephi modify the thinking of his day, might have little meaning to a non-sailor. But for one who has engineered oceangoing sailing vessels, it provides important evidence that the Book of Mormon is true. How could Joseph Smith have known that the Omanis built some of the best oceangoing vessels of their era? However, even their ships were not designed to endure a Pacific crossing.

The Raft Myth

Despite the great odds against even a well-constructed ancient sailing ship surviving a passage to the Americas, some have thought that Nephi constructed a large raft. This idea would see Nephi tying logs together to form a raft, boarding it with dozens of people, and drifting his way to the promised land. However, like a raft, this idea holds no water.

In light of Nephi's record, the idea of a raft seems greatly out of place. One must remember that while camped anywhere along the seashore in southern Arabia, Nephi would have seen the impressive sailing vessels of his day passing offshore on their way to trade for frankincense at Khor Rori. It should also be remembered that our all-knowing Lord instructed Nephi to follow his divine design, a design superior to how other men were building ships, so that "I [the Lord] may carry thy people across these waters" (1 Nephi 17:8). Would the Lord's blueprint for an improved ship to cross the great oceans be a raft?

Undoubtedly, Joseph Smith, the translator of the Book of Mormon, knew the difference between a *raft that drifts* and *a sailing ship that can be steered, guided, and sailed* (1 Nephi 18:22). Consider these definitions from Noah Webster's 1828 American Dictionary of the English Language:

> "*raft*: from floating, sweeping along, or . . . to fasten together horizontally and float down a stream; a float."

> "*ship*: a peculiar structure, adapted to navigating, or floating on water by means of a sail. In an appropriate sense, a building of a structure or form fitting for navigation, furnished with a bowsprit and three masts, a main-mast, a fore-mast and a mizen masts, each of which is composed of a lower-mast, a top-mast and a top-gallant-mast, and square rigged."[1]

Certainly, Nephi's ship did not have the advanced features of a nineteenth-century sailing vessel. However, it should be clear that Joseph Smith knew the difference between a raft that drifts and a sailing ship. Further, Nephi's own words confirm that he built a ship that he could "steer" (1 Nephi 18:13), "guide," and "sail" (1 Nephi 18:22). Sailing ships are maneuverable by having keels, rudders, adjustable riggings, and narrow hulls that allow the ships to be sailed in a specific direction. A raft, even suited with a sail, is as the definition states—a "float." With a wide-flat base, a raft drifts in the ocean like a bottle. Thor Heyerdahl understood this principle when he embarked from Peru aboard his raft the Kon-Tiki. The explorer had the Kon-Tiki towed by a tug into the Humboldt Current. Heyerdahl had studied the flow of the current and knew that the current would float the Kon-Tiki directly into the path of eastern Polynesia Islands. When his crew finally spotted an island they tried to make landing, but could not reach the island because the current pushed the raft further out to sea.[2] When the Kon-Tiki approached a second island, its crew could not steer the raft safely passed the island's coral reef that then destroyed the Kon-Tiki.[3]

According to the raft idea, Nephi navigated a float across the dangerous currents of the East Indies and Asia Pacific archipelagos and successfully negotiated dockings at several uncharted bays where the family would have needed to restock fresh water and other necessary supplies. In reality, a raft would have never made it out of the Indian Ocean. If a raft could have stayed together long enough to round the tip of India, it would have been driven back toward Africa by the west-going current.[4]

Further, the raft idea does not explain how Nephi and all his family went "down into the ship, with all our loading and our seeds, and whatsoever thing we had brought with us" (1 Nephi 18:6). The most likely meaning of this verse is that Nephi and his family

Nephi's ship appears to have had a lower deck that one could go "down" into with provisions.

members stored their provisions, personal items, and bedding below deck, something that is not possible on a raft.

William Revell Phillips writes: "No trees grow in Oman that could provide suitable planking for Nephi's ship, either today or probably in the past. Trees are very scarce in the Dhofar, and those of significant size tend to yield gnarly, punky wood."[5] Phillips could have added that the Sycamore figs which grow at Dhofar, ones that would have been used in the construction of a theoretical raft, are softwoods and when placed in water will become waterlogged and sink.

During calm seas, a small party can endure aboard a raft for some time. However, when the weather turns, they are doomed. For this reason, Thor Heyerdahl intentionally launched his Kon-Tiki during the calm period of the year to avoid Antarctic gales and hurricanes.[6] To have had any chance to reach even as far as India from Oman, a raft would have needed to be launched during the stormy summer monsoons, the only time when the north Indian Ocean currents flow east toward India from Arabia. During any other season of the year, the Indian Ocean current reverses and flows toward Africa,[7] and during the

monsoon season. the northern Indian Ocean suffers from constant high seas and strong winds. Marco Polo wrote of the destructive storms of the Indian Ocean and the effect they had on the sailing ships of Arabia: "And you can take my word that many of them sink, because the Indian Ocean is often very stormy."[8] Indeed, if Nephi's ship were even a finely crafted raft, instead of praising its virtues, his older brothers would have been "exceedingly afraid" at the thought of boarding a raft that offered no protections from the sea, instead of calling the ship "exceedingly fine" (1 Nephi 18:4).

No large raft with dozens of people sitting on its logs could have survived the four-day "great and terrible tempest," a "great storm" that became "exceedingly sore" (1 Nephi 18:13–15). Jack London describes being in a typhoon off the coast of Japan. The storm Laman steered Nephi's ship into would have been of similar destructive force.

> It was on the deck that the force of the wind could be fully appreciated, especially after leaving the stifling fo'castle. It seemed to stand up against you like a wall, making it almost impossible to move on the heaving decks or to

69

breathe as the fierce gusts came dashing by. The schooner was hove to under jib, foresail, and mainsail. We proceeded to lower the foresail and make it fast. The night was dark, greatly impeding our labor. Still, though not a star or the moon could pierce the black masses of storm clouds that obscured the sky as they swept along before the gale, nature aided us in a measure. A soft light emanated from the movement of the ocean. Each night sea, all phosphorescent and glowing with the tiny lights of myriads of animalculae threatened to overwhelm us with a deluge of fire. Higher and higher, thinner and thinner, the crest grew as it began to curve and overtop preparatory to breaking, until with a roar it fell over the bulwarks, a mass of soft glowing light and tons of water which sent the sailors sprawling in all directions and left in each nook and cranny little specks of light that glowed and trembled till the next sea [wave] washed them away, depositing new ones in their places. Sometimes several seas following each other with great rapidity and thundering down on our decks filled them full to the bulwarks, but soon they were discharged through the lee scuppers.

To reef the mainsail we were forced to run off before the gale under the single reefed jib. By the time we had finished the wind had forced up such a tremendous sea that it was impossible to heave her to. Away we flew on the wings of the storm through the muck and flying spray. A wind sheer to starboard, then another to port as the enormous seas [waves] struck the schooner astern and nearly broached her to. As day broke we took in the jib, leaving not a sail unfurled. Since we had begun scudding she had ceased to take the seas over her bow, but amidships they broke fast and furious. It was a dry storm in the matter of rain, but the force of the wind filled the air with fine spray, which flew as high as the cross trees and cut the face like a knife, making it impossible to see over a hundred yards ahead. The sea was a dark lead color as with long, slow, majestic roll it was heaped up by the wind into liquid mountains of foam. The wild antics of the schooner were sickening as she forged along. She would almost stop, as though climbing a mountain, then rapidly rolling to right and left as she gained the summit of a huge sea, she steadied herself and paused for a moment as though affrighted as the yawning precipice before her. Like an avalanche, she shot forward and down as the sea astern struck her with the force of a thousand battering rams, burying her bow to the catheads in the milky foam at the bottom that came on deck in all directions – forward, astern, to right and left, through the hawspipes and over the rail.[9]

It seems appropriate to dismiss the idea that Nephi sailed to the promised land on a raft.

Our Vision of Nephi's Ship

Convinced that Nephi required a strong and fully navigable vessel, we have engineered what we believe is a ship that could have made a crossing from Arabia to Chile and that could have been constructed using the materials and technologies available at Khor Rori in the sixth century BC. Is it consistent with what is known about the design of ancient Omani ships? Yes. But, by definition, its divine modifications would make her a remarkably advanced ship for its time.

As we discuss the attributes of our model for Nephi's ship, the reader might not be familiar with maritime terminology. For this reason, we have placed a list of seamanship terms in the back of the book. To begin with, Nephi's ship would have needed a fine entry (bow piece or front of ship) with enough bearing (steady direction when moving forward in the sea) to run safely in a big sea (large waves). She would have to carry her beam to the transom in order to make her easy to build (see page 41). With a long straight run to a shapely transom, this would allow her to carry sail.

She likely would have had a mean (average or midpoint) depth (lowest point of the ship below the waterline) of about half the greatest cross beam (greatest width of the ship). Likely, she would have a ratio of length to beam of 4 to 1, meaning that the greatest width of the ship was one quarter her length. These were the successful shipbuilding standards in antiquity. Beyond these measures, the designers of old would be baffled by the terms bandied about by modern designers.

The two traditional methods of planking a vessel are clinker-built (or lap strake) and carvel. (A strake is a strip of planking in a wooden vessel running longitudinally along the vessel's side, bottom or the turn of the bilge, usually from one end of the vessel to the other.) The greatest difference between the two is the way the seams are shaped and fastened. The clinker-built depends on the accuracy of the bevel edge on the lapped area (where the planks overlap).

The carvel depends on precisely matching the smooth edges of the plank so that the planks butt up against each other, edge to edge, gaining support from the frame and forming a smooth hull. This was the method possibly employed on Nephi's vessel regardless of how it was fastened, albeit wood pegs, iron nails, or mortise and tenon. All dhows (wooden Arab ships) are

and have always been carvel planked. This would have been the planking process observed by Nephi at Khor Rori. However, due to its size, the hull construction of Nephi's ship may very well have been fashioned after the Greeks, such as built with dados or biscuits between the planks. Otherwise, it is almost impossible for a 120-foot vessel to be built to edge-to-edge

Pointed entry of a traditional Arab ship.

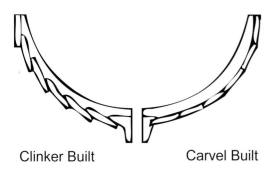

Clinker Built   Carvel Built

tolerances of 1/64 inch along the strakes, subsequently tightening with the swell in salt water.

The planking plan: the boat has fewer planks at the pointy end than at the fat part in the midship centerline. Therefore, planks are reduced in number as one goes forward. Thus, it is necessary to periodically create what are called "joggles" (sawn planks fitted to the reduced planking). The builder joggles planks in order to accomplish his work. Before the planking gets too pointy, joggle it. This is done for strength as well as design. The question begs to be asked, "Who taught Nephi how to create a planking plan or how to joggle?"

If the planking was teak from India, which it most likely was, it would be impervious to toredos or worms that consume any other uncoated wood

Example of joggling planks.

below the waterline. To use anything else but teak in tropical waters would have been a recipe for disaster. Above the waterline, the vessel could and would be a mix of softer woods, particularly in the hull interior as is done in the construction of today's vessels. The hull would have needed curves, thus steam-bent strakes or planks would have been necessary.

As noted, the vessel would have had a length to beam ratio of approximately 4 to 1, which is the norm for antique sail packets, whereas a more recent Clipper ship, for example, would have a length to beam ratio of 5 to 1. The depth of the hull from the main deck to the base line (bottom of the ship) would be half the beam's length (at that point of the ship).

Planking of an Arab dhow.

Bulwarks on Arab wooden ship.

*Traditional shipwright painting
Plimsoll line on Arab dhow.*

*Massive weight of a large wooden sailing
ship is due to the thick timbers needed in
its construction. Notice the screw driver
on the 8" x 12" beam.*

Unlike most ships of Nephi's time, the Lord's design appears to have included an upper deck. We know this was almost certainly the case because they "went down" into the ship (below deck, 1 Nephi 18:8). Even with all their provisions aboard, they still had room to dance (1 Nephi 18:9). With young children aboard, the bulwarks (siding of a ship on the upper deck) would likely have been waist high for an adult at a minimum.

The draft (the depth of water a ship reaches when loaded) of Nephi's ship would likely have equaled one fifteenth ($\frac{1}{15}$) the length of the waterline (a line painted along the sides of a modern ship, indicating the legal limit to which a ship may be loaded, known as a Plimsoll mark or line). These are the basic rules that from antiquity to today still hold true and are used by modern day naval architects.

Ship with lateen sails and a flying sail.

The masts or spars (logs that support the sails) would have been limited by the length of the dhow (Arab ship) that carried the trek logs from India to Khor Rori. The hills of Bountiful above Khor Rori did not have native hardwood trees of the type that would be straight and tall enough to be suitable for masts and spars. This is the reason for the limit of 65 to 82 feet in their length and the necessity for more than one mast to drive this likely

73

more than 500-ton loaded vessel across two oceans with enough square footage of sail to make that happen. The vessel would have needed at least 5,000 square feet of sail area for her size.

Someone, perhaps the Lord, would have advised Nephi as to whether the rig should have square sails, or a lateen (or satee) rig (triangular sail on a long spar hoisted at an angle from a low mast). A square sail rig sails more efficiently downwind (sailing in the direction the wind is blowing), whereas a lateen rig is more efficient going to weather or beating (tacking toward the direction of the wind). We assume either rig could have been used. There are areas of Nephi's voyage where the vessel would have to go to weather (tack, which is turning the forward part of the ship in the direction of the wind). They could have had flying sails (triangular sails extended over the bow on a removable jibboom) to help point high into the wind. Large sweeps (oars) were commonly used on vessels of this period in light air (wind) and for maneuvering in and out of an anchorage. Because the computer simulator has Nephi's ship sailing to weather in parts of both the Indian Ocean and the Pacific Coast of South America, we favor the idea that Nephi used fore and aft sails.

Where could Nephi obtain the idea for lateen sails when most scholars believe that ships of antiquity were rigged exclusively with square sails? One possible answer is that the Lord could have inspired the shape of the sail as one of the modifications of the ship so that it could more effectively carry the family across the many waters (1 Nephi 17:8). It is also possible that lateen sails were already in use in southern Arabia at Nephi's time. Both the date of introduction and origin of the lateen sail, whether in the Mediterranean Sea or Indian Ocean, are debated. Frank remembers visiting the London Maritime (Industrial Museum in West Kensington) in 2007, where a lateen rig display was dated to 1000 BC. Ali Al-Shahri, a rock art specialist who has lectured at Brigham Young University, has documented rock art in the hills surrounding Khor Rori. The rock art has been dated

Two examples of lateen sails from Ali Al-Shahri's collection of rock art in the area around Khor Rori.

to approximately 1000 BC.[10] His extensive documenting of the rock art in the hills around Khor Rori provides a remarkable documentation that lateen sails were used in the first millennium BC at Khor Rori. We can muse whether their first use might have been on Nephi's ship. But whether or not, we believe the Omanis were using flying sails.

On another important matter for Nephi's ship, pine tar or any resinous wood would make a tar to fill the gaps in the decks and interior for finishing. Pitch, bitumen, or lime and fat would make a hull coating, all of which were abundant at Khor Rori.

The vessel likely would need two skiffs or launches (small boats) and a set of some sort of davits to launch and recover the two small boats, most likely off the stern. A davit is a crane made of a swinging boom with blocks and tackle, usually mounted in pairs, which may be swung over the side of a ship to lower and recover small launch. These small boats would be needed for recovering persons in case someone went over the side. The skiff or gig (small boat designed for speed) would also be necessary to go ashore for water and other provisions when the vessel would be at anchor. Also, both skiffs could be used as

Illustration of skiffs used to service anchored dhows. Illustration by Jose Flores.

the storing, the vital balancing, the piloting, the discipline, the land falls, the maintenance, and repair of a vessel that there had to be experienced shipbuilders and mariners involved in this venture.

Displacement is the weight of a mass of water pushed aside by the intrusion of a ship's hull. The likely displacement of Nephi's vessel could be calculated using this formula:

Length x Beam x Draft divided by 35 cu. ft. (1 ton of water) x .65 (constant) = approx. tons displacement (dead weight).

So:

120 ft. length x 30 ft. of width x 8 ft. of beam / 35 cu. ft. x .65 = 535 tons displacement.

A vessel of this size would not be beach launchable either empty or fully loaded.

propulsion aids in the doldrums or calms, for landings and departures through reef passes, and to and from potential harbor sites where they could take on provisions.

Most likely the ground tackle (anchor and its gear) for Nephi's ship would be two stone anchors, one port and one starboard, in addition to one spare anchor to replace either if lost. The spare anchor would have

to be properly secured on the main deck in a most seaworthy manner, because in heavy weather, the potential exists for a loose anchor to damage the vessel to the extent that the ship could even be lost.

There is no doubt in our minds, however, that as Nephi constructed his ship, he needed experienced help. There is so much involved in the construction, the rigging,

Length 120 feet

Width 30 Feet

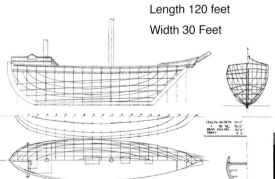

Proposed Dimensions of Nephi's Ship, Drawings by Frank Linehan

*Ancient Indian Ocean vessel
with quarter rudder.*

Yet it could not be much smaller and make the trip with perhaps up to seventy people aboard. Each of the anchors alone would have weighed a minimum of a ton in order to hold safely a vessel of this size and tonnage in any kind of severe weather.

Nephi's Quarter Rudder and What It Tells Us about Nephi's Ship

A large sailing ship capable of reaching the New World from southern Arabia would have been a very complex vessel. Some might think an ancient sailing ship was low-tech and something a novice could construct, but nothing could be further from the truth. A vessel capable of enduring a transit of the Indian and Pacific Oceans would have to have incorporated the very best shipwright skills of its time, a body of knowledge that had been handed down from father to son over centuries of shipbuilding. To illustrate this point, let's discuss in detail just one of dozens of critical parts of Nephi's ship: its rudder.

A simple steering oar would not have worked for Nephi's passage to the New World because it is imprecise. A steering oar could be placed at various locations on a ship; in many cases, it was hung off or lashed to the stern. In contrast, Nephi's and the brother of Jared's vessels required the more precise and advanced quarter rudders that already had been developed by their eras.

Forty-five hundred years ago, the quarter rudder development spread throughout the ancient seagoing world. The quarter rudder is also called a side rudder. We will use the term quarter rudder rather than

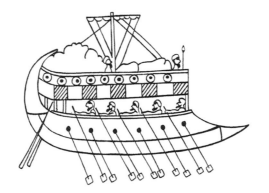

Quarter rudders on Phoenician ship.

the other term only because it denotes the location where the rudder was placed on the vessel, at the rear quarter of the ship. The quarter rudder was actually two rudders, one attached to each side of the ship. It was a very effective and simple way of steering a ship. The development went through many changes in design during the next two thousand years; it became more refined and thus was capable of steering large vessels. Technologically, it was the state of the art for steering ships in the ancient world. Ultimately it was replaced by the rudder as we know it today. This occurred because the quarter rudder couldn't evolve to fit the more advanced construction and more complex vessel designs that came out of shipyards three thousand years later.

All Greek, Roman, Omani, and Indian designs employed the quarter rudder, yet even to this day, we still do not exactly know how they attached or mounted the rudder. Even in Aristotle's *Mechanica* where he discusses the rudder and its functions, there is no mention of the design and attachment to the vessel. This means the ancients were more technologically advanced than some give them credit for. The rudder attachment becomes paramount, particularly in heavy weather,

ships, but also served to promote stability similar to today's daggerboards (center board of a sailing boat).

The reason the attachment of the quarter rudder is of such interest is because of the necessity to hoist the rudder out of the water and the requirement to keep that rudder from swinging side to side in heavy weather. Obviously, this is a matter that was solved by shipwrights of the time. It is not a design problem Nephi could have solved while building his first ship without the assistance of a skilled shipwright. Yet without a stable quarter rudder he could not have steered his ship to the New World. Nephi's vessel would be too large to even consider a single point attachment as presented by Plato in his *Alcibiades*. Plato's description of moving the tiller inward and outward can be interpreted in many ways and is hardly proof of its attachment. Further, the Greeks point out that the helmsman of large vessels only had to use one hand on the tiller to maneuver the ship. This tells us they knew where to design the center of fulcrum (turning point) in order to overcome the moment of inertia of the vessel.

It is pretty much common knowledge that the ancient quarter rudders were designed

and placed between thirty and forty-five degrees from the vertical. This we know from Greek and Roman records. This angle of range reduced the stress on the mounts, in addition to being the most effective angle for maneuvers. The angle also reduced the hydrodynamic lift and immersion surface of the blade, thus reducing turbulence (cavitation) and drag of the rudder. Deep immersion would cause greater drag of the vessel and also cause greater possibility for structural failure of the rudder and/or its mounts. If the rudder were mounted at a

Repairing quarter rudder on the
Phoenicia. *Courtesy of Phoenicia.org.*

because loss of the rudder generally means loss of the ship. The hydrodynamic forces on the quarter rudder versus later-period rudders are dramatically different due to the location and design of the vessel's stern. We know that their quarter rudder was of a more sophisticated design than heretofore thought. It not only steered their

Quarter rudder on the **Phoenicia.**
Courtesy of Phoenicia.org.

too shallow angle, every time the helmsman turned the rudder it would cause the blade to lift, thus loosing the rudder's inherent steering advantage. Optimum immersion would have been about seventy percent. Deeper would have caused more drag.

These quarter rudders had more design-thought in them than today's modern center hung pintle and gudgeon designs. The ancients may not have understood all the engineering mechanics of their designs, but rather through years of observation they likely polished the construction of mountings, angles of repose, blade design, depth of immersion, and weight of the rudder. These rudders would have weighed several tons, as would have Nephi's. They probably would have to be of this weight, otherwise in heavy weather, without mechanical assistance, these quarter rudders would have been truly unwieldable for even the strongest helmsman.

The rudders would have to be adjustable in terms of their depth in the water due to the change of the ship's draft because of the addition of more ballast or cargo. A rudder has to be at just the right depth and angle to the stern. Thus, if the vessel were changing her draft quite often, as per a cargo vessel, then the rudder would need to be angle adjustable. This principle also applies to Nephi's vessel just from the standpoint of the rudder becoming water logged and weighing more as the trip progressed across the Indian Ocean and the Pacific Ocean. In other words, when the trip began, the rudder—due to more buoyancy—would have been floating at a steeper angle. As the rudder became more water-soaked, it would move downward at a closer angle relative to its fulcrum center (the support about which the rudder levers pivot). This would make the rudder much more difficult to actuate.

When that occurred, the master would want a spare and would seek to pull in somewhere sheltered in order to change it out. Undoubtedly, Nephi's vessel carried a spare quarter rudder, if not two. The spares would need to be secured on deck somewhere for ease of accessibility. A lower freeboard (the vertical length between the waterline and the top of the hull) would require a smaller rudder, but a greater freeboard, as in Nephi's ocean-going ship, would require a larger rudder. The greater freeboard and larger rudder would be necessary in order to transit the rough seas of the lower latitudes of the South Pacific with such a large number of passengers and their provisions. This greater freeboard on Nephi's vessel negates the hypothesis of a single point attachment of the quarter rudder on his vessel. If the vessel encountered a wave that caused the ship to roll and lift, the strain on the rudder would be such that only a two-point attachment system could spread the strain to both beams and prevent failure.

The rudders' transverse beams would have been anchored into beams for strength of construction and to spread the load of both rudders being in water at the same time. The lower beam would have to have been stouter structurally to carry the weight of the rudder plus absorb the forces of the sea pushing into the hull of the vessel. In addition, if Nephi's vessel went in stern (rear) first to the beach where there was no docking facilities in order to unload passengers and cargo, it would have been necessary to be able to pull up the rudders so as not to sustain damage. This supports the need for a twin beam double-lashing system that would protect the rudder when hitting a submerged object or running aground, because one lashing would break, and the rudder would pivot up on the other lashing. In addition, it also was necessary to pull the rudders up in certain points of sail to increase the speed of the vessel. The rudder mounts would require a design that would enable them to lift the heavy rudders out of the sea. Further, the mounts needed to be of sufficient strength to endure the loading and stress transmitted to the vessel from the forces of the sea in everyday sailing, plus have the ability to not sustain damage in a storm that could result in the loss of vessel and passengers. The rudders would have to be designed such that in a storm they would enhance the stability of the vessel.

All aforementioned factors needed to be taken into account by local shipwrights when designing and building Nephi's vessel. When the reader considers all the issues that were encountered in the design and building of Nephi's vessel, it gives one a much greater appreciation for their accomplishment.

Without going into the calculations, we can hypothesize that Nephi's rudders were not lighter than a quarter of a ton but not greater than three tons. His crew would have needed tackle of some form in order to manage adjustments to height and angle of the rudder. His crew would use this tackle to change out the rudder due to damage or waterlog or in order to beach the vessel for reason of bottom scraping

and fouling. These issues would have been encountered about halfway through the voyage, so this would necessitate the rudder being designed to be raised. If the rudders weighed a couple tons each, it would not be possible for a even couple of sailors to lift the rudder from their own strength alone. We should say here that it has also been documented that some vessels carried different size and design of rudders to facilitate different sailing conditions and in order to balance the rig. Smaller rudders would work with correspondingly smaller forces and torques. They could be lashed into place without specialized mounting. To prevent rudders from slipping in their lashings or mountings, they would need to be tapered in their shaft so that they would be thicker toward the head of the shaft that the tiller was attached to. We hypothesize that Nephi had both types of rudders and their corresponding attachments, due to the length of his voyage and the unknown conditions that they were going to encounter.

Nephi needed a steering system that would allow the rudder shaft to rotate partially forward when an upper lashing broke after hitting a submerged object. This hypothesis is suggested by the routes that Nephi and company took through waters where

this was bound to happen. Therefore, the crew would need to have been skilled at pulling one rudder out of the water and unshipping it from its mount by rigging tackle from the mast and/or yard arm to pull it to the vertical. This is no small undertaking and requires the skill of experienced seamen. Simply controlling the swaying mass, if it had to be done at sea, required great skill and seamanship.

The technology associated with a rudder sophisticated enough to guide a ship from Arabia to the New World was well known to the shipwrights of Nephi's period. What we have tried to show the reader is that it was not a simple undertaking to build a vessel and transit fifteen thousand miles across two oceans. But though not simple, it was completely accomplishable with the professional help of that day and age. In addition, we hope we have made the case that the ancients were a great deal smarter and craftier than we give them credit for in our day and age. Their designs were well thought out and the sailors of that age were very skilled.

We of this dispensation owe much to the ancients who surely assisted Nephi with his construction and voyage to the New World. They are the unknowns who

Crew working aboard a pearl ship, Bahrain National Museum.

and rig would need to be repaired immediately in order to not lose the vessel, no matter if it were day or night. This is how it has been for millennia—both in antiquity as well as today. It is also a sailing fact that people get hurt in heavy weather sailing and need to be taken care of.

Once underway, frequent maintenance and repair would have included scrubbing the decks; wetting the decks down in the tropics; wetting down the skiff or launches; "stoning the decks" weekly (sand the deck with abrasive flat stones to clean off grease, blood, and so on); cleaning the berthing; cleaning the galley, stove, and cookware; getting wood for the stove; getting water from the barrels to cook with; checking the potable water storage; checking food supplies; restocking food; checking and repairing rigging and sails; checking and

helped make possible the voyage to provide a gospel legacy that has been given to us for our age.

Sailing aboard Nephi's Great Ship

It should be apparent that we believe that at least some trained crew would have been required in order to have made a safe and successful voyage. Nephi's voyage could not occur by happenstance or with a complete group of untrained novices. Too many seriously negative events would have happened en route. Some of the waters that Nephi and company transited are known to be very treacherous. When sailing a

large sailing ship with gaffs (spars), heavy canvas, thick manila lines, and so on, it is all a crew can do to eat, sleep, and sail. No one has time to dance and make merry (1Nephi 18:9) unless in port or in a dead calm. This again tells us there was probably a professional crew doing the work behind the scenes during Nephi's voyage. Fortunately, Khor Rori was the main port for the frankincense trade and, thus, there would have been an ample source of skilled seamen.

Here are some considerations. When sailing in heavy weather, damages to the hull

Manning the sails required trained and experienced crewmen. Illustration by Jose Flores.

repairing vessel scantlings or hull; repairing coatings as necessary; applying where necessary tar or fat on the rigging and spars; and replacing rigging or sails as needed, weather providing. Likely, each day in some aspect or another, the wooden sailing vessel would have required maintenance and repair on it and the rig. It would be a perpetual task on a two- or three-mast rig of the size to transport approximately seventy persons across the Indian and Pacific oceans.

The necessity of having some persons aboard who understood the arts of manning sails, steering the ship, sailing with and against the wind, and repairing the ship at sea require—in our minds—some persons aboard Nephi's ship were experienced sailors, perhaps even sailors Nephi converted while at Bountiful (D&C 33:8). We believe to crew Nephi's vessel would have taken at least three men for each traditional four-hour watch during a twelve-hour period: two men aft at the tiller and one man forward as lookout. That is nine men for the three watches, yet even this does not include some type of sailing master who would have to supervise the crew. It also does not include a ship's carpenter and sail maker. Cotton canvas sails require frequent repair and that is why a sail maker was part of major crews. He would be as vital as the ship's carpenter who literally would be slowly rebuilding the ship during the course of voyage.

When the sails became wet, they would be extremely heavy to handle, and it would have required all hands on deck. That's a likely minimum core crew of thirteen experienced seamen to crew a 120-foot, two-mast, square sail or fore and aft rig sailing vessel. However, it would have taken at least eight men alone to raise the main spar. This total number of crew, of which thirteen would be experienced seamen, compares well to the twenty-man crew aboard Severin's much smaller *Sohar*, eight of them forming the core of the team. Severin's writes of his eight-man core, "They would have to be prime seamen, accustomed to shiphandling, because they would have to teach the rest of the crew how to sail the vessel using the very special rig of an Arab *boom*. Throughout the voyage the main work of *Sohar*, the handling of sails, the adjusting of the rigging, and the general maintenance of the ship, would fall on the shoulders of the Omani sailors . . . to back them up would be other volunteers, mostly European, who had specific technical skills."[11]

Three of Severin's eight Omani sailors served as "watch leaders" during the voyage. Members of the non-Omani crew were assigned positions of navigator, purser, diver, and ship cook. Severin was the ship's captain for the voyage. Three of the non-Omani voluneeters who sailed on *Sohar* were marine scientists keen on having an opportunity to perform experiments along the way. However, Severin made it clear that everyone on board was a member of the crew and responsible for the ship. "'I'm afraid we can only ship aboard about half of that stuff,' I told the three scientists, gesturing at their piles of equipment. 'Your first job is to select what equipment is not essential, and leave it behind, or send it back home to your universities. Afterwards, we will find room for what is left and stow it aboard. As soon as that is done, I want you to help out with the general loading and rigging of the ship.'

"'But we've come as scientists . . . ,' began Andrew.

"'Not on *Sohar*, I'm afraid,' I broke in firmly. 'Everyone is first and foremost a sailor, or the ship can't operate. I want all of you to handle ropes and riggings, and to stand watches. Sailors first, scientists second.'"[12]

Of course, we can only speculate the number of people it took to fill the crew of Nephi's ship. However, it is most reasonable to assume that Nephi needed a core of "prime seamen" to safely operate his large ship. We believe the crew of the *Sohar* provides a reasonable model for how Nephi could have acquired the seamanship skills and experience necessary to reach the promised land. Our proposed model would be a core crew of approximately thirteen seasoned Omani sailors who were supported by every physically fit member of Lehi's family. Even the three surprised scientists on the *Sohar* can represent reluctant members of Lehi's family who found themselves having to pull their share of the workload.

How large a crew did it traditionally take to man an Omani ship the size we think was Nephi's? According to the Omani Ministry of Heritage and Culture, a traditional wooden Omani sailing ship required a crew of 25–40 persons. A typical crew would have consisted of:

Nawkhuda (captain) 1

mu'allin (pilot or navigator) 1

karrani (clerk or keeper of accounts) 1

sarhang (boatswain or mate) 1

sukkani (helmsman) 2–3

bahriyah (seaman) 10–15

tabbakh (cook) 1–2

batili (boatkeeper in large vessels towing a mashwah or small vessel) 1

walad (boy) 2–3[13]

Even in modern sailing vessels with automatic pilots, a twenty-four-hour-a-day watch is necessary. This report that we received from Jody Lemmon aboard the *Banyan* points this out.

A Rough Night aboard the Banyan

Sat. 6 Jun 2009

We are all doing well.

I started sending the "Spots"; let me know when you start receiving them. We are moving along at a decent rate. The wind has been shifting a lot from the Southeast to almost due East. I have had to get up 4–8 times a night to adjust the sails for the past 3 nights. When the wind shifts the sails begin to flap violently and the whole boat shudders and shakes, a most unpleasant experience. Among the various sail changes is the wing and wing configuration. This involves swinging the main sail all the way out to one side while the jib or headsail is swung out and poled to the opposite side. This allows our course to follow straight downwind. The problem with this setup is that when the wind changes, the main can become back winded. When that happens, the entire sail flaps violently—not fun.

At sunset yesterday we were sailing wing and wing and the main back winded. Luckily no one was on deck, because the preventer that was rigged to stop the boom from swinging across the boat and destroying anything in its path became disconnected. There is a canvas canopy that covers the cockpit and is removable to allow the boom's position to be carefully changed. When the preventer failed, the boom swung across the entire boat and ripped the canvas's connection points out. For some amazing reason only two of the button fasteners actually were torn from the canvas, the other 12 or so appeared completely undamaged.

Once we heard the violence occurring topside we all crept up the stairs to find out what was happening. As we poked our heads out we could see the boom swinging about freely, a great danger on a rolling boat in the middle of the sea. We grabbed the main sheet and hauled with all of our might to tame the wild beast. Once everything was under control I crawled up onto the fore deck to investigate the cause of all the excitement. The preventer shackle, seemed perfectly fine. A very bizarre situation. I reattached the shackle and let the main sheet out. Needless to say from now on we use an extra line to secure the main, a backup preventer, if you will. One can only imagine what would happen if one of us was standing on deck when the giant boom decided to go on a free-for-all.

We should see land in about 2½ days. The idea seams surreal. We all have our own wishes and desires that only land can satisfy. The excitement is beginning to well up inside of all of us as we approach a place that is both magical and foreboding. The beauty of the tropical islands will be something incredible to behold after so much blue. We are all starved for a view that only land can provide.

I, personally, am a bit nervous about the reefs we will be skirting and the obstacles ahead of us. The Tuamotu atolls lie between the Marquesas and Tahiti. This treacherous area of the ocean has claimed many a vessel due to the uncharted and hidden reefs. The task of traveling between so many islands, where the highest point of land may be only a few feet, is daunting in itself. Compound this with the narrow reef passages one must navigate to get to a protected lagoon and the task becomes daunting. Many of the passages can have currents up to 6 knots during the rush of high and low tide. Our timing will be critical and a watchful eye aloft will be indispensable in the spotting of submerged reefs. We have been studying the charts and pilot guides for the reefs and passages, but only experience can provide peace of mind. I just hope the learning curve does not prove to be too disastrous . . .

Jody

Frank made some sobering comments on Jody's report: "Those boys are breaking the Cardinal Sailing Rule, and that is 'someone is always on watch' regardless of how tranquil the conditions appear. You can never turn your back on the sea." Frank sent this comment to Jody's father (Bruce), because the South Pacific claims several yachts each year, and sailing at night is particularly treacherous.

Of course, any crew has to know with immediate exactness what to do under various sea conditions. If hit by a sudden gale, the crew would have only minutes to shorten the sails or the sails would be ripped apart or the ship capsized. The crew had to have the savvy to know how to handle giant rogue waves and other hazards of the sea.

Conrad recalls an experience he had while on a fishing boat returning from Alaska. While traveling through Seymour Narrows on the down side of Ripple Rock, his vessel was forced by a freighter into a monster whirlpool full of shooting logs. But for the grace of God, the logs would have pierced his hull had it not been by a quick maneuver of the engineer and Conrad who were on the helm. They reversed one propeller for a moment to get the bow of the vessel facing up and out and then switched back to the forward position. They gave both engines full throttle, which after making one rotation on the lip of the whirlpool, they had just enough power to push the vessel out of a dire situation that would have swallowed the vessel and all hands aboard. Can we imagine trying to handle such a whirlpool or a treacherous shore-bound current in an ancient sailing ship with an unseasoned crew? Surely, Nephi's crew consisted

of either experienced Omani sailors or a "family crew" (bloodline males, servants, and so on) who had considerable practice sailing or, most likely, the full crew came from both of these sources.

The challenge of the sea is what brings out the best in a sailor and draws him back to sea. Even a rather normal day at sea requires the seaman's skill and wit. Over time, the two forces of ocean and sailor blend together. We received this email from our friend Jody Lemmon.[14]

Aboard the Banyan with Jody Lemmon

Hello there,

We are currently crossing the famed Tehuantepec! Yesterday evening we loaded the boat full of 5000 pesos (approx. $370.00) worth of groceries from the Super Che in Huatulco and shoved off. It was sad leaving the odd little marina. The governing authority is Enrique and his attendance seemed to be a guest appearance at times rather than a full-time presence. The marina is truly the last refuge for sailors heading south past the Tehuantepec. It also acts as a final southing point for many sailors. The mixed group of people present in the marina was quite intriguing.

A German couple arrived shortly after us from the south. Their dilapidated vessel seemed to have been to the far reaches of the world so we invited them over for a refreshment and some story swapping. It turned out that they had left Germany 3½ years ago. They headed to South America and then decided on a whim to round

Cape Horn. They did so and at times faced 80-knot winds. Once they reached the Horn they found about 20 boats "holed up" waiting for a weather window to cross into the Antarctic! A wild and cold world indeed down there. From Tierra Del Fuego they headed north to Peru, then launched across to the Galapagos. Once there they headed straight for Costa Rica. From Costa Rica they skirted the coast past El Salvador and ended up in Huatulco.

We left yesterday evening, despite Captain Pete's belief that we should wait until morning. We motored all night through calm seas. It began to feel a bit weird, but nothing too strange.

We passed our night shifts as we hugged the coast until 3 am. Then, we aimed southeast and began to cross the Tehuantepec. At 8 a.m. the wind finally kicked in and I awoke with a throbbing sore throat and a fever. Perfect timing. I clambered up on deck and Sean and I hoisted the main to the second reef point and the jib in an appropriate balance. As the morning wore on the winds increased. We found ourselves 20 miles from land in 25 knots of wind!!! The books all say that one should traverse passage within one mile or less of land, but the people we spoke with said that the region was completely fouled with fishing nets and hugging the coast would increase our crossing time by 6 hours.

Well, we decided to reef down the main to the 3rd reef and doused the genoa in exchange for the cutter/storm sail. We, then, proceeded along through the increasing maelstrom. I worried that we were in store for a wild and wet ride. Water was beginning to splash onto the deck, so all weather side ports were closed forthwith. Our speed was between 5 and 5.5 knots on a beam reach. As the morning turned into day the waves began to increase coming at us from the shore side direction, which was very odd indeed. At about this time I crawled below to try and sleep off my fever.

I awoke an hour later to the gentle slapping of waves against the hull. The wind had dropped to 10 knots!!! I leaped up the stairs and promptly hoisted all the canvas we have on board.

Jody

It is our opinion that Nephi's party probably made landfall at least three or four times to replenish water and fruit. Otherwise, the whole company could have been dropping like flies from scurvy before they arrived in the New World. The minimum amount of food per person would be 1.5 pounds per person per day. If you stored the ship for 120 days for 70 persons at 1.5 pounds per day, this would equal 6.75 tons of food for the journey. This would not include fruit that would be required to combat scurvy. Finding fruit would have been no problem while transiting through Indonesia, Micronesia, Polynesia, Australia, and New Zealand. However, it required finding and navigating into a safe harbor. Fortunately, they had the Liahona.

A very bad day aboard the *Banyan* illustrates how dangerous landing on an island for provisions could have been. Jody Lemmon is an experienced sailor aboard an exquisite boat that he brought into Tuamotu atolls under the control of power (motor), not sails. His experience again highlights the training and experience Nephi's crew must have.

June 18, 2009

Tuamotu atolls

We just entered our first Tuamotu. It was quite possibly the worst experience we have had so far. My tide log claimed that low tide was 30 minutes before our arrival. We should have had slack tide. We pulled up to a small fishing boat with natives and asked in sign language if it was okay to go through the reef pass. It was about 1 hour before dark. The fishermen all waved and pointed into the pass with thumbs up. We decided to go for it.

As we entered the narrow pass we could see water flowing out of the lagoon. We figured it would be okay so we made our way against the 2-knot current into the channel. The channel runs about 1 mile long and is about 50 feet wide. As we made our way along the narrow channel the current began to increase. By about the half waypoint I realized that the current was really becoming strong, but I was trapped and couldn't turn around. So we kept pushing on toward the end of the narrow channel, where we could

turn into the deep lagoon. As we reached the critical point we could see a terrible current ripping around the bend and into the channel. As I neared the turn the current whipped up to 6 knots. I had to punch the throttle into full bore and handle the wheel with a death grip. It took about 5 minutes to make it through this terrible rip current where one mistake would have thrown the boat onto the dry reef. It was the most harrowing experience I have had so far aboard the Banyan. Even with the engine on full bore we only made headway of about 2 knots. We crept along with the bow swinging wildly until we made it into the deep water of the lagoon. Once there we thought the trouble was over. I was trembling all over from the intensity of the situation.

We all looked at each other relieved. I then turned our course toward the backside of the small island ring where we could find an anchorage. As we motored along all of a sudden we smashed into solid ground. We all got thrown forward and the boat lurched to a halt.

After all of that I had run aground on a coral head! My nerves had been completely shot and I blew our course and crashed. I then was able to get us off of the coral head and back into deep water. We then motored over to the anchorage and attempted to anchor in 70 ft of water. The first try was unsuccessful as the anchor drug and we were in danger of hitting ground again. By this time the sun was setting and we were nearing dark. We quickly pulled up the anchor and moved further into the lagoon amongst the oyster farming buoys. We dropped

anchor again and it held, luckily. I quickly dove over the side hoping that enough light would be left to check for damage. The keel sustained moderate scrapes and the rudder was scratched up the side. As I neared the propeller I could see that the blades had hit the coral head as well. Each blade was bent slightly in perfect unison. Under power there was no rattling or shaking, so I can only hope the prop is still somewhat balanced. I screwed up big time, but at least I didn't lose the entire boat. My first atoll proved to be a real horror. I feel very intimidated by these reef passes. I am quite nervous to leave the pass now after such a horrible experience. I don't think we will be stopping at any more of the Tuamotu's. We will head straight to Tahiti where we will stop for a bit to gather our senses and put the boat back in order.

I'm really upset at myself. I hope the prop will hold out, considering you guys just went through so much to get a new one. I wonder if I can take it off and have it re-bent back into position in Tahiti, or if I should just leave it until New Zealand. The blades all seem to be bent evenly and when I ran the engine I could feel no shaking. I even put the boat in gear and put my hand on the shaft inside the boat to feel for any vibration. It felt fine.

This all happened about 30 minutes ago, my spirits are really low right now. We are in a huge lagoon in the middle of the Pacific Ocean lined by a death reef. I am really nervous about going out again. We will have to go ashore and check with someone, hopefully dependable, about when we should attempt to leave this trap.

Jody

In times of heavy weather of fifteen- to twenty-foot seas, a crew must secure everything. That means everything has to be tied down. Even cupboards must be latched. Otherwise, everything will be thrown about like missiles. In such sea conditions, cooking in the ship's sand pits would not be possible.

A crew's work proceeds without stop 24/7. Would Nephi's brothers and Ishmael's family know this? Could they have done it without some skilled seamen aboard? We sincerely doubt it. For example, who taught Nephi and the family how to load the ship? The cargo of stores and personal possessions would need to be loaded through a hatch on the main deck that would be weather tight. This cargo would need to be loaded so that it would not shift in heavy weather or in a storm and cause the loss of the vessel. Further, cargo had to be loaded in a manner to allow access and proper bracing and be secured against movement that could damage the hull.

Let's take up another question: How would they sleep? Historically, sailors used hammocks. There would be bunks for some of the privileged, such as the captain, heads of families, owners, and so on, but the bulk of the crew would have lain down on the deck with bed rolls.

85

Food and water likely would need to be rationed quite severely at times for a voyage of Nephi's length, unless the company pulled in for land fall at least three times. Toward the end of the voyage, it is quite possible that food and water did not suffice.

Winds tend to be fluky or ever-changing in some areas when sailing along the southern latitudes. Constant sail changes in trim and reefing would be the norm. Reefing is the practice of shortening the sail to prevent it from being blown out by heavier airs and would have been perpetually required, both day and night. Generally at night they would have to shorten or change sails for rig safety. Sail changes at night would need to be done by seasoned, skilled sailors who intuitively knew where the tripping hazards were and where all the rigging was secured. Likely, there would only be one small lamp on deck, and that might be for the Liahona. Otherwise, you want everything as dark as possible so that your eyes could become accustomed to the night and so that the watch's night vision would not be affected. Further, the watch navigated by the stars.

Landsmen, generally with difficulty, would attempt to walk the deck of a vessel with no lights among all the tripping hazards of bitts, rings, pad eyes, blocks, lines, spars, and all other matter of equipage on a wet, rolling, and night-shrouded deck. Only a seasoned sailor could work safely in such an environment.

We hope you are starting to understand the size, scope, and dangers of Nephi's endeavor. It was truly monumental in its undertaking.

Repairing the ship

As noted earlier, a wooden sailing ship is in need of constant repair. Even without the impact of hitting a reef or being attacked by another ship, a wooden vessel is being constantly weakened and must be continuously repaired to maintain its strength. A scene from the book *Master Commander*, a British commander focuses on his ship being severely damaged by a French warship. He had to decide whether to head for port to be refitted or to attempt refitting at sea while chasing the French vessel. He elected to repair the heavily damaged warship at sea. Undoubtedly, Nephi's ship also experienced some kind of significant damage during the great and terrible four-day storm that was about to swallow his ship into the depths of the sea (1 Nephi 17:14–15), as well as from countless other events in the months ahead. To understand the complexity and precise balance required in building and maintaining a ship, we return to the *Banyan*'s troubles of Jody Lemmon at the dangerous Tuamotu atoll.

June 20, 2009

Hey guys, well here is what we did and found out today. The coral head smashed the rudder. It punctured into the foam core about one inch deep by two inches wide. We first filled in the hole with underwater epoxy. I then realized how the propeller got damaged. The rudder got jammed over so hard it actually hit the propeller, thus chewing a bite out of the rudder and bending the propeller blades. I then had Matt turn the wheel, while I was under water. The rudder would turn to starboard fully, but only to port about 2 inches. This was at 8 a.m. this morning.

I then opened up the lockers to get access to the steering area. Once I inspected the various components I found that the sheer pin that holds the steering linkage wheel together was completely bent. I took the whole steering linkage apart and inspected the wheel. The sheer pin was bent beyond repair and the slot in the bronze where it fit was totally smashed and bent. We found that turning the steering wheel still turned the rudder, but it had bent so much that it could barely go past center on the starboard side. I tried to bend the pin and re-seat the whole wheel back onto the rudder shaft with no success. I, then, decided to completely abandon the pin and use a bolt to hold the wheel in place. I had to drill a 3/8-inch hole into the side of the steel rudder shaft. After a long time I finally got the hole drilled and put the 3/8 bolt through the wheel into the pin. Then we cranked down the four bolts that held the wheel around the rudder shaft. Now the pressure of the rudder in relation to the steering wheel all depends on a 3/8-inch bolt, and the friction of four bolts that just clamp the wheel around the shaft. Once I put it all together I realized it was off by a bit, so we tried to re-adjust the little wheels where the cables go, so one of them wouldn't hit the rudder shaft wheel. That didn't work because it messed up the alignment between the two little wheels and the cable fell off. I, then, had to use the metal grinder and grind down these four bolt heads to about 1/2 their original height. This allowed free movement to occur without any of the pieces hitting each other when the wheel was turned.

The next problem I found was that the auto pilot arm attachment to the rudder shaft had also been damaged. The 3/8-inch bolt that held the arm attachment from the rudder shaft to the electric arm was completely sheared off level with the shaft. I took the whole arrangement off and tried to figure out how to get the broken bolt out of the shaft. By this point it was 5 p.m. 8 hours of straight work in the death hole. Mikey had brought us a cold drink at about 2 p.m. and we ate 3 pieces of breadfruit. That was all we had eaten all day. I decided to take a break and have some cabbage and canned tuna salad, which Mike had prepared.

During the day a catamaran had pulled into the lagoon and dropped anchor next to us. They said that they had had a heck of a time as well, but the current was only at about 3 knots as opposed to our 6 knots. He said that it was also a harrowing experience, he had to use both of his engines in a back an fourth manner to avoid being caught broad side to the current and being swept onto the reef. During the day they had gone to shore and by speaking French were able to talk to the weather station manager. He said that tomorrow at 1 p.m. would be a good time to leave. We will follow the catamaran out tomorrow at that time.

Back to the sheered bolt problem. I once again climbed into my tiny hole, this time with a head-lamp, as it was almost dark. I decided to try and drill a couple of holes into the center of the sheered-off steel bolt. This proved to be very difficult. I, then, got a chisel and a hammer and tried to at least get some sort of a groove into the bolt. As I was smashing the hammer the broken bolt actually moved a little bit. It was amazing; the bolt was slightly loose in the threads. I, then, spend the next hour using a hammer and chisel to move the small piece of bolt around and around by tiny little increments. Finally, I was able to use vice grips and I triumphantly unscrewed the sheered-off bolt. Amazingly, Mikey was able to find a same sized bolt to match our broken one, amongst our spares, and I re-attached our autopilot arm and screwed in the new bolt to hold the arm securely in place, just like it was originally!

Now, our problem revolves around the bent propeller and the fact that only one 3/8-inch bolt is holding our steering system in place to our rudder shaft. Once we get to Papeete, I will get a tap and die set to drill a new hole and threads into the shaft in a new location. That way two bolts will share the pressure. The sheer pin is now useless. Hopefully, this new system will work. At least we are back in action after about 12 hours of intense work in a grease pit. I just hope that the poorpropeller shaft doesn't get too loose. She now has a fare bit of play as opposed to how she was when we hauled the boat out of the water back in Long Beach. Running aground on a reef is really a damaging affair. I hope this episode will never be repeated! At least we are good to go for now and can make our way directly to Papeete, where some much needed supplies and safety await!

Jody

Who Might Have Conducted the Sea Trials of Nephi's Vessel?

Having reflagged (changed ownership or re-commissioned overhauled ships) and drydocked many ships, Frank explains the absolute necessity of sea trials before a ship is ready for her first voyage. "It has taken me almost forty years of experience to learn how to conduct a ship's sea trial. No one can obtain knowledge like that overnight. Where I am heading with this is that somebody who was a very skilled mariner surely went out with Nephi's ship on her maiden voyage and 'shook her down,' in marine jargon.

"That master seaman had to determine that Nephi's ship had the correct amount of ballast and that it was placed correctly and properly secured for heavy weather. He would essentially ask many questions: Was the rig set up and tuned right? Were the sails sized properly and cut right? Was all the running rigging rigged and sized adequately? Were both masts properly stepped and positioned to the keel? Was the rudder properly sized for the vessel and secured to the stern frame in such a manner that it would not be lost in heavy weather? In all points of wind, did the boat have weather helm [tendency of the ship to turn into the wind] or lee helm [tendency of the ship to turn away from the wind] with all the canvas flying? Was the ground tackle adequate to hold the vessel in a 'blow'? At what point of sail would the ship sail most efficiently under various ranges of wind? Most important would be thorough checks to see that the vessel was watertight in all sea conditions. Quite possibly, one watertight bulkhead [a partition separating areas] would be forward [toward the front of the ship] only a few feet aft [back] of the bow. This would be called the collision bulkhead. If the vessel hit something, this bulkhead, along with the heavy keel, would prevent the ship from sinking. This would have been particularly necessary if transiting through Polynesia and Micronesia with their myriad of reefs.

"At the end of the sea trial, this master mariner would have a list of deficiencies that would require repair and alteration. Many repairs and adjustments would need to be done on an adjacent dhow or similar vessel that likely was twice as large as the norm with double the sailing rig for that day and age. The fellow who conducted the sea trial would have been a capable, well-experienced seaman and boat builder."

How Did Nephi Navigate His Ship?

As we know, Nephi had one huge advantage over other ancient mariners: he had the Liahona that functioned as a compass, as well as many other things, and was the means for receiving new communications from the Lord. From what the Book of Mormon tells us, the Liahona pointed the direction to follow to reach the promised land. However, it likely did not calculate one's current position on earth, like a GPS (Global Positioning System) would do. So, can we ask, how did Nephi know that his ship had been forced backward (1 Nephi 18:13–14) in the four-day storm they encountered during the initial stage of their voyage? Because Nephi states "time and distance," he would have had to know how to calculate his latitude position. In Nephi's day, such information and related methodology for knowing it was a guarded secret known in the Mideast only to the Arabs, Phoenicians, and Egyptians. However, it should be remembered that Nephi spent eight years in the Arabian desert, apparently converted people while there, and subsequently spent up to possibly two years building his ship, all the while rubbing shoulders with the greatest seagoing captains of his time at Khor

Arabs calculated latitude by measuring the angle of the stars to the horizon.

Rori. As such, we believe that Nephi had a unique opportunity to have learned how to calculate latitude, which is yet another remarkable insight into the historicity of the Book of Mormon. Severin explains how the ancient Arabs mariners calculated their latitude:

> Just how did an early Arab navigator measure his position? How did he lay off his course? The instrument he used was no more than a wooden tablet [called a Kamal] about 3 inches wide with a hole in the middle of it; through this hole ran a piece of string with a knot in it. The navigator placed the knot between his teeth, stretched out the string until it was taut, and closing one eye held the tablet so that one edge of it touched the horizon. He then checked the height of the Pole Star against the side or the upper edge of the tablet.[15]

There is no doubt that the earliest open-sea mariners used the stars to navigate. However, an intriguing question begs to be answered: *could Nephi have acquired or copied ancient maritime charts while he was at the port at Khor Rori?* What has been unknown to Western civilization until a few hundred years ago are the methods the ancients used to accurately locate their current positions around the world. Ancient charts of unknown origin that have very accurate depiction of landmarks, shorelines, rivers, mountains, and lakes have been a source of wonder for hundreds of years.

For example, Crichton Miller in his book *The Golden Thread of Time* offers real evidence of the meaning and use of the ancient Celtic Cross as a navigation device. A derivation of the so-called Celtic Cross as well as other various means for keeping accurate time and spherical mathematics were used by Celts, Egyptians, Minoans, Phoenicians, Chinese, Arabs, and Greeks. These devices and methods made it possible for mariners to locate where they had traveled and thus allowed them to return again to their homeports. Although there is evidence that ancient mariners had a fairly accurate knowledge of the size and shape of the earth, the real problem until the invention of earth-orbiting satellites was how to construct a complete and accurate chart of the entire surface of the earth.

Navigators of yesterday had to have some kind of charts and logs to refer to in order to dodge heavy weather prevalent at certain times of the year in latitudes they covered in their voyages. This is not something novice navigators would know. Thankfully, we know the Spirit and Liahona were involved in guiding Nephi. We also suggest that someone was aboard Nephi's ship with enough knowledge of the seas to assist the vessel to cross two of the largest oceans on earth. Perhaps one of Nephi's converts (see D&C 33:7–8) would be a remarkable individual and as competent a navigator as existed during his age.

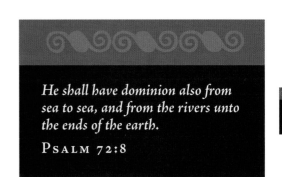

He shall have dominion also from sea to sea, and from the rivers unto the ends of the earth.

PSALM 72:8

Notes

1. Webster, *American Dictionary of the English Language*, "Vessel."

2. Thor Heyerdahl, *Kon-Tiki*, trans. F.H. Lyon (New York: Washington Square Press, 1973), 169.

3. Ibid., 206.

4. Severin, *Sindbad Voyage*, 156.

5. Wm. Revell Phillips, "Mughsayl, Another Candidate for Land Bountiful," *Journal of Book of Mormon Studies* 16, no. 2 (2007): 55.

6. Thor Heyerdahl, 29.

7. No author mentioned, "Aerographer/Meteorology," Integrated Publishing, http://www.tpub.com/weather3/1-13.htm, accessed 29 January 2009.

8. Severin, *Sindbab Voyage*, 20.

9. Jack London, *The Works of Jack London*, "Story of a Typhoon Off the Coast of Japan" (Stamford, Connecticut: Longmeadow Press, 1994), 439–40.

10. Nayeem, *The Rock Art of Arabia*, 447.

11. Severin, *Sindbad Voyage*, 73.

12. Ibid., 84.

13. Omani Ministry of National Heritage and Culture, Oman, *Oman, a Seafaring Nation*, 96.

14. Bruce and Jody Lemmon, sailing on his 43-foot sloop.

15. Severin, *Sindbad Voyage*, 92.

The Banyan escapes the atoll

June 20, 2009 afternoon

Hey guys. Well we just made it out of the dreaded lagoon. The catamaran guy picked me up at 1 p.m. in his dingy so we could motor over and check out the pass. This was the time that the weather station operator had told him to leave. Once we approached the narrow opening into the lagoon we could see a stiff current pouring out of the lagoon. We decided to wait 3 more hours and then try to leave. The catamaran left at 4 p.m. and then radioed us after he safely left and was in the open ocean with an "all is okay, the current is only 2 knots" radio transmission. We then fired up the engine and tried to pull the anchor up. But of course it was stuck on a coral head of some sort. Matt jumped in with the scuba tank and dove down 70 ft to untangle the mess. After two tries we were able to pull up the anchor. We then headed out of the channel with little problem.

The wind is now completely calm. I am very nervous about running the engine. I just poked my head into the engine room to look at the drive shaft and I can see and feel a slight wobbling in it. I'm not sure if it is being caused by the bent propeller blades or if the actual shaft is bent. Either way we are in a bit of a bind. My plan is to run the motor at low rpms for the next hour so we can get clear of the island before nightfall. Then we will have to sail in these light airs as best as we can. The wind meter is reading .5 knots off our stern. Not a good situation. It could take a couple of weeks to get to Papeete if this wind stays down. We did hear along the grape vine that in 2 days the calm conditions will dissipate and some wind should be coming our direction. We must all whistle for wind!

Anyway, mom and dad. Here is what the situation is as I can tell.

Once we get to Papeete I will take the prop off and try to get someone to either bend it back into place or cut off the bent parts and just make it smaller. Then if the shaft is still wobbling after we put it back on a dilemma will have to be traversed. I can either look into hauling the boat out of the water in Papeete and getting a new shaft and cutlass bearing installed, which could be a real challenge. Or we can get a new propeller via Jess or have the damaged one fixed, and use the engine very sparingly, sail as much as possible and once the dingy engine is fixed use that as a backup. Then we will just stay in Tahiti for a couple of months and just sail straight to New Zealand with only a couple of stops. That way we will only use the engine to go into and out of harbours. Once in New Zealand we could haul the boat and get everything squared away. My only concern is if the shaft is bent can the transmission get screwed up; or is the only worry having the cutlass bearing burn out?

I will try to get some answers to these questions once we are in Papeete. We could also look into having Jess bring a new drive shaft and cutlass bearing, if they don't carry such things in Papeete. Then we could just haul the boat and change everything quickly. Well, that's the situation.

Jody

Comments by father and boat owner from Long Beach, California:

The weather shows tomorrow 15–18 knots all day and night, increasing to 23 knots on Monday. Banyan can take that kind of wind without flinching. Hopefully, Papeete will have the necessary parts. Personally I don't think the shaft is bent—it's a 1¼-inch thick stainless steel piece of hardened metal. The cutlass bearing is probably ruined along with the prop. The cutlass bearing keeps the prop shaft spinning where she is suppose to spin, sort of how the main bearing in an engine keeps the crankshaft in place—it looks kinda like a donut.

Bruce Lemmon

The Following Day's Report:

June 21, 09 this morning

Thanks for the nice words, Dad! I feel as if we are dragging our way into Papeete with our tail between our legs. We sailed all last night in about 5–6 knots of wind and amazingly made 3 knots over ground. This morning at 5 a.m. the wind kicked up to 10–12 knots and we are now up to hull speed, 6.5 knots. It is really wonderful to be sailing and not having to think about the motor breaking at any second. We should hopefully be there in a couple of days, if the wind stays with us. As far as the replacement of the shaft and cutlass bearing are concerned, I will look into that business once we are there and see how readily available things are. They must have a good amount of parts due to the large number of vessels in the area and it being the biggest port in the South Pacific. Either way, we will get everything squared away before we shove off into the labyrinth of coral islands that awaits us. It does make me feel better to think that other captains have run aground shortly after commissioning their new vessels. At least I made it this far . . . I kept telling myself that other people have done the exact same thing or worse. However, it really doesn't help the humiliation at the moment. One feels as if they did the worst of all possible things when they crash their boats into solid ground, especially a hard substrate like a coral head.

I ran the engine for 3 hours last night to get clear of the small atoll next to our unlucky atoll. I checked the shaft and was vigilant about any burning smell, but all was okay. Needless to say it was a great relief when we shut the engine down and the roar was replaced by the calm simplicity of sailing. I hope to be able to sail right to the entrance of Papeete harbor and then just motor for less than an hour to get her safely at anchor! Then, it's time to get down to business. Repairs, ahh the endless repairs.

It was quite amusing the other day when the French Canadian catamaran gentlemen came over in his dinghy to visit us. Matt and I had been in the engine hole of the boat for about 8 hours and we were covered head to toe in grease. Our faces were blackened and we had cuts and scrapes all over our arms. As the dinghy approached we emerged, as if out of some unholy grease pit and gave our greetings. Of course, our only contribution to the conversation was in regards to the damage that was done and the slow and painful progress we were making to get everything back into working order. The man simply asked, " Buut zhow are yuz goings to leave dis place?" We replied, " Oh, we will get her going again." He, then, simply said, "Zats fine" and didn't want to even talk about anything to do with repairs or damages again. He quickly changed the subject to how amazing his Galapagos $1500 US charter cruise was around the islands. It was quite amusing to see how he avoided any topics having to do with anything remotely close to a difficulty or a problem. He asked, "Soo zhow wass yours stay en ze Marquesas, Nuka Hiva?" We replied," Well, our starter motor broke 2 days from the island so we were mostly concerned with repairing it. He, of course, gave a sort of scowl and said, "Dis is the existence of boat life, no?" We all looked at each other and nodded our heads in the affirmative!

Jody

The following report from the *Banyan* voyage to the South Pacific illustrates the need for constant repairs to a sailing ship and the value of having a shipyard in which to make repairs. It also provides an example of how costly a small error in navigating can be, such as hitting a coral reef of the atoll. Of course, Nephi did not have the luxury of having shipyards en route and where he could stop and make repairs. Hopefully, the repairs Nephi made during his voyage to the promised land would have been of a minor nature, thus reinforcing the need for his ship being of fine workmanship and for his need to have been trained as an excellent captain or to have such help aboard to avoid any number of mistakes that would have damaged the ship during storms and while adjusting to changes in wind and sea conditions.

July 30, 2009

Hey guys,

Hopefully, the boat will be back in the water tomorrow. After the machine shop tested the shaft it was found to be 3 millimeters off. If the bent area was fixed it would then make the other end of the shaft bend in the opposite direction. The shipyard owner took me to the machine shop and we talked about it. Since the shaft would still be bent the cutlass bearing would wear unevenly. This was unacceptable. So, the other option was, of course, to install a whole new shaft.

This is going to cost a little over a thousand bucks . . . so, I went ahead and did it. That is that. We have repaired the rudder and ground out a lot of little bubbles in the paint on the hull. The next step was to apply epoxy. The hull looks really good. Later today we will put the bottom paint on and if all goes as planned the new shaft will be installed and we will be able to be back in the water by tomorrow. The propeller you sent works better than the old one. That worked out well.

The two cutlass bearings you sent out to me are not the right size. The shaft size is correct, but the outside diameter is way too big. I went around to four different shops yesterday trying to buy the correct size. None of them had the exact size either. I found one with the right shaft size, but a little bigger outside diameter (only 2 millimeters). The machine shop is going to mill it down to the proper size. At least every problem is getting addressed. Thank goodness for machine shops!

As far as battery chargers go, my plan is this—

I will need a new small 30-amp 110-battery charger. Once someone flies out to New Zealand they can bring it. I, also, need a new "Echo Charge" unit. It was fried out during the knock down, but I didn't notice it until now. It's only about 3 inches by 3 inches.

That's it so far for our needs from your end and these items are not imperative. No need to worry about it now. A friend may meet us in Fiji . . . we will see. We are good for a couple of months.

Once we get to New Zealand I will buy a 220-battery charger that we can use at the marina. So that's it . . .

Everything is working out just fine. I will have to try to spend as little money as possible until we get to New Zealand.

Here's a little thing I just wrote about the shipyard:

The downtown Papeete shipyard is our new home. Banyan is now perched precariously on stilts surrounded by a muddy swamp of dirt and grime. This shipyard is run by a formidable Frenchman whose mannerisms are, at first, somewhat offensive. This characteristic became increasingly present when he discovered oily bilge water deposited all around our boat (from yesterday).

Since we have overcome so many obstacles thus far we felt this would be a "no brainer." We quickly took it in stride and mended our offence with a slight flourish of the hand as we deposited oil-absorbing mats onto the oil slick. Problem solved.

As our days here have progressed our once gloomy and downright depressing first impressions of the boatyard have given way. You see, at first we found ourselves repulsed by the filth, noise, and discomfort; but, now amazingly enough, we have come to appreciate this drastic change in our lifestyle. Our mornings begin at 7:30 a.m. with the commencement of loud banging noises. The sounds of metal hammers on metal boats, men yelling and metal grinders grinding quickly sinks into our consciousness. We are soon up and ready to meet another workday.

The hustle and bustle of a modern shipyard can be compared to a small city, where each inhabitant has his own specific specialty. Of course, many employees play many different roles in this complex game of boat repair. Some seem to enjoy doing more than one job. For instance, after our mechanic was successfully able to dislodge our propeller shaft he immediately found a new job applying bottom paint to the catamaran next door. Cranes, trucks, and giant boatlifts are constantly moving about emitting all sorts of creaks and groans and smoke and clouds of dust. Dust is something that simply must be taken in. Living in the shipyard becomes a constant struggle to remove the accumulation of dust and grime from our bodies. After 3 days here we truly appreciate the cleanliness of the oceanic world and have found we can get used to anything.

Jody

He [Lehi] spake unto them concerning their rebellions upon the waters, and the mercies of God in sparing their lives, that they were not swallowed in the sea.

2 NEPHI 1:2

LAMAN'S MUTINY

THERE SEEMS to be little good to report about the Book of Mormon character named Laman, Nephi's oldest brother. We know that he was a recalcitrant character (1 Nephi 2:11–13, 4:4), lazy (1 Nephi 17:18), and violent (1 Nephi 7:16, 16:37, 17:48)—all characteristics that, when placed in the context of a long voyage to the promised land, explain why he caused multiple rebellions aboard the ship during his family's voyage (2 Nephi 1:2).

Laman's first insurrection on the sea is the only one that was detailed in Nephi's text. We will refer to this event as "Laman's Mutiny." To try to understand Laman's actions, it may help to see that a large sailing ship has to be a "house of order," or it will not survive the challenges of the open sea. An orderly ship requires (1) a strict chain of command, (2) a disciplined crew, and (3) constant hard work to maintain the vessel and the readiness of her crew. As the captain of his ship, Nephi must have understood this principle and would have taken his responsibilities seriously. On the other hand, Laman probably had no stomach for being a member of his younger brother's disciplined crew and within days, his emotional steam-pot went off in rebellion. As recorded in the Book of Mormon, here is the order of events of Laman's mutiny.

1. Each member of the crew (family) boarded the ship, each with their personal belongings according to their age (1 Nephi 18:6). This information is important for it clearly shows there was a strict order and discipline on ship. Everyone was responsible for their items, and the storing of the items was processed in an orderly fashion. Nephi's ship was a ship of order and rules.

2. They set sail and were driven toward the promised land (1 Nephi 18:8). Likely, the ship left Oman at the end of the northeast monsoons, heading first south, then eastward toward the Pacific. South of the equator in the Indian Ocean, strong westerly winds and intense gales are common during this time of the year.

3. For many days the passage seemed to be going well. So much so that Nephi's brothers and the sons of Ishmael "began to dance, and to sing, and to speak with much rudeness, yea, even that they did forget by what power they had been brought thither; yea, they were lifted up unto exceeding rudeness" (1 Nephi 18:9).

4. Because of the behavior of the crew, Nephi "began to fear exceedingly" that "because of our iniquity, that we should be swallowed up in the depths of the sea" (1 Nephi 18:10).

5. As captain of the ship, Nephi spoke "to them with much soberness" (1 Nephi 18:10).

6. Laman and Lemuel reacted angrily to Nephi's words: "We will not that our younger brother shall be a ruler over us" (1 Nephi 18:10). They bound Nephi with cords and treated him harshly (1 Nephi 18:10).

7. As a result, the Liahona stopped working and the captain-less ship floundered into the great and terrible tempest (1 Nephi 18:12–13). Thus, their defiance of the Lord and their commandeering of the ship nearly cost the lives of the entire party.

Sailing Conditions before the Mutiny

At first, it appears that things were going well for the crew. Steady winds were blowing the new ship in the right direction. Under such favorable conditions, the captain needed to keep the crew busy or boredom would engulf the ship. Idle hands lead to mischief and a poorly maintained ship. Dana writes in *Two Years Before the Mast*: "As we had now a long 'spell' of fine weather, without any incident to break the monotony of our lives, there can be no better place to describe the duties, regulations, and customs of an American merchantman, of which ours was a fair specimen."[1] In other words, an effective captain must enforce the duties, regulations, and customs of the ship during fair weather or foul sea conditions. It seems that Nephi's brothers and the sons of Ishmael thought otherwise, seeing good sailing conditions as a time for partying and rudeness. While the wind blew favorably and the sun shone bright, the thoughts came strong: *Why do extra work? Why respect Nephi's rules?* As expected, their behavior soon led to reveling and a total disregard for the Lord's rules and the need to call upon the Savior to protect them on the waters.

Role of the Captain

We believe that Nephi appears to have been tutored in the critical role of a ship's commander. A profound line from the submarine film *K-19* is, "A ship can have only one captain and the burden of command rests solely on his shoulders." Nephi's role was a difficult role, especially for a younger brother. However, the captain's role and rule is absolutely necessary for the safe operations of a complicated and large sailing ship. A captain's responsibilities bring with it respect, yet the role of leadership on board a ship is a lonely calling that requires a strong hand. Dana writes:

> The captain, in the first place, is lord paramount. He stands no watch, comes and goes when he pleases, and is accountable to no one, and must be obeyed in everything, without a question, even from his chief officer. He has the power to turn his officers off duty, and even to break them and make them do duty as sailors in the forecastle [upper deck forward of the fore mast]. . . . he has no companion but his own dignity, and no pleasures, unless he

94

differs from most of his kind, but the consciousness of possessing supreme power, and, occasionally, the exercise of it."[2]

Nephi's role aboard his ship might not have been exactly that of a nineteenth century American captain, but his leadership posture would have been similar in nature. Regardless of the era, a captain functions as the overseer who watches guard over the ship. He/she has to maintain discipline and keep the ship and its crew in good order. He engages in "no pleasures" with the sailors for he has to be obeyed. In this regard, Nephi did not participate in the merry-making aboard the ship. Seeing that perhaps some of the crew were not performing their duties, Nephi could be genuinely concerned for the welfare of the ship and his extended family. He realized that if the crew did not maintain their seaworthiness, they all would be "swallowed up in the depths of the sea" (1 Nephi 18:10). Understanding his role as captain, Nephi would have realized that it was his responsibility to "speak to them [his crew] with much soberness" (1 Nephi 18:10). As seamen with many years of sea experience, we see this account as highly informative regarding the order of things on Nephi's ship.

Ship's Steward

Another thorn in Laman's side could have been the role of the ship's steward, the crew member who reports only to the captain. Just as the captain watches over the ship, the steward guards its precious provisions. An ocean passage is like crossing a great desert in that every drop of drinking water has to be rationed, protected, and monitored for freshness. As the poet penned about the ocean, "Water, water everywhere, and not a drop to drink." The usage of fresh water aboard a ship has to be controlled with exactness. Likewise, food stores must be safeguarded against those of weak willpower. Dana provides us with this description: "The steward is the captain's servant, and has charge of the pantry, from which everyone, even the mate himself, is excluded. These distinctions usually find him an enemy in the mate [perhaps Laman in our scenario], who does not like to have any one on board who is not entirely under his control; the crew do not consider him as one of their number, so he is left to the mercy of the captain."[3]

If Nephi could have trusted anyone aboard his ship to protect its precious provisions, perhaps it might have been his faithful brother Sam. During the days of dancing

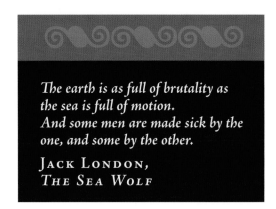

The earth is as full of brutality as the sea is full of motion. And some men are made sick by the one, and some by the other.

JACK LONDON, THE SEA WOLF

and singing, we can envision Laman going to Sam and asking for more refreshments, grape juice, and extra food. In response, we can see Sam saying, "Nephi told me not to . . . ." We can picture Laman steaming off, cursing again the name of Nephi.

Laman the Mutineer

Knowing Laman's predisposition to rebel against authority and his laziness and violent temper, we think we can diagnose the root cause of Laman's mutiny and marvel at the Book of Mormon's accurate depiction of the behavior aboard Nephi's ship. Let's start by recalling Laman's resentment to Nephi's leadership. On land, Nephi's leadership would have been easier for the rebellious older brother to accept. However, in the close quarters of a ship, it must have been unbearable for a man of such ill character. Nephi knew his

95

oldest brother's flaws and possibly would have tried to appease this contemptuous brother by giving him leadership responsibilities comparable to what is known today as a second mate. The position would have meant that Laman might have held a degree of respect on board ship. Except for the captain and steward, every member of the crew would have had to report to him, yet the second mate was still required to work beside the rest of the men and women. Without the option of throwing his eldest brother overboard, giving Laman a leadership responsibility may have been the next best alternative Nephi could apply to keep the peace. Even so, the role of ship's second mate would not have been easy to bear for the defiant Laman. That position still required that he obey every direct command of Nephi. Dana noted:

> The second mate's is proverbially a dog's berth [place where sailors sleep]. He is neither officer nor man. The men do not respect him as an officer, and he is obliged to go aloft [above the deck] to reef [reduce sail] and furl [roll] the topsails, and to put his hands into the tar and slush [grease from boiled meat fat], with the rest. The crew call him the "sailor's waiter," as he has to furnish them with spun-yarn [rope from twisting together two or three

ropes], marlin [small spun-yard], and all other stuffs that they need in their work, and has charge of the boatswain's [man in charge of rigging's] locker, which includes serving-boards [flat boards for working smaller ropes], marlin-spikes [iron-pins used for fid and a heaver], etc, etc. He is expected by the captain to maintain his dignity and to enforce obedience, and still is kept at a great distance from the [first] mate, and obliged to work with the crew. He is one to whom little is given and of whom much is required.[4]

Having to work along with the others while still taking orders from his younger brother surely would have eaten away at Laman's rebellious heart.

An equal force in driving Laman to rebellion was his apparent extreme laziness. He thought he would die during the family's relatively short trip from Jerusalem to the valley of Lemuel; he complained to his father that it would be too hard a task to get the plates from Laban; he refused to help Nephi in building his ship; and in the New World he allowed his children to become filthy and illiterate. In other words, Laman was not an ideal crew member, and this would be manifest by his allowing crew members to desert their duties and leading them in song and dance,

and make merriment, particularly if he were in a position of some kind of ship authority. Nothing could be more foreign from the nature of good seamanship. Dana explained:

> Before I end my explanations, it may be well to define a day's work, and to correct a mistake prevalent among landsmen about a sailor's life. Nothing is more common than to hear people say—"Are not sailors very idle at sea?—what can they find to do?" This is a very natural mistake, and being very frequently made, it is one which every sailor feels interested in having corrected. In the first place, then, the discipline of the ship requires every man to be at work upon *something* when he is on deck, except at night and on Sundays. Except at these times, you will never see a man, on board a well-ordered vessel, standing idle on deck, sitting down, or leaning over the side. It is the officers' duty to keep everyone at work, even if there is nothing to be done but to scrape the rust from the chain cables. In no state prison are the convicts more regularly set to work, and more closely watched. No conversation is allowed among the crew at their duty, and though they frequently do talk when aloft [above deck], or when near one another, yet they always stop when an officer is nigh.

With regard to the work upon which the men are put, it is a matter which probably would not be understood by one who has not been at sea. When I first left port, and found that we were kept regularly employed for a week or two, I supposed that we were getting the vessel into sea trim, and that it would soon be over, and we should have nothing to do but to sail the ship; but I found that it continued so for two years, and at the end of the two years there was as much to be done as ever. As has often been said, a ship is like a lady's watch, always out of repair.[5]

It would be the captain's (Nephi) responsibility to keep the ship in good order, and his "duty to keep everyone at work," including his lazy eldest brother. Laman might have lacked humility and a good work ethic, but he did not lack a violent temper. He had already tried to kill his brother on several occasions and he had even proposed killing his father (1 Nephi 16:37). After many days at sea, Laman must have realized that he faced a long emotional voyage under his brother's command and that the work would never cease. Like his behavior in the wilderness, Laman's temper was feathered by murmuring. The tougher the captain, the more the mumbling against him. Can you picture Laman conjuring up tall tales about Nephi to others in the crew? Or possibly twisting the story of why Laban died and who was to blame for Ishmael's demise? Jack London portrays one sailor's ramblings against his captain.

"Ah, my boy,"—he shook his head ominously at me,—" 't is the worst schooner ye could iv selected; nor were ye drunk at the time, as was I. 'T is sealin' is the sailor's paradise—on other ships than this. The mate was the first, but the first [to die], but, mark me words, there'll be more dead men before the trip is done with. Hist, now, between you an' meself an' the stanchion there, this Wolf Larsen [the captain of the *Ghost*] is a regulr devil, an' the *Ghost*'ll be a hell-ship like she's always be'n since he had hold iv her. Don't I know? Don't I know? Don't I remember him in Hakodate two years gone, when he hand a row an' shot four iv his men? Wasn't I a-layin' on the *Emma L.*, not three hundred yards away? An' killed 'im a man the same year he kill with a blow iv his fist. Yes, sir, beast he is, this Wolf Larsen—the great big beast mentioned iv in Revelations; an' no good end will he ever come to. But I've said nothin' to ye, mind ye; I've whispered never a word; for old fat Louis'll live the voyage out, if the last mother's son of yez go to the fishes.

"Wolf Larsen!" he snorted a moment later. "Listen to the word, will ye! Wolf—'t is what he is. He's not black-hearted, like some men. 'T is no heart he has at all. Wolf, 't is what he is. D'ye wonder he's well named?"

"But if he is so well known for what he is," I queried, "how is it that he can get men to ship with him?"

"An' how is it ye can get men to do anything on God's earth an' sea?" Louis demanded with Celtic fire. "How d' ye find me aboard if 't wasn't that I was drunk as a pig when I put me name down."[6]

Certainly, the passage to the promised land was an extremely difficult voyage on many levels. It was a constant measure of the spiritual, mental, emotional, and physical strength and willpower of everyone aboard. Consider the feat of Jody Lemmon's crew aboard their modern sailing ship in the Pacific:

Sun, 26 Apr 2009

Well the ocean is a real mess now. You are a very fortunate man to have avoided this mess. We are still about 160 miles from our turning point to the Galapagos and have been through a very uncomfortable night. The winds are still out of the east north east, but they are now pushing up to 30 knots. Fun stuff. We sailed all night with just a fraction of the main up. We at least are going with the winds, but there is a solid 3 meter south swell running, so we are going into a ground swell and being pushed by about a 2 meter wind swell, which makes for a very uncomfortable ride. Mikey got sea sick last night trying to cook dinner and had to abandon the final stages, so Matt picked up the reigns. I felt all right and was able to sleep on and off until my shift at 4 a.m. It is 9 a.m. now and about an hour ago I tried to cook up some cream of wheat, but I couldn't do it due to sea sickness. . . . So I took one of your magic pills, ate a banana, some pineapple, and a granola bar and I feel much better. It's pretty nasty out here, high winds, the decks are awash and the boat is lurching from side to side so that each rail is alternately under water. We have been playing with our sail configuration and angle to the swell all morning trying to get the best possible ride out of her, but it all seams to be unfruitful.

At least the sea sickness pill has kicked in, I just had a sketchy shower on deck and Matt is drying out the cast Iron skillet. So we are maintaining a sense of civility amidst the Chaos!

Jody

We suspect that even after conquering the extreme challenges of the Arabian wilderness, the daughters of Lehi and Ishmael would have certainly preferred their tents on the shores of Bountiful to the cramped quarters and lack of privacy aboard Nephi's ship. Since Nephi's ship was new, the family might have been spared the weevils, cockroaches, and rats that plague wooden sailing ships. However, the duties of the women would have been as rigorous as those of the men, and their responsibilities would be assigned and accounted for by captain Nephi. For example, who prepared the food as the ship rocked back and forth in rough seas? Who cleaned the vomit of the seasick from the floor of the lower deck or cared for the elderly Lehi and Sariah (1 Nephi 18:17)? Who kept the small children calm, safe, and out of the way of the sailors? And who added their muscle to the ropes when the men needed help in raising the heavy spars? These tasks were undoubtedly filled by the women aboard the ship. Also, we know from their experiences in the wilderness, some of them had a propensity to speak their mind and complain (1 Nephi 16:35; 17:2).

We do not seek to judge any of the women aboard the ship. Indeed, Nephi did not negatively write of their complaints or murmurings or hardships, other than to say what he did. Still, we expect that under the trying conditions the women experienced during the voyage, some of them also likely joined in the rebellions. For example, take the simplest chore, such as washing clothes. In Patrick O'Brian's novel, *The Wine-Dark Sea*, he writes of a medical doctor asking for fresh water:

> "Jack!" cried Stephen, coming in to their strangely late and even twilit dinner, "did you know that those active mariners have brought a large number of hogsheads aboard, and they filled with fresh water?"
>
> "Have they, indeed?" asked Jack. "You amaze me."
>
> "They have, too. May I have some to sponge my patients and have their clothes washed at last?"
>
> "Well, I suppose you may have a little for sponging them—a very small bowl would be enough, I am sure—but as for washing clothes—washing clothes. . . . That would be a most shocking expenditure, you know. Salt does herrings no harm, nor lobsters, and my shirt has not been washed in fresh water since Heaven

knows low long. It is like coarse emery-paper."[7]

With her skin burned from the sun and her hair dry as straw from the wind and salt water, we do not picture Laman's wife with a "truly happy camper attitude." Instead, perhaps he faced many times a hail of complaints from her about captain Nephi. But whether or not his wife added to Laman's problems, something finally triggered Laman's anger and rage to the point that he led a violent mutiny against his righteous brother.

In conclusion, on this point, building Nephi's ship was a very arduous challenge—and sailing on her was also a very arduous challenge that was problematic and dangerous. You can believe whatever you may, but anyone who has set sail across an ocean can tell you that it is nonsense to believe that Nephi left Arabia with an untrained crew. Certainly, each physically able adult member of the family had some assigned sailing tasks that were practiced before the ship finally left Khor Rori for the New World. The very fact that his older brothers and the sons of Ishmael believed they could mutiny against Captain Nephi shows that they also thought they had enough seamanship skills to man the ship without his leadership and without the aid of the Liahona. They were wrong. Obviously, these family members would see themselves more in authority than any servants or Omani sailors who likely were also aboard.

It is our belief that Nephi's brief account of their time at sea should be appreciated as a small window into many kinds of trials that the men and women aboard Nephi's ship, including Laman, suffered during their voyage. To gloss over their voyage without fully understanding the incredible challenges Nephi and his family had to overcome is to overlook their hard work, their acquired seamanship skills, and their great courage. For months on end, 24/7, they sailed toward an unknown destiny. Their challenges were both physical and psychological.

When Christopher Columbus's crew had sailed into the unknown, and only after a fraction of the distance of Nephi's voyage, his crew desired to turn back for Barcelona, Spain. Nephi's family would have sailed for months into what must have seemed an endless unknown. Samuel Eliot Morison writes of Columbus:

> It became more and more difficult to maintain morale. The fleet had now been three weeks without sight of land; probably no man aboard had ever equaled that record. Only those who have experienced it, know what wear and tear shipmates inflict on each other's tempers during a long sea voyage. Ashore you may hate your boss or despise your fellow workers, but you are with them only from nine to five. Even in a boy's school or military training camp, there are some means to gain privacy for short intervals. But on a vessel like these caravels, where men even had to ease themselves in public, it is impossible to get away from your mates except by sleep; and even then they fall over you or wake you up to ask silly questions, such as, where did you leave that marlin-spike last watch? In a really long voyage such as this, which is full of anxiety and disappointment, especially if there is no stiff weather to keep them busy, the men invariably form gangs and cliques, work up hatreds against each other and their officers, brood over imaginary wrongs and unintended slights, and fancy that they are shipmates with some of the world's worst scoundrels.[8]

The journey of those aboard Nephi's ship was a constant struggle against many deadly forces of nature. Dana's description is useful on this matter:

99

Another method of employing the crew is, "setting up" rigging. Whenever any of the standing rigging becomes slack, (which is continually happening,) the seizings [fastening ropes of same size] and coverings must be taken off, tackle got up, and after the rigging is bowsed [pulled] well taught, the seizings and coverings replaced; which is a very nice piece of work. There is also such a connection between different parts of a vessel, that one rope can seldom be touched without altering another. You cannot stay a mast aft [near end of ship] by the back stays [large ropes that support the mast], without slacking up the head stays, etc. etc. If we add to this all the tarring, greasing, oiling, varnishing, painting, scraping, and scrubbing which is required in the course of a long voyage, and also remember this is all to be done in addition to watching at night, steering, reefing [taking in sail], furling [rolling sail], bracing, making and setting sails, and pulling, hauling and climbing in every direction, one will hardly ask, "What can a sailor find to do at sea?"[9]

The life of a sailor at sea requires his never-ending vigilance. The length and challenges of Nephi's great voyage far surpassed those faced by Columbus; however, the parallels between the two men and their voyages are quite interesting. Both men were visionaries commanding men of lesser spirit. Morison writes of Columbus:

> Their [the crews] issue with their commander was the eternal one between imagination and doubt, between the spirit that creates and the spirit that denies [Laman and Lemuel]. Oftentimes the doubters are right, for mankind has a hundred foolish notions for every sound one; it is at times of crisis, when unpredictable forces are dissolving society, that the do-nothings are tragically wrong. There are tides in the affairs of men, and this was one of them.[10]

Like Columbus, Nephi encouraged his family to continue their struggle to reach a promised land. In his case, the journey from Jerusalem to a new home surely had lasted more than ten years. Despite being surrounded by doubters and deniers, both Columbus and Nephi were marvelously obedient to their duty. Morison continues:

> And so, on October 10, when the fleet was steering straight for the Bahamas, and the nearest land was less than 200 miles ahead, all the smoldering discontent of the men flared up into open mutiny. They had done enough and more than enough; the ships should and must turn back. . . . What Columbus noted down (the Las Casas abstracted) is short and to the point, and not ungenerous to the men:

> "Here the people could stand it no longer, complained of the long voyage; but the Admiral cheered them as best he could, holding out good hope of the advantages they might have; and he added that it was useless to complain, since he had come to go to the Indies, and so had to continue until he found them, with the help of Our Lord."[11]

It is not hard imagining Nephi using similar words to hold off the rebellions that he faced during the voyage to the promised land. While Nephi knew that it was the Lord who preserved them upon the waters, Columbus was no less aware of his Deliverer. Morison writes: "Columbus always loved to apply the Sacred Scriptures to his own life and adventures; . . . .

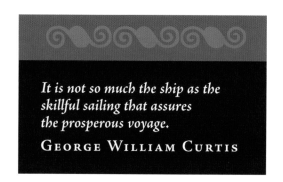

It is not so much the ship as the skillful sailing that assures the prosperous voyage.

GEORGE WILLIAM CURTIS

The really significant thing about these entries for September 22–23, as Charcot points out, was the men's uneasiness over scudding free for so many days on end, which proves that they had no previous experience of the trade winds. Columbus knew little if anything more than they; his serenity came from an inward assurance and confidence in God, not from superior knowledge."[12]

Indeed, Columbus was to a degree a type of Nephi in his day. Angelo Trevisan wrote of the Admiral, "*Christophoro Colombo Zenovese homo de alta et procera statura rosso de grande ingegno et faza longa.* [Christopher Columbus, Genoses, a tall man and *strong stature*, ruddy, of *great creative talent*, and with a long face]" (italics added for emphasis).

Notes

1. Dana, *Two Years Before the Mast*, 50.
2. Ibid.
3. Ibid., 51.
4. Ibid.
5. Ibid., 54.
6. Jack London, *The Works of Jack London*, 250–51.
7. Patrick O'Brian, *The Wine-Dark Sea* (London: Harper Collins, 1993), 104.
8. Morison, *Admiral of the Ocean Sea*, 209.
9. Dana, *Two Years Before the Mast*, 55.
10. Morison, *Admiral of the Ocean Sea*, 215.
11. Ibid., 215–16.
12. Ibid., 206.

During a long sea voyage, one experiences scores of emotions. Certainly, those aboard Nephi's ship experienced many fearful and sad moments. They had left their homeland forever and were sailing on what must have seemed a truly endless sea. To provide the reader a sense of the kind of emotions that must have been aboard Nephi's ship, Frank suggested we add the following poem. Having spent many a Christmas aboard ship, this poem touched him:

Christmas at Sea
Robert Lewis Stevenson

The sheets were frozen hard, and they cut the naked hand;
The decks were like a slide, where a seaman scarce could stand;
The wind was anor'wester, blowing squally off the sea;
And cliffs and spouting breakers were the only things a-lee.

They heard the surf a-roaring before the break of day;
But 'twas only with the peep of light we saw how ill we lay.
We tumbled every hand on deck instanter, with a shout,
And we gave her the maintops'l, and stood by to go about.

All day we tacked and tacked between the South Head and the North;
All day we hauled the frozen sheets, and got no further forth;
All day as cold as charity, in bitter pain and dread,
For very life and nature we tacked from head to head.

We gave the South a wider berth, for there the tide-race roared;
But every tack we made we brought the North Head close aboard:
So's we saw the cliffs and houses, and the breakers running high,
And the coastguard in his garden, with his glass against his eye.

The frost was on the village roofs as white as ocean foam;
The good red fires were burning bright in every 'longshore home;
The windows sparkled clear, and the chimneys volleyed out;
And I vow we sniffed the victuals as the vessel went about.

The bells upon the church were rung with a mighty jovial cheer;
For it's just that I should tell you how (of all days in the year)
This day of our adversity was blessed Christmas morn,
And the house above the coastguard's was the house where I was born.

O well I saw the pleasant room, the pleasant faces there,
My mother's silver spectacles, my father's silver hair;
And well I saw the firelight, like a flight of homely elves,
Go dancing round the china-plates that stand upon the shelves.

And well I knew the talk they had, the talk that was of me,
Of the shadow on the household and the son that went to sea;
And O the wicked fool I seemed, in every kind of way,
To be here and hauling frozen ropes on blessed Christmas Day.

They lit the high sea-light, and the dark began to fall.
"All hands to loose topgallant sails," I heard the captain call.
"By the Lord, she'll never stand it," our first mate, Jackson, cried.
. . ."It's the one way or the other, Mr. Jackson," he replied.

She staggered to her bearings, but the sails were new and good,
And the ship smelt up to windward just as though she understood.
As the winter's day was ending, in the entry of the night,
We cleared the weary headland, and passed below the light.

And they heaved a mighty breath, every soul on board but me,
As they saw her nose again pointing handsome out to sea;
But all that I could think of, in the darkness and the cold,
Was just that I was leaving home and my folks were growing old.

Ruins on Isle of the Sun, Lake Titicaca, Bolivia. Photograph by Matthew Potter.

CHAPTER FOUR

And when they had taken up the anchors, they committed themselves unto the sea, and loosed the rudder bands, and hoisted up the mainsail to the wind . . .

ACTS 27:40

NEPHI'S VOYAGE

THE FIRST STEP in reconstructing a possible route for Nephi's voyage is to determine its harbor of origin and then its final destination. In chapter one, it was proposed that the probable place where Nephi built his ship, conducted sea trials, trained his crew (and was trained himself), and finally set sail away from the dry lands of Arabia was the famous frankincense harbor of Khor Rori. To determine where Lehi's family first set foot in the promised land, we turned to modern revelation as well as to empirical research. Elder James E. Talmage of the

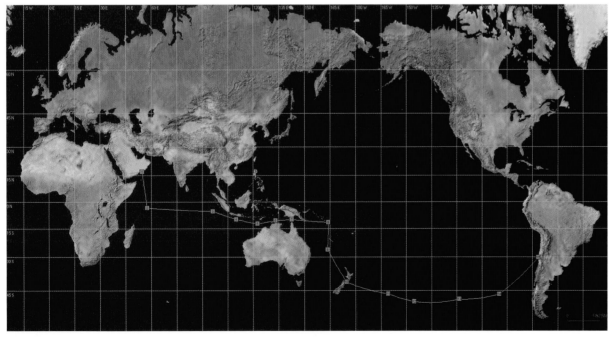

Map of simulated voyage of Nephi's ship.

Quorum of the Twelve said:

> The migrating colony [those aboard Nephi's ship] journeyed by slow stages for about eight years in the desert, during which time Lehi and his faithful younger son Nephi received many revelations of the Divine word and will, through which the purpose of their own exodus was made known, as were also the portending vicissitudes of the nation from which they had become expatriated by the Lord's command. Eventually they reached the shores of the Arabian sea, where, divinely directed, they built a vessel, in which they were carried by the wind and current across the ocean to the western coast of South America.[1]

The prevailing view of some early Church members who knew the Prophet Joseph Smith is that they believed it had been revealed to the Prophet that Nephi's ship landed in Chile. Two influential Apostles of the Church, Elder Orson Pratt and Elder Franklin D. Richards, taught that the Prophet received a revelation that Nephi's ship landed at 30 degrees south latitude on the western shores of South America. Both Apostles knew Joseph Smith. Some evidence supporting this are the words written in the "handwriting of Frederick G. Williams, Counselor to the Prophet, and on the same page with the body of an undoubted revelation that had been typeset and received earlier. Some of President Williams's handwritten words were, 'Lehi . . . landed on the continent of South America in Chili [Chile] thirty degrees latitude.'"[2] The Church included a footnote that Nephi landed in Chile in the 1879 edition of the Book of Mormon.[3]

Perhaps one of the reasons Elder Parley P. Pratt of the Quorum of the Twelve Apostles and his companion Rufus Allen went to Valparaiso, Chile, in 1851 on their historic mission to South America is that from knowing of the reference to Chile as the landing site of Lehi, they wanted to visit the general area and introduce the restored gospel to his descendants. While en route in September 1851, he wrote to his family and said, "We study Spanish every day. It is a beautiful language, and wonderfully adapted to . . . the Lamanites."[4] In March 1852 in a letter to President Brigham Young, he wrote, "Four-fifths, or perhaps nine-tenths of the vast population of Peru, as well as of most other countries of Spanish America, are of the *blood of Lehi*" (italics by Elder Pratt).[5]

In his *History of the Church in Peru*, Dale Christensen, former mission president [1984–1987], quotes from General Authorities:

"On October 29, 1959, a conference was held with some 300 people in attendance (in Santiago, Chile). At this meeting Elder Harold B. Lee presented the names of the Andes Mission Presidency . . . The following excerpts are from a stirring address given in the morning session of the Conference by Elder Harold B. Lee of the Council of the Twelve Apostles. . . . 'There have been a flood of memories and thoughts running through my mind . . . where the followers of Lehi landed . . . no one knows exactly where this location was. In the wisdom of the Lord it has not been definitely revealed. We know that at the time of the crucifixion of the Lord, the whole face of the earth was changed and the arrangements of mountains and valleys and rivers may not be the same as they were before that time. But from the writings of the Prophet Joseph Smith and of other inspired men, it seems that all are in agreement that the followers of Lehi came to the western shores of South America.'"[6]

In March 1970, George was serving a mission in the small city of Juliaca on the northern side of the Lake Titicaca Basin.

At that time, the Peruvian Altiplano cities of Juliaca and Puno were still part of the Bolivian Mission. That month, Elder Steve Farnsworth, the mission's public relations representative, received a surprising response to a letter he had sent with a copy of a mission paper called "Mormon" to the President of the Church at the time. Mission President Keith Roberts had the letter included in the mission's monthly newsletter. He introduced President Smith's correspondence in these words: "The following letter from President Joseph Fielding Smith was received by Elder Steve Farnsworth in March 1970. It was written March 18, 1970. I think that it is an important statement for this Mission and should be part of your permanent record. Read it often and it will give you a boost in your work."

Dear Brother Farnsworth,

Thank you for your kind letter of March 11, 1970, which just arrived from Bolivia together with a copy of the paper called "Mormon."

I am very pleased to know that you are having wonderful success in your field of labor. No doubt a paper in Spanish in that country dealing with the doctrines of the Church would be a great help to you. There is no reason that I know that you should not have remarkable success in that field which at one time was the central country occupied by the people in the Book of Mormon times as we learn from the Book of Mormon. It is my judgment that the missionaries would have remarkable success in this section of the country.*

It is indeed a pleasure for me to get a communication from that Land which at one time was headquarters of the Church in Book of Mormon history.

May the Lord continue to bless you and your companions and open the doors before you that you may teach the people. I humbly pray.*

Sincerely your brother,

Joseph Fielding Smith, President

JFS.re

In his history of the Church in Peru, Dale Christensen continues:

"In June 1968, Elder Harold B. Lee talked about his experiences in organizing the Andes Mission and said, 'I remember standing at the pulpit in the archway between the living room and the dining room. As I spoke to the congregation, I

George before his Peruvian candidate for the temple at Bountiful (Cahuachi, Nazca), with missionary companion David Richardson. Photograph by Matthew Potter.

was impressed by the Spirit of the Lord, in a way in which I had seldom been impressed before, to tell the people that the land of Peru had been one of the most important lands in all the history and development of the people of the Book of Mormon.' He subsequently commented that he wondered if Lehi and his family had perhaps landed on or near the coasts of Peru."

Dale Christensen provides another entry of keen interest:

"April 24, 1969 (Thursday): Today Elder Hinckley [Gordon B. Hinckley, then of the Quorum of the Twelve Apostles] met with the missionaries from the Quito and Guayaquil Zones at the Villa Flora Chapel. As Elder Hinckley bore witness of the divinity of the Savior and mentioned his great love for Him, he wept openly as did most of the missionaries present. Elder Hinckley also told the missionaries that he felt that the spirits of some of the great ancient American Prophets had been present at that meeting, inasmuch as they are interested in seeing that their descendants receive the message of the restored Gospel. The Spirit bore witness to those who were present that the Lord had indeed spoken through one of his special witnesses and that the feelings which Elder Hinckley had expressed were true and correct."

Peruvian woman weaving. Photograph by Mylene d'Auriol.

Another entry from Dale Christensen reads:

"Elder Hinckley at the organization of Lima, Peru stake, 1970: 'I look into the faces of you people and I see the blood of those who walked this land anciently, and who at that time found great favor with the Lord, but because of wickedness and indulgence they lost that favor. Because of their wickedness they were oppressed and driven and killed. I also see forbearers of others who are here today. There is in the veins of hundreds who sit here a mixture of those two great peoples, the descendants of Father Lehi that found favor in the sight of God, and the Spanish who came here in the name of Christianity. Now I would like to say to you today that you are a people of prophecy, and this is a day of fulfilled prophecy, and God is remembering the promises made of old.'"

Christensen further notes:

"1986 dedication of the Lima Temple, Elder Hinckley: 'Surely father Lehi has wept with sorrow over his posterity. Surely he weeps today with gladness, for in his holy house there will be experienced the fullness of the priesthood to the blessing, not only of those of this and future generations, but also to the blessing of those of previous generations.'"

Here is another of his historical notes quoting a 1986 temple dedication commentary from *Church News*:

"In remarks before the dedicatory prayer, President Hinckley spoke of 'another congregation' looking down on the proceedings. 'I always feel during a dedication that I am standing in two spheres with a very thin veil.' He told of past trips in Peru and Bolivia when he had seen the children of Lehi in poverty, oppressed in spirit by the scarcity of gospel truth among them, and cried within himself, 'How long, oh Lord, how long?' 'The day has arrived. Lehi, Sariah, Nephi, and others in that other sphere are rejoicing. This is the day of salvation for generations.'"[7]

In his book *Nephi in the Promised Land*, George has documented extraordinary compelling evidence leading to the claim that the history of the Book of Mormon transpired in Peru and nearby surrounding locales. Indeed, given the current body of germane archaeological, ethnological, and anthropological evidence, it appears that Nephi's promised land could only have been South America and nowhere else in the New World. For this and other reasons, we place Nephi's ship landing at 30 degrees south latitude in Chile in compliance with the Frederick G. Williams' text.

Surviving a Lengthy Sea Voyage

Regardless of the size of Nephi's ship, at some points along the voyage the party needed to stop to restock their provisions. The most precious of their supplies would have been fresh water. We assume that Nephi also brought aboard his bow that could have allowed him to hunt on shore for game, seabirds, and any other sources of meat to restock their stores. Other members of the family might have explored the shoreline for shellfish and pools and shallows for netting fish. Their days onshore would not have been rest stops, rather a time for repairing the ship and its sails. All the same, getting their land legs back and finding relief of sea sickness and the physical fatigue from the rigors of sailing meant that time on dry land would have renewed their spirits and bodies.

Sailing from Khor Rori to Chile

Sailors all know that in transiting the sea, the shortest distance between two points is not a straight line but rather an arc. Those of you who remember your geometry know this. A straight line on a chart in

navigation jargon is referred to as a "rhumb line."

Using the *Visual Passage Planner 2* simulator, we were not surprised to find that the most favorable route to Chile from southern Arabia is via the stormy winds of the Pacific "roaring forties." At first, one might doubt the wisdom of submitting a wooden sailing ship to the high winds and rough seas of the southern forties (latitude). However, experienced Pacific sailors know that taking a large wooden sailing ship against the currents or along a route with lesser winds (an equator passage) would be disastrous. One principle about sailing the Pacific is always true—any voyage across that massive ocean is a long one, and without substantial provisions and a well-planned route, dying of thirst or hunger before reaching land is a likely outcome. A Hawaiian voyaging proverb explains: *Poho pono na pe'a heke a ku ana*, "A full sail helped him to arrive."[8] In other words, without the favorable current and high winds of the southern Pacific, Nephi's vessel likely would have been a ghost ship before it reached South America.

Sailing south around India would mean entering equatorial waters. Unless Nephi's timing was just right, between the months of January and February his ship could not have sailed south-eastward of Sri Lanka. In the Indian Ocean south of India, March is the changeover month when the north-east monsoon dies down and is replaced by the stronger south-west monsoon winds. South of the equator during the north-east monsoon, winds blow in an eastward direction toward the Pacific. Outside this time window, Nephi's ship had a good chance of becoming stranded at sea in doldrums and slowly drifting backward toward Africa in the west-going current.[9]

Sea travel near the equator, otherwise known by sailors as the "doldrums, or horse latitudes" (for having to eat your horses before you reached land), can be filled with a multitude of weather experiences. Temperatures range in the upper eighties and lower nineties with humidity at near 100 percent. Wind is light to sparse. At the equator, the wind comes together from opposite quadrants and causes uplifts that result in light wind between mini bad-weather cells that are very dense, dark, full of moisture, and electrical energy. The air around these mini storms is full of ozone from the lightning that comes thundering from within. Lighting appears in both bolt and sheet form that can be startling the first time one is confronted with such a gauntlet. The wind and rain just ahead and inside these storm cells are a power-punch that can be very damaging to a vessel, especially its electronics. With a high risk of being struck by lightning, an equatorial storm is an area to be navigated around, usually to the trailing edge.

On the first leg of the *Visual Passage Planner 2* simulation of Nephi's voyage, the simulator predicts that the Liahona would have pointed south-southeast across the equator in order to reach the trade winds that would shift and carry the vessel in an easterly direction. In the modern era, sailing across the equator has become a rite-of-passage. In modern sailing lore, the first time sailors cross the equator they are awarded the title, "Shellback," and become members of King Neptune's Court. This title is held in high esteem by other Shellbacks. All other seamen are known as "pollywogs."

As soon as a vessel crosses the equator, the winds and currents will shift and the seas will become confused. However, the further south of the equator one goes, the more the trade winds become steady in direction and velocity, and the person will notice that all the northern star patterns are gone and that the Southern Cross is paramount.

Nephi's crew appears to have been confident of the ship's construction. Indeed, his "brethren" declared the workmanship of the ship was exceedingly fine (1 Nephi 18:4). It is clear that the family left the port well "prepared [in] all things, much fruits and meat from the wilderness, and honey in abundance, and provisions according to that which the Lord had commanded us" (1 Nephi 18:6). Nephi wrote that having "gone down into the ship, and had taken with us our provisions and things which had been commanded us, we did put forth into the sea" (1 Nephi 18:8).

Once aboard, we believe they tied off and sailed with confidence through the natural breakwater at Khor Rori and entered the open waters of the Indian Ocean. Once under sail, they "were driven forth before the winds toward the promised land" (1 Nephi 18:8). In other words, the winds were behind them, so they did not flounder in the winds and waves and find themselves wrecked along a nearby beach.

Their Last Hours in Arabia

In today's world, before a vessel gets under way on a long international voyage, traditionally the crew, families, and friends have a going-away party. It is believed that one of the origins of the word *wake* comes from the party to see loved ones off in the wake of their vessel. Perhaps a large group of well-wishers gathered to bid Nephi and his family farewell also. Among such a group would have been friends that the family met at Khor Rori, shipwrights who had helped Nephi build his ship, and perhaps even converts Lehi and Nephi might have made at Khor Rori (D&C 33:7–8), as well as family members of the Omani sailors who likely joined Nephi's crew or who taught the family how to sail. In the hours before boarding the ship to set sail, we imaginatively see Lehi leading the family and friends in a fervent prayer to express gratitude for their ship, the help of their friends, and to ask the Lord for good weather, good health upon the waters, and safe passage to the promised land.

If Omani sailors were aboard Nephi's ship, then it would have been a very tearful good-bye. We speculate that possibly these men, who knew the quality of Nephi's ship and the valuable resources that went into it, as well as the innovative concepts the Lord guided Nephi to accomplish, might have been willing to man the crew in exchange for the ship once it reached its destination. Nephi does not tell us what happened to the ship once it landed in Chile, so we are free to speculate that it is possible it could have headed out on a possible return to Oman. The sailors who man the vessels that travel the world seas as well as their families are a close society. On the other hand, if the Omani crew members embarked with the understanding that they would stay with the Lehites in the promised land, then their farewell at Khor Rori would have meant a final good-bye and would have been a deeply emotional experience.

Departure begins with high expectations and good wishes for a safe and easy voyage. Anchor is weighed at or near high slack (even) tide. Sails are set. The watch is set and the crew begins the routine of the watch. Heading out to sea generally is a time of quiet reflection. One remembers loved ones on shore and will have a prayer in his or her heart that all will be safe while they are gone to sea. There also can be underlying fear with the awarenss that some of the crew may be lost at sea. What were the thoughts aboard Nephi's ship as the group departed?

During the first days at sea beyond sight of the shore, generally all there is to see in any direction is water. Your ship is a tiny island that keeps you and everyone else on board

111

alive. Perhaps land will not be seen again for weeks on end, and so the ship and crew begin to settle into their new element and the seemingly endless waters of the great deep. Severin writes of the first days at sea:

> It is a general rule that the first days of a venture like the Sindbad Voyage are among the most frustrating. This is the time when new ropes snap, poorly tied knots come undone or jam hopelessly tight, sails rip, fittings break off, and hours are wasted in search for items that have been buried in the last-minute rush of packing and loading. Also the crew is at a low ebb. The surge of excitement at the departure has faded, and a reaction sets in. Men who have not yet found their sea legs lurch and slip. The unlucky few retch and vomit over the rail as the ship begins to move with the waves and swell. Surreptitiously the crew members study one another, fully aware of the months that lie ahead which will be spent cooped up together in a confined little wooden world.[10]

Nephi's ship was of good workmanship and undoubtedly made from the strongest hardwoods. However, the constant "song of the ship" reminded everyone aboard that the ship faced a constant test of strength to see if it could survive against the forces of the sea. Severin wrote:

> The sounds about a medieval Arab sailing ship are unique. The groaning and creaking of timber and rope, the constant background of our lives, had begun to assume special characteristics. There was the high-pitched creak of the coconut fibre ropes holding the mast, the sound unlike that made by any other type of rope, and which varied with the degree and rhythm of the rolling of the ship. Then there was the soft, regular thump of the tiller nudging against the tiller lines with each wave that passed under the ship, followed by an occasional gentle clatter of the blocks as the steersman adjusted the tiller. From high above came a soft, rubbing sound as the great spars nuzzled the masts, each spar bandaged against jacket. Dozens of wooden joints talked gently in every part of the hull, as the ship shouldered her way through the waves. The large planks of the lower deck crept up and down against one another in sympathy with the slight flexing of the hull, and in my cabin even a slight change in the wind direction or speed could be detected without even going up on *Sohar*'s deck. The whisper of water along the side of the hull told the speed of the ship, and *Sohar*'s angle of heel was marked by little beads of moisture which seeped through the uncaulked planks at the water level outside.[11]

Long Days aboard the Ship

The cook or cooks have lots of fresh fruit, vegetables, meat, chicken, milk, butter, bread, and so on for the first week or so. After that, in today's world the cook relies on fresh fish, dried fruit, dried vegetables, dried milk, salted meat, canned food, and homemade bread to feed the crew. Fresh water is always a problem for replenishment on a long voyage. Water may be collected from rain. Going ashore on some remote island is risky at best, unless the location is known to be safe as well as the water. In modern times, chlorine is placed into drinking water to kill possible bugs. Modern vessels have water making equipment which removes salt from the salt water. And, as we all know, mealtime is very important for the well-being of morale. Good food lifts the spirit of any mortal.

While a vessel is near land, wind shifts are common. After a vessel sails away from land, the wind becomes steady in direction and will tend to vary in tenacity and direction primarily only with a change in the weather cell. Many times the vessel will remain on the same tack for days, with reefing and shaking out of sails dependent only on wind speed. Smart crews will reef (reduce) sails at night while most of the crew is below sleeping. Nighttime at the helm is spent holding the ship's heading on a compass-course set by the captain. If one is on watch, sail tending is also required because of shifts in the wind's direction or speed. Modern vessels have autopilots to hold the heading. Some are electric and hydraulic driven. Modern navigation systems are integrated with the GPS (Global Positioning System). This combination of systems can be programmed to direct the vessel to travel from waypoint to waypoint along the passage.

While off watch, the crew's duties consist of sleeping, repairing the vessel, preparing food, sharing sea knowledge, standing by for a sail change, or fishing for food. Fishing is usually best within two hundred miles from land. Whales, dolphins, tuna, marlin, shark, and many kinds of other fish are usually found near land, islands, reefs, and atolls. Flying fish can be present most anywhere and will often land on decks of the boats. We envision Nephi assigning small children the fun task of gathering flying fish and proudly delivering the strange creatures to the galley.

Body Care

Being on the ocean in the tropics for many days will cause wind- and sunburn on exposed skin. Skin may become split at the joints of fingers. The inside of the mouth and nose can be sunburned and become very painful. Ears can burn and crack. Eyes can burn and be damaged from sun and salt. Leg strength can diminish. Some of the crew may lose their desire to eat or drink water, which will cause serious problems if not corrected. A captain is responsible for the health and welfare of the crew. We see this reality reflected in the Book of Mormon. Nephi records some sickness of his parents (1 Nephi 18:17).

The captain needs to be proactive at all times, seeing and correcting health problems before they get out of hand. Strains, cuts, bruises, muscle soreness, broken bones, bowel irregularities, sore teeth, and earaches are common problems. There can be depression, melancholia, or a mental withdrawal that strikes some crew members from time to time. Major injuries must be taken care of, using the best skill on board. In today's world, the radio is of great help in contacting medical personal for advice, which can make the difference between life and death. Caring for the sick or injured aboard ship is always paramount.

The captain can actively care for the sick. However, there is little he can do about the revolting smell below deck on a wood ship. Severin writes of the *Sohar*:

> Mohammed Ismail, my head shipwright, was not worried by the smell of rotten eggs. He just shrugged, and said that the bilges of wooden trading ships always smelled like that. I tried to console myself with the fact that I had once read that wood warships in the eighteenth century smelled so powerfully below deck that a junior midshipman would be sent to walk the lengthen of the lower decks carrying a silver spoon. When he reappeared on deck he gave the spoon to the captain for inspection; if the spoon had tarnished, it was judged to be time to scour the hull. It seemed to me that *Sohar* and an eighteenth-century warship had at least one feature in common—the stench.[12]

The stench below deck on the *Sohar* was because Tim Severin used sand and dates instead of rock for ballast. With rock there is no H_2S—in other words, stench. Still, foul air below deck is a common reason why during periods of good weather sailors like to sleep on deck. On ship, the sunrise and moonrises, along with their sets, are beautiful. Once in a great while, there would be a sunset or moonset with a moonrise or sunrise. Sometimes, during the night there would be no moon. During such times, if there was no cloud cover, a person actually can read by starlight. And, of course, during any night of smooth sailing, the day-and-night rush of water over the hull has a healing effect on the troubles one carries through life. Oh, that it were so for the Lehites.

Even in calm weather, however, sleep would never have been guaranteed. Consider this night aboard the *Banyan*:

June 5, '09

500 miles to Marquesas.

All is well; we are now making good time and should be there in 4 days or so. The jib sail's sheet chaffed through again last night at about 3 a.m. So we had a moonlight adventure getting her all squared away until we could fix everything properly in the morning light. Needless to say, the night was very uncomfortable and we didn't sleep well. We also had a late night visitor when a rather large, 6 inch long, flying fish flew into our cabin through an open window. Mike jumped out of bed and scrambled on the floor wrestling with the little guy. He soon had him and flung him out a window into the pitch-black sea. After that a most unpleasant smell of fish wafted throughout the boat and into my little bunk. Not a very nice aroma to be sure. Jody

When Things Turn Bad

To understand just how terrified Lehi and his family could have been during the great tempest and other storms they experienced, let us consider the faith-promoting experience of Conrad. As noted before, Conrad has twice survived hurricanes, which are tempests at sea. One of those took place between Skowl Arm and Vallenar Point at the north end of Dixon Entrance, Alaska, and resulted in breaking all of the windows out of the pilothouse. This caused flooding and shifting of the purse seine net and skiff that were on the stern, which made it very difficult to navigate and steer. Conrad was the only person on board who was not too seasick to function. He spent five hours at the helm, soaked to the bone, cold, and eating salt water that was being slammed through his teeth. Salt burned his eyes to near blindness, yet all the time he knew if he made a mistake all would be lost. When he had the vessel safely maneuvered out of the heavy wind and sea into Tongass Narrows, the captain had to physically carry Conrad from the helm to give him relief. The owner credited Conrad with saving the vessel and crew. That storm took several of his friends to their death who were traveling in a nearby vessel. That vessel's only survivor was a young lad found the following morning by a searching fleet of fishing vessels and the Coast Guard. When found, the young boy was with his dead uncle, the boat's captain; both were floating on top of a hatch cover. Perhaps they had made a mistake or their bodies failed to cope or maybe their vessel just broke apart. The boy was in such shock that he could not tell anyone what had happened.

Conrad again experienced a second great storm a few weeks later in the Dixon Entrance and Hechet Strait between Alaska and Canada while traveling to Seattle on board a Power Scow. He spent two days battling a storm that broke the lashing on a load of obsolete fish-processing machinery. The storm threatened to tear apart the vessel's bin boards and main deck. Conrad and crew were sent to see if they could re-lash the machinery, but to no avail. During the worst part of the storm, the vessel took a very hard and fast roll that broke every piece of glassware on board. Forks and knifes were found stuck an inch into the wooden bulkheads. All of the crew had many bumps and bruises and several had broken bones.

What Might Have Gone Wrong during Nephi's Voyage?

We have proposed that Nephi's ship left in January with the north-east monsoons. They sailed for many days until Laman and others bound Nephi and took over the helm. Without the Liahona and sufficient navigating skills, they likely set a course that took them directly into the tempest that drove the ship backward (westward) for four days. This is exactly what could occur in the Indian Ocean during this dangerous time of the year. A nearly identical fate happened to Severin's replica of Sindbad's ship. Notice the similarities between Nephi's account and what Severin writes:

After *Sohar* sailed from Galle [Sri Lanka] on 22 February, eastbound for Sumatra and the entrance to the Malacca Strait. It was a distance of about 900 miles in a direct line across the Indian Ocean, and I hoped to make the passage in less than a month if the wind favoured us. This was the shortest, direct track toward the lands of South-east Asia, and the route that had been used by Arab ships since the eighth century. But everything depended on the arrival of the monsoon: March was the changeover time when the north-east monsoons gradually died

away and was replaced by the stronger south-west monsoon. On the way to Sumatra any north-east wind would be a head wind, and would be made worse by the west-going current. The combination of head wind and head current would be too much for *Sohar* to make progress eastward, but as soon as the south-west monsoon came everything would change. The wind would turn in our favour, the current would eventually reverse direction, and an eastbound ship could proceed swiftly and comfortably. The golden rule for this sector of the voyage had been laid down by the early Arab navigators. It was to wait for the south-west monsoon before sailing to Sumatra, the land the Arabs called the Land of Gold.

But this year the south-west monsoon was late, disastrously late. We left Sri Lanka at the time when the last of the north-east winds should have been fading, and we sailed hoping to pick up the leading edge of the south-west monsoon as it was drawn across the Equator. In theory we should have experienced unsettled weather, changing winds and brief calms, which would turn into a warm, wet, south-westerly breeze. Instead the unfavorable headwinds continued. Day after day the wind blew from the north-east, interspersed with periods of calm. *Sohar* beat back and forth, gaining a little

ground, but promptly lost it when the winds died away and the current set her back along her track. On the chart the ship's path made a futile series of zigzags and circles, getting no nearer Sumatra as the weeks passed. It was very frustrating. Seeking to pick up the south-west monsoon earlier, I risked taking *Sohar* farther and farther south, almost to the Equator, but to no avail. The unfavourable conditions: headwinds and calm, adverse current and sign of a change.

The last fling of the north-east monsoon had a vicious sting. The Pilot Book warned that the changeover season, from north-east to south-west monsoon, was a dangerous period. There was a risk of sudden gales, quick changes of wind direction, and unstable conditions. At dusk on 3 March the air had an ominous feel. All day it had been swelteringly hot; now there was a sullen, thundery atmosphere, and a spectacular display of evening cloud was building up on the horizon, a mass of cumulus cloud boiling up into great pyramids and billows. The sea around us turned a harsh silver, but beneath the thunder heads it was the colour of lead.

The first squall hit at dusk. The impact was like a slap from an open hand, delivered. The ship shied away, and the sail shivered at the blow. A moment later, and the main weight of the squall hit us. Already off-balance from the first impact, the ship began to tilt. The huge sails, pushed by the sudden increase in pressure, began to force *Sohar's* head downwind and she began to heel more steeply, in a massive cant. Everything became unstable. We lost our footing on the sloping deck. Men grabbed for ropes as handholds. With an alarming crash, all the items left lying carelessly about during day's calm slid into the scuppers in an untidy mess of saucepans, tin plates, mugs, hand torches and baskets of fruit, loose dates rolling like marbles. *Sohar* was at an unhappy angle. The force exerted on her rigging was enormous. She lurched and staggered, and the wind brought a hissing curtain of rain across us.

Now the Omanis were at their best. They knew how to handle the situation. With a stamping rush of running feet, all eight of the Omanis raced to the poop deck. They were yelling excitedly, and bubbling with activity. Abdullah grabbed the tiller from Andrew, and with Musalam's help forced the rudder over so that *Sohar's* head began to swing ponderously upwind. At the same time Khamis Navy and Saleh laid hold of the mizzen sheet and eased it off a fraction. The other four Omanis went to the heavy double mainsheets.

With shouts of encouragement they eased out the massive ropes so that the wind began to spill from the mainsail, and the intolerable pressure on the ship was lessened. The great sail bellied and flapped. Massive, soggy thumps of wet canvas reverberated above the hiss of the rain and the clamour of the wind. *Sohar* straightened up, poked her bowsprit toward the wind and, like an acrobat relaxing his muscles, the sinews of the riggings slackened. Again a squall struck. Again *Sohar* tried to wheel away under the blast. And again the Omanis balanced tiller and sail to protect her from the strain. They juggled with the controls of the recalcitrant ship, coaxing her back into a safe attitude. The Omanis were grinning with glee. This was what they enjoyed: the challenge of the sea. The risk of capsize, of ballast shifting, of sails bursting, of a spar breaking loose and coming crashing down on deck, all the dangers and exhilaration of a boom under the stress of weather.[13]

As soon as the storms passed, the *Sohar* was stuck in windless doldrums waiting for the coming of the south-west monsoon. Let us now recall the order of events that happened to Nephi's ship and see that they were parallel events to what the *Sohar's* experienced.

Nephi's family boarded his ship and "put forth into the sea" and were "driven forth before the wind toward the promised land." This being "driven" suggests that the north-east monsoon was still in effect and Nephi was commanded to get as early a start as possible, perhaps near our proposed January 1 departure date. This date would ensure that they crossed the Pacific before the dead of winter in the Southern Hemisphere.

After "many days" of following the Liahona south of the equator, our simulator predicts that Nephi would have passed the south tip of India. Having initially experienced only favorable winds, Laman and the others stage a rebellion, thinking that he could captain the ship. The Liahona stops functioning (1 Nephi 18:12). Before the rebellion, the still functioning compass likely had the ship on a perfect course toward the east and favorable wind conditions south of the equator. However, perhaps Laman tried to steer the ship northward in an effort to return to land, perhaps even hinder Nephi's objective of reaching the promised land. He had made a similar effort while in the wilderness (1 Nephi 16:35–37).

Not only did Lehi's family end up in a

terrible storm, perhaps similar to the one experienced by the *Sohar*, but also they were driven back to the west for four days (1 Nephi 18:14), just as the *Sohar* had been driven westward from the northeast monsoon and the westward flow of the current. And just as the storm nearly caused the *Sohar* to capsize, Nephi's ship was nearly "swallowed up in the depths of the sea" (1 Nephi 18:15).

Nephi wrote that when the storm finally passed, "the winds did cease, and the storm did cease, and there was a great calm" (1 Nephi 18:21).

Enduring the "Great Calm"

Undoubtedly all aboard Nephi's ship were grateful for the passing of the bitter tempest that nearly sent them to a watery grave. In the days that followed, as they neared the equator they may well have experienced a different kind of "calm" than the one the Lord immediately provided to end the tempest that nearly destroyed them. As Severin related, during this same time of the year the sea off southern India is subject to dangers of storms and long calms or windless doldrums. These doldrums can be almost as difficult to endure on deck as below deck in the sweltering and foul smelling quarters of the ship. Severin describes the days his crew was trapped in doldrums of the Indian Ocean:

The psychological pressures and strains of being becalmed or frustrated by headwinds was an experience very different from the normal difficulties encountered at sea. Yet in their own way these strains were just as wearing. Instead of short periods of the fear of shipwreck or capsizing in the clamour of a gale, we were facing the long, slow, gnawing doubts of boredom, frustration and the ultimate possibility of thirst. There we were, becalmed in the doldrums, hundreds of miles from land, in a very empty part of the world's oceans.[14]

In the third week of March *Sohar* lay in a calm so flat that she stood in the shimmer of her own reflection. She was the very picture of stillness. Only a faint ripple radiated out from her hull, which now showed darker patches where the white lime of the anti-fouling had flaked away. Her sails hung limp, sagging loosely from the spars without a breath of wind to fill them. The sea was like hammered steel, and in the water around her rudder post we could see the striped shapes of the pilot fish waving their fins with just the slightest effort to keep station under the becalmed ship. On deck it was so hot that even three months in the topics had not prepared us for the scorching heat of the calm. Each day the sun arched so high that it stood vertically above the mast, blazing down so that the flaccid sails gave barely a margin of shadow which the crew followed for shelter as they tried to escape the heat. The deck itself was baked until it became too hot to touch, and bare feet which had not worn shoes for twelve or more weeks now wore sandals.[15]

Simulating Nephi's Voyage to the Promised Land—and Captain's Log

Using *Visual Passage Planner 2*, we will take you on a simulated voyage that occurred some 2,600 years ago. The capabilities of the computer software simulator are remarkable. The simulator's charts are for January, February, and March, which we think are the months that one could transit the Indian Ocean to get into the southern Pacific while it was still warm. Further, the summer would be the only time one would want to sail the "roaring forties" due to the frequency of storms in the winter. The simulator will identify what most likely were the oceanic conditions at that time of year and the routing a sailing vessel would take or be guided to take in crossing those waters.

117

In addition to the computer's simulated routing, we have added a "Captain's Log" to help clarify sailing and traveling conditions they likely endured. Of course, our attempt to create Nephi's log is fictional and is more like a journal than an actual ancient captain's log. However, we hope that readers will find the exercise not only educational but that it also will provide them insights into some of the likely challenges our Book of Mormon mariners overcame.

Passage Summary Report

Passage Filename: C:\PROGRAM FILES\ VISUAL PASSAGE PLANNER 2\NEPHI.PP2

Passage Creation Date: 4/10/2009

Pilot Chart Data Used: Actual dates based on departure specified

Vessel Profile Used: C:\Program Files\ Visual Passage Planner 2\NoName.vp

Minimum Speed Set: 0.50 Knots

Fuel Consumption Set: 0.00 Units/Hour

Currents: ON

Current Values Used: Average All

Wind Values Used: Average All

Waypoint #	Latitude	Longitude Date
1	N17°1.78'	E54°34.99'
2	S3°28.70'	E57°32.12'
3	S5°19.58'	E96°11.01'
4	S9°57.06'	E109°51.12'
5	S12°23.24'	E122°30.55'
6	S10°36.42'	E133°11.32'
7	S9°59.03'	E142°33.69'
8	S11°32.04'	E164°0.68'
9	S26°13.87'	E163°32.63'
10	S41°28.04'	E174°44.99'
11	S46°17.25'	W160°48.11'
12	S49°19.71'	W145°21.06'
13	S48°23.96'	W118°24.07'
14	S46°25.90'	W94°32.26'
15	S30°10.54'	W71°34.88'

General Information	Data
Calculated Great Circle Distance	14801.5 NM
Calculated Rhumbline Distance	14821.1 NM
Actual Distance Traveled due to Beating	14852.5 NM
Elapsed Time to Complete Passage	74.2 Days
Fuel Consumption	0.0 Units
Average Boat Speed	8.3 Knots
Boat Speed Made Good	8.3 Knots

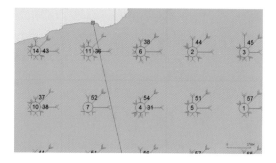

LEG 1

Departure Date 1 January circa 587 BC

VESSEL PERFORMANCE AND WEATHER CONDITIONS REPORT

Start N17° 1.78' E54° 34.99' [Khor Rori Harbor, Oman]

End S3° 28.70' E57° 32' [1,300 miles southwest of southern tip of India]

Elapsed Time to Complete Leg 1: 5.6 Days

Calculated Great Circle Distance: 1242.8 Nautical Miles, [1426.7 miles]

Actual Distance Travel due to Beating [waves effect]: 1242.8 Nautical Miles

Average Boat Speed: 9.2 Knots

Boat Speed Made Good: 9. Knots

Average Wind Speed: 11.1 Knots [1 Knot = 1 Nautical Mile per Hour]

Average Wind Direction from True North: 035.4°

Average Current Drift: 0.7 Knots at **Average Current Set:** 220.7°

Average Wave Height: 3.9 feet

Average Sea Temperature: 78.8 F

Average Air Temperature: 78.3 F

Average Percentage Risk of Calms: 1.9%

Average Percentage Risk of Gales: 0.1%

Captain's Log: Leg One

The Lord has been with us since departing land. We are in our fourth day upon the many waters of the sea. Our final sight of land was the great cliffs that protect the harbor at Khor Rori. Our friends stood on the cliffs and waved their farewells as we passed between the towering cliffs and entered the sea. Praise be to God that our ship handles well in open waters. The strong steady northeast winds drive us toward the south, but we hold our heading in the direction the Liahona points. The dates, meat, water, and grain we have stored and used for ballast have balanced the ship so that she sets deep in the water. So far, we have experienced only minor leaks that we have successfully sealed. She is a good ship and everyone seems confident that, as the Lord promised, his design will be strong enough to carry us safely to the promised land. We hope our final destiny will come soon, yet we are confident in the Lord. Still, Laman is complaining about the inconvenience of being in cramped quarters. Many aboard find it hard to sleep because of the constant motion of the ship and the smell below deck. Some find it hard to eat, and when they do they vomit within minutes.

Still, we praise the Lord, for we have been favored with a constant northeast monsoon wind, which, as the captains at Khor Rori taught, would take us swiftly to the southern seas. The Liahona remains steady. All is well, but amidst such blessings I am afraid some have forgotten who designed this ship and guides us and protects us upon the waters. Some boast about being great sailors. What must God be thinking?

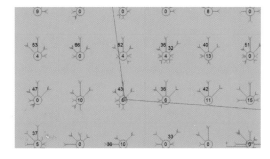

LEG 2

VESSEL PERFORMANCE AND WEATHER CONDITIONS REPORT

Start S3o 28.70' E57o 32.12' [1300 miles southwest of southern tip of India]

End S5o 19.58' E96o 11.01' [200 miles south of Western Indonesia]

Elapsed Time to Complete Leg 2: 12.9 Days

Calculated Great Circle Distance: 2314.4 Nautical Miles, [1 NM = 6067.115 feet]

Actual Distance Travel due to Beating: 2314.4 Nautical Miles

Average Boat Speed: 7.5 Knots

Boat Speed Made Good: 7.5 Knots

Average Wind Speed: 8.6 Knots

Average Wind Direction from True North: 245.8o

Average Current Drift: 1.0 Knots at **Average Current Set:** 112.6o

Average Wave Height: 4.2 feet

Average Sea Temperature: 82.1 F

Average Air Temperature: 80.8 F

Average Percentage Risk of Calms: 10.4% [High]16

Average Percentage Risk of Gales: 0%

Captain's Log: Leg Two

The wind has shifted to becoming more from the west. I made a course change to the east. The Lord is our light upon the waters, and he has delivered us from the jaws of the deep. As I feared, my brothers' actions became increasingly rude and boisterous. Their merriment continues and is disgusting. They dance in a manner that is crude and immodest. It is only because our Lord is so patient and merciful that he has not battered this ship upon rocks or caused a great sea beast to crush it.

My worst fears were realized when I saw the Liahona no longer functioning. The Lord's Spirit withdrew. Without him we were becoming lost upon the waters. I ordered the rudder to be steadied East South. My elder brothers cursed me and ordered the sons of Ishmael to ignore my orders.

I had no choice but to take action. I confronted them. Laman became angry and tried to strike me. We wrestled to the deck, where Lemuel and the sons of Ishmael joined in against me. Together they beat me and tied me to the mast. Half conscious, I could hear the boisterous songs they composed of how they were mighty sailors upon the waters, fearing neither God nor sea. I sensed that the wind had shifted and was coming from the west-southwest. Laman had reset the rudder and was heading the ship on a north-northwest course. His plan was to return to land. The captains at Khor Rori warned me to avoid the dangerous waters in this part of the sea. They told how many vessels had been lost in great storms on the lee shores of the islands they call Indonesia. I tried to warn Laman, but he would not listen.

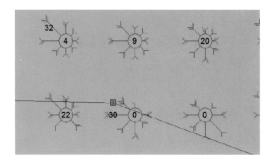

LEG 3

VESSEL PERFORMANCE AND WEATHER CONDITIONS REPORT

Start S5 19.58' E96o 11.01' [200 miles south of Western Indonesia]

End S9o 57.06' E109o 51.12' [along central Indonesian shoreline]

Elapsed Time to Complete Leg 3: 4.9 Days [+ 4 Days Mutiny + 10 Days calm]

Calculated Great Circle Distance: 858.6 Nautical Miles, [986.6 miles]

Actual Distance Travel due to Beating: 858.6 Nautical Miles

Average Boat Speed: 7.4 Knots

Boat Speed Made Good: 7.4 Knots

Average Wind Speed: 9.5 Knots

Average Wind Direction from True North: 242.8o

Average Current Drift: 0.6 Knots at **Average Current Set:** 165.7o

Average Wave Height: 3.5 feet

Average Sea Temperature: 82.5F

Average Air Temperature: 81.6 F

Average Percentage Risk of Calms: 5.6%]*

Average Percentage Risk of Gales: 0.8%

* For leg three, the probability of a calm and a gale are slightly more than for Leg Two. This leads us to think that the tempest and calm Nephi wrote about may have occurred during the beginning of Leg Three.

Captain's Log: Leg Three

Only a few hours in sailing into the dangerous waters, a large wave crashed against the side of the ship. The wave drenched me in it foamy broth. Then I knew it. My brothers ignored the warnings of the Omani members of our crew, and without the Liahona, my brothers had allowed the ship to drift into stormy waters. Once we were engaged within the first grasps of the storm and they, being ignorant of the seamanship skills required of a captain, did not know how to read the wind or waves and they remained in control of the ship. Laman ordered all of our crew to do as he said. My elder brothers did not recognize they had entered the jaws of a great storm, nor did they know the direction they needed to steer the ship to free us from the storm's grip. "Don't worry, it will pass," they shouted to each other. I begged them to release me, for I feared the Lord would find us unworthy of a promised land and destroy us before we ever reached our destiny.

By nightfall, the situation became critical. All adults, including women, were ordered to the deck to try to take in the sails. Rain fell in heavy sheets and the wind's endless howling mocked Laman's efforts to control the ship. One sail was torn apart and the others stretched out of shape before they were properly reefed. The ship was taking on water and being driven back by the force of the southwest winds and waves. It was only a matter of time before the forces of the storm would top the ship and send her along with all of us to the bottom of the sea. Day and night the mighty tempest punished our ship. My parents were gravely ill and everyone else either too tired, sick, or afraid to move. I continued asking my brothers to release me, but they would have none of it. All I could do was to pray for the salvation of my family.

The following day, the storm became even stronger and I could see from the expressions on my brothers' faces that they began to fear that they would soon be facing the judgment bar of the Almighty. It was then that I realized the tempest would not destroy us, but was sent as another warning to my wayward brothers and in-laws. Finally, after four days of trying to fight against God and the tempest, my brothers and their allies repented and released me. I manned the rudder and took command of the ship. The Liahona functioned again, and I prayed to the Lord. After I prayed, the storm ceased, and there was a great calm witnessing to all that our God is in charge. He is our protector. I again steered the ship in the direction the Lord indicated.

Within hours, we were away from the storm. I ordered all hands on deck. Before mending the ship, we prayed and thanked the Lord for our delivery. Some were somewhat defiant, telling the family I had been lucky in finding our way out of the storm. Instead of praying, they stayed below deck. Immediately, the Liahona stopped working again. The wind left our sails and the ship came slowly to rest, not making so much as a ripple of progress in the water.

The favorable wind was lost; indeed, there was no wind at all. The heat and reflection of the bright light off the water was unbearable. The captains at Khor Rori had taught me that gales were not the greatest fear of a seaman. It was the opposite— the great calms. We had no wind, which also meant there was no rain to replenish our drinking water. If the winds do not come, we could become a ship of the dead unless the Lord steps in again. After being becalmed for three days, everyone sensed our fate. Even Laman started to humble himself and began cooperating.

To keep the family's spirits up, I kept everyone busy in drying out our provisions that had become soaked during the storm. I engaged them in many repairs that were needed. The ship's rigging and sails were in terrible shape. However, keeping the family busy was a two-edge sword. It helped with morale, but in the warm, humid weather of this silent sea, we needed more drinking water and this caused our stores of water to be fearfully low. We fasted and prayed, but not the faintest breath filled our sails. We fasted and prayed again. Soon the wind became alive again. First, there were only small breaths of wind that filled the sails and the ship started slipping through the sea. Then the winds shifted to the normal winds coming from the west and we sailed for many days, finally coming upon the coastline of a large body of land. Be it a great forgotten island or a new land, I cannot determine. What I do know is the land is on our north and the Liahona points steadily to the east. We were all hoping this was our land of promise. But it is not because the Liahona tells us otherwise. We were directed by the Liahona to stop and restore our water supply and to find some fresh fruits. This will please those who have been complaining that we have had no fresh food. It also pleases me to stop, for my sick parents need a rest.

We were directed to a safe cove where we anchored ship. It felt good to place our feet upon this strange land. It was blessed with many kinds of trees, a land greener than we have ever imagined. Fresh water was abundant from springs and small rivers. We netted fish in the shallows and rested our bodies. We found many colorful wild flowers in varieties and quantities beyond what we had known in the land of Jerusalem. It felt good to be upon a land our God had created. Laman and Lemuel insisted on settling here, but the Liahona directed otherwise. We must go on. Perhaps it was well that this was not to be our new land. As we explored hills around our temporary port, we discovered snakes large enough to swallow a goat and large lizards that reminded us of stories of dragons. Most curious of all were what we called the little orange people. These were apes, nearly the size of a man. They can stand on two feet while on the ground, but prefer living up in the forest. What wonders are the creations of our Lord.

With our provisions replenished, we set sail again. However, it was not without some voiced murmurings.

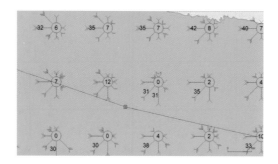

LEG 4

VESSEL PERFORMANCE AND WEATHER CONDITIONS REPORT

Start S9o 57.06' E109o 51.12' [along central Indonesian shoreline]

End S12o 33.99' E122o 51.23' [near east Indonesia]

Elapsed Time to Complete Leg 4: 4.3 Days

Calculated Great Circle Distance: 780.9 Nautical Miles, [897.3 miles]

Actual Distance Travel due to Beating: 780.9 Nautical Miles

Average Boat Speed: 7.4 Knots

Boat Speed Made Good: 7.4 Knots

Average Wind Speed: 9.9 Knots

Average Wind Direction from True North: 244.3o

Average Current Drift: 0.7 Knots at
Average Current Set: 244.3o

Average Wave Height: 3.7 feet

Average Sea Temperature: 83.1 F

Average Air Temperature: 83.3 F

Average Percentage Risk of Calms: 4.8%

Average Percentage Risk of Gales: 1.1%

Captain's Log: Leg Four

Thanks to the Lord, we continue to make good progress toward the promised land. Winds are steadily blowing us in an easterly course as we do our best to steer the ship in the direction indicated by the Liahona. The ship remains seaworthy, with no significant leaks. The wave height remains the same. During the last few days the passage has not been difficult and most of the family are now well and are now able to hold their food. We butchered the last of the goats. The women cooked the feast on deck in the sand box they use for cooking. I find it remarkable how women can prepare good meals in such conditions, even baking bread in the sand. From here on, we will need to turn to the sea for fish if we are to supplement our salted meat. We need the rest of the goats for milk. We have saved the fat of the goats to anoint our skin to help protect us from the sun. Praise the Lord that he had us build a deck so women and children could find refuge from the sunrays. We continue to see land to our north, but the Liahona continues to separate us further and further from it.

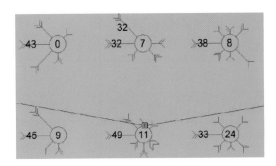

LEG 5

VESSEL PERFORMANCE AND WEATHER CONDITIONS REPORT

Start S12o 33.99' E122o 51.23' [near eastern tip of Indonesia]

End S10o 36.42' E133o 11.32' [northern Australia]

Elapsed Time to Complete Leg 5: 3.5 Days

Calculated Great Circle Distance: 636.9 Nautical Miles, [731.2 miles]

Actual Distance Travel due to Beating: 636.9 Nautical Miles

Average Boat Speed: 7.6 Knots

Boat Speed Made Good: 7.6 Knots

Average Wind Speed: 9.6 Knots

Average Wind Direction from True North: 244.6o

Average Current Drift: 0.6 Knots at
Average Current Set: 186.3o

Average Wave Height: 3.5 feet

Average Sea Temperature: 82.8 F

Average Air Temperature: 83.6 F

Average Percentage Risk of Calms: 8.7%

Average Percentage Risk of Gales: 1.2%

Captain's Log: Leg Five

Winds have decreased somewhat, but the height of the waves remain about the same. Progress is smooth and our speed even has increased a little. No land is to be seen, so our Lord must favor us with a homeland further east. I pray it is close, for the exposure to the sea is hard on us. We bathe in water we draw from the sea, so our skin and clothes are saturated in fine salt. Almost everyone has sores on their lips and burns and rashes on their skin. We made nets in an attempt to catch fish, but we have had no success. However, the children throw nets at sea birds that come to rest on the ship. To everyone's surprise, at times they succeed and their families are rewarded with a dinner of fresh meat. We attend to our prayers as we honor the Lord. The Liahona is our faithful friend.

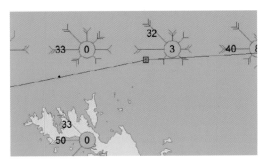

LEG 6

VESSEL PERFORMANCE AND WEATHER CONDITIONS REPORT

Start S10o 36.42' E133o 11.32' [northern Australia]

End S9o 559.03' E142o 33.69' [northeastern tip of Australia]

Elapsed Time to Complete Leg 6: 2.2 Days

Calculated Great Circle Distance: 554.6 Nautical Miles, [636.7 miles]

Actual Distance Travel due to Beating: 554.6 Nautical Miles

Average Boat Speed: 10.3 Knots

Boat Speed Made Good: 10.3 Knots

Average Wind Speed: 11.8 Knots

Average Wind Direction from True North: 288.5o

Average Current Drift: 0.3 Knots at
Average Current Set: 077.4o

Average Wave Height: 3.6 feet

Average Sea Temperature: 83.0 F

Average Air Temperature: 81.9 F

Average Percentage Risk of Calms: 8.9%

Average Percentage Risk of Gales: 1.0

Captain's Log: Leg Six

The Lord strengthens the wind and we are making good progress. Despite stiff wind, seas are smooth and our ship splits the seas with little effort. The sails are stretching and will soon need to be replaced by another of the sets our women made in Arabia. On occasions, we think we see land mass far to the south. The sea is a light blue, leading us to believe the depth of water below may be shallow. Perhaps we are nearing the promised land. At times, dolphins swim beside our ship as if the Lord has provided sea angels to escort us. While dragging our nets behind us, we finally caught a large shark. We have agreed that it was delicious. My son caught a seabird. The shark was better.

We sail with more and more confidence. The men of the family have helped form a commendable team of sailors. There have been no gales and no calms. Perhaps the worst is behind us. Praise be to the Lord.

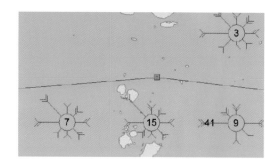

LEG 7:

VESSEL PERFORMANCE AND WEATHER CONDITIONS REPORT

Start S9o 59.03' E142o 33.69' [north-eastern tip of Australia]

End S11o 32.04' E164o 0.68 [Solomon Islands]

Elapsed Time to Complete Leg 7: 7.0 Days

Calculated Great Circle Distance: 1267.5 Nautical Miles, [1455.1 miles]

Actual Distance Travel due to Beating: 1267.5 Nautical Miles

Average Boat Speed: 7.5 Knots

Boat Speed Made Good: 7.5 Knots

Average Wind Speed: 11.0 Knots

Average Wind Direction from True North: 233.6o

Average Current Drift: 0.5 Knots at
Average Current Set: 172.0o

Average Wave Height: 3.8 feet

Average Sea Temperature: 83.8 F

Average Air Temperature: 82.5 F

Average Percentage Risk of Calms: 6.5%

Average Percentage Risk of Gales: 1.7%

Captain's Log: Leg Seven

Though our speed has decreased, we are making good progress and the Lord has strengthened our sails. They continue to hold the wind and drive us toward the promised land. The waves are shifting their direction, leading me to think we are moving away from land and deeper into the sea. I never imagined the Lord's oceans were so vast. His world is so grand. How can our new homeland be much farther? A small leak has appeared just below the waterline. We plugged it with rope and grease of sheep's fat. The leak is holding. Rains have replenished our drinking water.

Two days ago, a great fish came to the surface of the sea and swam for some time next to the ship. It was nearly as long as our entire vessel. Panic took hold among the family. Some screamed like a child that the fish would crush our ship with its great tail. It gave some another opportunity to curse my name and blame me for the family's possible death.

Such little faith some have in the words of our Lord. Why don't they realize the Lord has promised us a safe passage if we keep his commandments. The great fish blew tall spouts of water from its head. The fish's great eyes looked at us in a curious fashion. Its great mouth seemed to smile at us, as the friendly beast slipped below the water and disappeared.

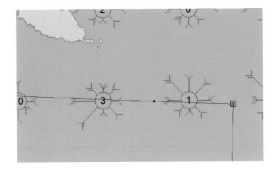

LEG 8

VESSEL PERFORMANCE AND WEATHER CONDITIONS REPORT

Start S11o 33.04' E164o 0.68' [Solomon Islands]

End S26o 13.87' E163o 32.83' [Tasman Sea]

Elapsed Time to Complete Leg 8: 5.5 Days

Calculated Great Circle Distance: 882.2 Nautical Miles, [1012.8 miles]

Actual Distance Travel due to Beating: 882.2 Nautical Miles

Average Boat Speed: 6.6 Knots

Boat Speed Made Good: 6.6 Knots

Average Wind Speed: 10.5 Knots

Average Wind Direction from True North: 079.6o

Average Current Drift: .6 Knots at **Average Current Set:** 194.7o

Average Wave Height: 5.3 feet

Average Sea Temperature: 81.4 F

Average Air Temperature: 81.4 F

Average Percentage Risk of Calms: 1.6%

Average Percentage Risk of Gales: 1.3%

Captain's Log: Leg Eight

The Liahona directed that we change our course to south. Our ship is moving now through the now dark blue waters of the great sea. Winds are stronger but not much speed is made. We were guided by the Lord in stopping at an island and filled the ship with much needed coconuts and refreshed our water and fruit. I believe the Lord's ship design has made our ship for such waters. Like a fast horse, the ship follows the Liahona's direction. Waves now come in large swells and several times each day the ship's bow plows deep into a wave, sending tall sprays of seawater across the deck. The Lord's will is taking us on a southerly course. The weather is pleasant. We are content despite the lack of fresh meat and the discomfort we experience from dry skin and sores. The women have made a coconut butter to put on our dry skin and sores. It seems to help. With others, I am also tired of eating dates and grain, but I shall not complain, rather glory that the Lord guided us to make such preparations. However, it seems that last night the Lord sent manna from heaven. In the morning we saw dozens of small fish lying on the ship's deck. The night watch told us they saw and heard them hit the deck through the night.

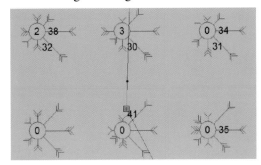

LEG 9

VESSEL PERFORMANCE AND WEATHER CONDITIONS REPORT

Start S26o 13.87' E163o 32.63' [Tasman Sea]

End S41o 28.04' E174o 44.99' [between New Zealand's North and South Island]

Elapsed Time to Complete Leg 9: 7.2 Days

Calculated Great Circle Distance: 1069.1 Nautical Miles, [1227.3 miles]

Actual Distance Travel due to Beating: 1118.4 Nautical Miles

Average Boat Speed: 6.5 Knots

Boat Speed Made Good: 6.2 Knots

Average Wind Speed: 14.7 Knots

Average Wind Direction from True North: 135.6o

Average Current Drift: .6 Knots at **Average Current Set:** 151.4o

Average Wave Height: 6.7 feet

Average Sea Temperature: 70.4 F

Average Air Temperature: 70.8 F

Average Percentage Risk of Calms: 2.2%

Average Percentage Risk of Gales: 1.6%

Captain's Log: Leg Nine

The Liahona has again directed us to change our course to southeast. On the sixth day, we spotted a long white cloud. For a day now, we have been sailing near a land of a long white cloud. We were directed to a safe harbor and anchored. The Spirit has warned me that it is time to make repairs. It has been seventy-eight days since we left Arabia. Our provisions are low and the continual pounding of large waves has caused several more leaks to appear. The ship is taking on water and the hull must be sealed before we continue. We must beach the vessel, repair its leaks, clean the hull, and apply a new coating of antifouling compound to protect the wood from sea worms. The standing rigging must be tightened and the sails need mending. God willing, the hull will be protected until we reach the promised land.

The land in which we find ourselves is naturally rich, with strange animals, no snakes, and unusual plants of a nature we have never seen before. There are varieties of flightless birds. These are easily caught with our nets. Some of these birds are so large they stand waist high against a man. We have found no signs of inhabitants.

Some have argued that we end our voyage here and now. However, they quickly changed their minds when a giant bird came to roost atop the mast. The avian monster had claws that could rip a man to pieces. As the great eagle peered down on the deck, the women quickly gathered the children and took refuge in the deck below. I took out my bow, and with the Lord's help the first arrow downed the giant. Everyone was amazed that a few fish and this amazingly large eagle provided a feast for everyone that night. Sam found a steaming hot spring not far from where we anchored. The hot spring emptied into a cool stream where we were finally able to refresh ourselves with a warm bath. Freed at last from the salt that baked our skins, many of us wondered how glorious must be the land the Lord has for us if this was not for us. However, the Liahona gave instructions, renewed the Lord's promise, and pointed to the east-southeast, out to sea and away from this land and its giant birds. Loaded with fish that we caught along the shore, birds we placed in cages, a full store of fresh water, and fodder, after fourteen days we set sail in the morning wind. We are tired. But, still, the Liahona directs us on.

[New Zealand's Haast eagle was the largest eagle ever to have lived and is the only eagle in the world to have been top predator of its ecosystem. It had a wingspan of eight feet. The giant bird became extinct around AD 1400.]

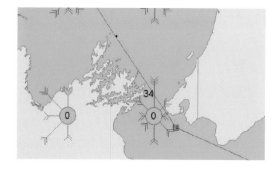

LEG 10

VESSEL PERFORMANCE AND WEATHER CONDITIONS REPORT

Start S41o 28.04' E174o 44.99' [between New Zealand's South and North Island]

End S46o 17.25' W160o 48.11' [1200 miles east of New Zealand - Roaring Forties]

Elapsed Time to Complete Leg 10: 5.0 Days

Calculated Great Circle Distance: 1091.3 Nautical Miles, [1125.8 miles]

Actual Distance Travel due to Beating: 1091.6 Nautical Miles

Average Boat Speed: 9.0 Knots

Boat Speed Made Good: 9.1 Knots

Average Wind Speed: 16.2 Knots

Average Wind Direction from True North: 194.4o

Average Current Drift: 1.2 Knots at
Average Current Set: 225.0o

Average Wave Height: 8.1 feet

Average Sea Temperature: 60.9 F

Average Air Temperature: 60.3 F

Average Percentage Risk of Calms: 1.2%

Average Percentage Risk of Gales: 4.4%

Captain's Log: Leg Ten

We passed some islands but were directed onward. We are five days into what has become an angry sea. The waves are as hills and valleys. The great waves push the ship high in the air, just to drop her down into ocean valleys where the sea surrounds us on all sides. It is cold, and we are all soaked from the spray of waves that crash over the bow. In these waters, the winds seem to never stop. They drive us hard toward the promised land, but at the same time, they chill our bodies. There is little rest. If not manning the ship, we are filling large pots to empty the hull that seems to fill with water as fast as we can empty it. It is impossible to cook, and we can eat only the remainder of our dates, coconuts, and fried fish. Food, however, is not on the minds of most, for they are sick from the constant rocking of the ship. I encourage the sick to eat, but some refuse. Many of the children cover their ears in an effort to reduce the constant roaring of the wind and grinding of the hull's timbers as the ship powers

onward through the waves. Some are angry and want to turn back to the land of the great eagles. They say if we continued in this angry sea, we will perish. I confronted them in front of the others, and they backed down. The Lord was with me and again witnesses to them that he was guiding me. I continue to reassure all that if we are faithful, the Lord will lead us to a choice land and will bless us greatly there.

We have not seen land the last four days. I wonder why we are in these angry waters. My thoughts are that the promised land is still far off. The Liahona has said the only way we can reach it before our fresh water and food gives out is from a quick passage through these hellish seas. I know the ship is strong enough to endure this punishing sea, for the Lord promised me that it would.

We have discovered the source of the little fish that arrived on the ship's deck. They fly out of the water like a bird and sometimes land aboard the ship. When the gales recede enough, I ask the children to collect them. After such a long time at sea, anything to help the children pass the time is welcome. Our new game is to see who can find the most fish each day from that which has landed on the ship's deck.

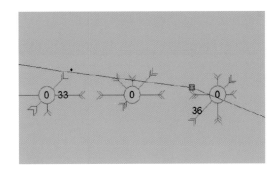

LEG 11

VESSEL PERFORMANCE AND WEATHER CONDITIONS REPORT

Start S46o 17.25' W160o 48.11' [1200 miles east of New Zealand - Roaring Forties]

End S49o 19.71' W145o 21.06' [2000 miles east of New Zealand - Roaring Forties]

Elapsed Time to Complete Leg 11: 2.6 Days

Calculated Great Circle Distance: 647.5 Nautical Miles, [743.3 miles]

Actual Distance Travel due to Beating: 647.7 Nautical Miles

Average Boat Speed: 10.4 Knots

Boat Speed Made Good: 10.4 Knots

Average Wind Speed: 19.5 Knots

Average Wind Direction from True North: 244.8o

Average Current Drift: 0.7 Knots at
Average Current Set: 166.6o

Average Wave Height: 9.6 feet

Average Sea Temperature: 54.0 F

Average Air Temperature: 53.2 F

Average Percentage Risk of Calms: 0.5%

Average Percentage Risk of Gales: 3.1%

Captain's Log: Leg Eleven

It is difficult to write because the waves have increased. We are cold, wet, many sick, and we are tired beyond what we thought possible. Even during the great tempest that we survived, we did not see such powerful waves. Thanks be to the Lord that the mighty winds are pushing us quickly, according to the instructions and directions given by the Liahona. Otherwise, some would not have the will to fight the sea. As always, some murmuring continues, however. Out of fear and not love of God, the rebellious members of my family are now keeping the commandments. The Liahona does not fail us; the Lord is our light. Praise be to our God.

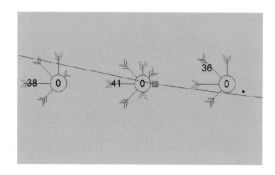

LEG 12

VESSEL PERFORMANCE AND WEATHER CONDITIONS REPORT

Start S49o 19.71' W145o 21.06' [2000 miles east of New Zealand - Roaring Forties]

End S48o 23.96' W118o 24.07' [Roaring Forties midway between Australia and Chile]

Elapsed Time to Complete Leg 12: 4.0 Days

Calculated Great Circle Distance: 1059.9 Nautical Miles, [1216.3 miles]

Actual Distance Travel due to Beating: 1059.9 Nautical Miles

Average Boat Speed: 11.1 Knots

Boat Speed Made Good: 11.1 Knots

Average Wind Speed: 21.7 Knots

Average Wind Direction from True North: 270.3o

Average Current Drift: 1.0 Knots at
Average Current Set: 090.00o

Average Wave Height: 9.8 feet

Average Sea Temperature: 50.7 F

Average Air Temperature: 50.7 F

Average Percentage Risk of Calms: 0.4%

Average Percentage Risk of Gales: 8.5%

Captain's Log: Leg Twelve

Sometimes I am so tired my hand shakes, but the ship continues toward the promised land. Each watch's helmsman are in a similar condition. Without the help of the Lord, I know none of us could make this journey alive. The wind is very strong. Only six of us, including my wife and one of my sisters and three of the Omani crew, are well enough to man the ship. The waves pound day and night. I have not slept for three days. I pray, if it be the Lord's will, the seas will lighten. My parents are gravely ill, and I pray that the Lord will preserve their lives until we reach the land of promise. Many are afraid and have lost hope. Despair blankets the faces of many.

Despite our perilous circumstances, I have not lost faith. When I consider the greatness of this sea, I begin to comprehend the powers of heaven. If the Lord can create such a great ocean, he can give us the strength to carry on. How great is our God who can form such seas. How strong is our God who can cause such wind that drives us on.

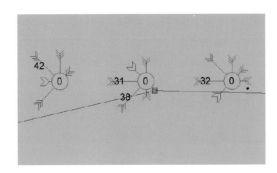

LEG 13

VESSEL PERFORMANCE AND WEATHER CONDITIONS REPORT

Start S48o 23.96' W118o 24.07' [Roaring Forties midway between Australia and Chile]

End S46o 25.90' W94o 32.26' [Roaring Forties 800 miles west of Chile]

Elapsed Time to Complete Leg 13: 3.5 Days

Calculated Great Circle Distance: 972.0 Nautical Miles, [1115.9 miles]

Actual Distance Travel due to Beating: 1072.4 Nautical Miles

Average Boat Speed: 11.5 Knots

Boat Speed Made Good: 11.6 Knots

Average Wind Speed: 22.5 Knots

Average Wind Direction from True North: 265.0o

Average Current Drift: 0.6 Knots at **Average Current Set:** 154.6o

Average Wave Height: 8.8 feet

Average Sea Temperature: 51.7 F

Average Air Temperature: 52.3 F

Average Percentage Risk of Calms: 0.2%

Average Percentage Risk of Gales: 11.4%

Captain's Log: Leg Thirteen

The winds have not eased. The Liahona has directed a course change to east from east-northeast. At times, the hand of the Lord seems so hard on his people. Three days past, a lengthy leak opened in the hull. We cannot seal it and we are taking on water. The task of bailing seawater has fallen upon our sick, while the others man the ship. They must force themselves to free the ship from a constant inflow of water or have us all sink into the depths.

I see the anger in eyes of some as they endure almost into exhaustion the gales that continually drive us eastward. I know it is only the hand of the Lord that keeps us afloat. How could it be otherwise? For the past three weeks, from sunset to sunset, the ship has endured the pounding of great waves. Its sails are stretched, but somehow they hold the raging winds and drive us forward. I know the ship is in need of repair. Her days are likely numbered, yet I remember the promise of the Lord that he will deliver my people to the promised land. We must be near our destiny, for the ship and its crew hardly feel alive.

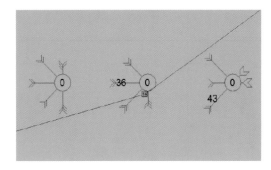

LEG 14

VESSEL PERFORMANCE AND WEATHER CONDITIONS REPORT

Start S46o 25.90' W94o 32.26' [Roaring Forties 800 miles west of Chile]

End S30o 10.54' W71o 34.88' [The Promised Land, 30 degrees south in Chile]

Elapsed Time to Complete Leg 14: 6.0 Days

Calculated Great Circle Distance: 1446.0 Nautical Miles, [1660.0 miles]

Actual Distance Travel due to Beating: 1446.2 Nautical Miles

Average Boat Speed: 10.0 Knots

Boat Speed Made Good: 10.0 Knots

Average Wind Speed: 14.5 Knots

Average Wind Direction from True North: 196.2o

Average Current Drift: 0.4 Knots at **Average Current Set:** 182.1o

Average Wave Height: 6.2 feet

Average Sea Temperature: 61.3 F

Average Air Temperature: 61.1 F

Average Percentage Risk of Calms: 1.0%

Average Percentage Risk of Gales: 6.6%

Captain's Log: Leg Fourteen

After eighteen days in the terrible southern seas, the Liahona directed our course to the northeast. Within a day's voyage toward the north, the winds have lightened significantly and the seas are more favorable. Giant waves no longer crash over the bow of the ship and her timbers no longer creak as if she would fall apart at any moment. The weather is warmer, bringing some relief from those suffering from the chills and fever. Five days ago, the Liahona directed us to change our course slightly more to the northeast.

Praise God! Today we have finally spotted land. Praise the Lord that it is a large land. It lies in a north–south orientation and the Liahona points us eastward. It is the land of promise. We have reached it! Our ship is weak, we are soaked to the bone, but the Lord has lightened the waves and brought us north into warmer waters. My father and mother have survived. During the past days the more part of the adults have been able to help man the ship. As we draw near to shore, the land looks much like the place we left three months ago. It looks arid, but in the distance are great mountains with snow resting on their summits. We are weak, tired, and afflicted with illnesses and sores. However, we are all joyful.

Thanks to our mighty God, the Liahona has directed us to a safe harbor in a bay with calm waters. We pitched our tents, tended to the sick, and gave thanks to him who brought us to our new home that we call the land of promise. Though I am grateful for having survived the great deaths of the sea, I sense some members of our family may be disappointed that we have arrived in a somewhat barren land. During our voyage, we visited lands with abundant vegetation and wild beasts for food. It can appear we crossed the many waters to arrive in a wilderness similar to that near where we dwelt before building our ship. But to our east stand towering mountains with snow covering their highest reaches. A river of sweet water flows down from the mountains and empties into the bay. Narrow stretches of vegetation grow on both sides of the river, but beyond this area of greenery all we see is a lifeless landscape. [The shoreline of northern Chile contains the driest desert on earth.]

Book of Mormon explorer Arthur Kocherhans standing at La Serena harbor, 30 degrees south, Chile.

The mountains beckon me. I am certain we will find rich valleys and pleasant meadows within this land. However, for the present, my family is too weak to travel on. We will remain here for a season, plant our seeds, and grow strong. We thank our Almighty God for his deliverance from his many waters and his many mercies to us. A new life now begins.

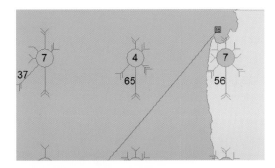

Summary of Computer Simulation of Nephi's circa 587 BC Voyage

Passage Filename: C:\PROGRAM FILES\ VISUAL PASSAGE PLANNER 2\NEPHI.PP2

Passage Creation Date: 4/10/2009

Pilot Chart Data Used: Actual dates based on departure specified

Vessel Profile Used: C:\Program Files\ Visual Passage Planner 2\NoName.vp

Minimum Speed Set: 0.50 Knots

Fuel Consumption Set: 0.00 Units/Hour

Currents: ON

Current Values Used: Average All

Wind Values Used: Average All

Total days sailing toward the promised land: 74.1 days (74)

Add four days when driven back in the great tempest: 78 days

Add ten days when adrift in the great calm: 88 days

Add another twenty-four days for stopovers for provisions and repairs: 112 days, roughly 15 weeks

Average Boat Speed: 8.4 Knots

Boat Speed Made Good: 8.3 Knots

Total length of voyage: 14,857 Nautical Miles [17,055.8 Miles]

Approximate arrival time per the simulation: last week of April

Apparent Wind Angle Information:

Numbers indicate percent of leg sailed at that column's relative wind angle. Relative wind angle given is the direction from which the wind comes. (See table below.)

Leg #	Beating (Apparent wind 0° to 45°)	Tight Reaching (Apparent wind 45° to 112.5°)	Broad Reaching (Apparent wind 112.6° to 157.5°)	Running (Apparent wind 157.6 to 180)
1	0% at 0 Knots	7% at 9.0 Knots	65% at 12.2 Knots	28% at 9.0 Knots
2	0% at 0 Knots	14% at 6.7 Knots	46% at 8.0 Knots	40% at 10.0 Knots
3	0% at 0 Knots	14% at 6.1 Knots	52% at 8.4 Knots	34% at 12.4 Knots
4	0% at 0 Knots	0% at 0 Knots	59% at 8.0 Knots	41% at 12.7 Knots
5	0% at 0 Knots	16% at 5.0 Knots	50% at 10.8 Knots	34% at 10.0 Knots
6	0% at 0 Knots	7% at 5.8 Knots	81% at 12.4 Knots	12% at 11.3 Knots
7	7% at 8.4 Knots	8% at 6.5 Knots	28% at 10.0 Knots	57% at 12.5 Knots
8	0% at 0 Knots	60% at 11.7 Knots	32% at 7.7 Knots	8% at 12.4 Knots
9	45% at 15.7 Knots	46% at 13.2 Knots	8% at 17.4 Knots	1% at 14.3 Knots
10	0% at 0 Knots	32% at 14.3 Knots	44% at 19.8 Knots	24% at 11.9 Knots
11	0% at 0 Knots	15% at 21.6 Knots	40% at 21.0 Knots	45% at 17.5 Knots
12	0% at 0 Knots	1% at 12.6 Knots	9% at 27.5 Knots	90% at 21.1 Knots
13	0% at 0 Knots	0% at 0 Knots	30% at 19.8 Knots	70% at 23.6 Knots
14	6% at 7.6 Knots	12% at 13.1 Knots	62% at 14.3 Knots	19% at 18.6 Knots

Notes

1. James E. Talmage, *The Vitality of Mormonism: Brief Essays on Distinctive Doctrines of The Church of Jesus Christ of Latter-day Saints* (Boston: Gorham Press, 1919), 133–34.

2. B.H. Roberts, *New Witnesses for God*, vol. 3 (Salt Lake City, UT: Deseret News, 1909), 501.

3. "Book of Mormon Geography," *Encyclopedia of Mormonism*, vol. 1, ed. Daniel H. Ludlow (New York: Macmillan, 1992).

4. Parley P. Pratt, *Autobiography of Parley P. Pratt* (Salt Lake City: Deseret Book), 388.

5. Ibid., 400.

6. Dale Christensen, "History of the Church in Peru," http://www.mission.net/peru/lima/south/page.php?pg_id=3753.

7. Ibid.

8. Mary Kawena Pukui, *'Olelo No'eau: Hawaiian Proverbs and Poetical Sayings* (Hawaii: Bishop Museum Press, 1983), 2.

9. Severin, *Sindbad Voyage*, 156.

10. Ibid., 89.

11. Ibid., 95–96.

12. Ibid., 80.

13. Ibid., 156–58.

14. Ibid., 167.

15. Ibid., 164.

16. Note that the computer simulation for leg two has nil probability of a gale and indicates that the risk of a calm is high.

Nephi's log was presented as a narrative. A modern captain's log is a technical report. Presented below is an example of a log for one of the ships Frank is responsible for:

```
CAPE INSCRIPTION DAILY REPORT
Thursday 22 April 2010

0600 Pre-cargo Ops and Safety meetings.
0630 Resume loading cargo.
1000 Finish loading cargo. Secure for
sea.
1300 Pilot aboard
1342 Last line
1430 Pilot away - Departure
1500 Safety Meeting for off-watch
personnel

REMARKS
Departure drafts F 24-06 A 32-08
Departure fuel: IFO 180 -  29,497 BBLS
/ 97%
ETA Bunker Port: 042030LT / 041130Z (-9
ZD) MAY

VOYPLAN DATA
ETA GUAM 042030LT / 041130Z (-9 ZD) MAY
MAX DRAFT 32.0 FT
ARR BUNKERS ONBD 20,183 BBLS / 66.5%
BUNKER STEM IFO 180 / 1,460 MT
BUNKER SKED 050800LT
ETD GUAM 060800LT / 052300Z MAY 2010
MAX DRAFT 32.5 FT
BUNKERS ONBD EST 29,757 BBLS / 98%
SOA 19.0K / DIS TO JAKARTA 2,613NM
ETA JAKARTA 112330LT / 111630Z (-7 ZD)
ARR BUNKERS ONBD 25,047 BBLS / 84%

Vr,
Master
```

Desert shoreline along South America's Pacific coast. Are the remains of Nephi's ship still to be found there? Photograph by Mylene d'Auriol Stoessel.

The Phoenicia, replica ship that sailed around Africa in 2010. Courtesy of Phoenicia.org.

THE VOYAGE OF THE MULEKITES

FOUR CENTURIES AFTER Nephi landed in the land of promise, his decendant, Mosiah led an exodus of the righteous away from what had become the wicked city of Nephi. After journeying in a wilderness, Mosiah's people came down into a populated land that the inhabitants called Zarahemla. Mosiah discovered that the people of Zarahemla had originally migrated from Jerusalem at the time when "Zedekiah, king of Judah, was carried away captive into Babylon" (Omni 1:15). The Book of Mormon says, "And they journeyed in the wilderness, and were brought by the hand of the Lord across the great waters" (Omni 1:15–16). Among the geographic features of the land of Zarahemla was an important river that the people of Zarahemla named Sidon (Alma 22:27).

The Book of Mormon provides clues as to the origin of the people of Zarahemla. They departed Jerusalem under the name of Mulek, the only surviving son of Zedekiah (Helaman 6:10, 8:21). It appears that the people of Mulek, the Mulekites, first disembarked from their ships in the promised land in the land northward, the area that had been originally inhabited by the more ancient Jaredites. We think the land northward is identifiable because the only known civilizations in the Americas that date to the time of the early Jaredites are found along the shoreline of Peru just north of its capital of Lima.[1]

Although the Mulekites left Jerusalem at the same general time as Lehi's party, it appears that their experience in reaching South America likely was quite different from Lehi's family. For example, Nephi

Model of Phoenician freighter.

and his helpers built a ship that was praised as being of good workmanship, and the voyage was a central theme in Nephite lore. However, there is no mention in the Book of Mormon of the Mulekites building a vessel or learning how to sail a ship. Likewise, to construct his ship, Nephi learned crafts, including smelting tools, working timbers, making cordage, and crafting sails. It would seem unlikely that Mulek, a royal prince of Judah, would have possessed any of these manual skills, nor would it have been appropriate for a prince to have indulged in physical labor such as manning the sails.

Hugh Nibley suggested that the Mulekites probably reached the New World by hiring the services of Phoenician mariners. In support of this idea, Nibley pointed to Phoenician names in the Book of Mormon, including the river Sidon that appears to have been named after the Phoenician harbor of Sidon.[2]

Another example of a Phoenician name occurs when Alma's son Corianton forsook his ministry and went after a harlot referred to as Isabel (Alma 39:3). In the goddess religion of the Phoenicians, Isabel was the name of the Patroness of Harlots.[3] Book of Mormon scholar John Sorenson agrees with Nibley:

The inhabitants of Zidon and Arvad were thy mariners: thy wise men, O Tyrus, that were in thee, were thy [ship's] pilots.

The ancients of Gebal and the wise men thereof were in thee thy calkers; all the ships of the sea with their mariners were in thee to occupy thy merchandise.

EZEKIEL 27: 8–9

It is very likely that non-Jews were in the crew of the vessel that brought Zedekiah's son Mulek to the New World (see Omni 1:15–16). A purely Israelite crew recruited in the Palestine homeland would have been possible during some periods, but at the time Mulek's party left, all the Mediterranean ports of the kingdom of Judah were in Babylonian hands. Most likely the crew of the ship (there could have been more than one, of course) were "Phoenician," itself a historical category that was by no means homogeneous.[4]

Lebanon's "Cedarland" website offers the following describing the nation's proud maritime legacy:

The best seafarers and ship builders of the ancient world were Phoenicians. The famous Lebanese cedar trees covering the slopes of mountains of their land was perfect material for construction of strong seaworthy ships. The Phoenicians made important contributions to trade, alphabet, language, mathematics, the invention of clear glass, marine construction, and marine science, having been credited with the division of a circle into 360 degrees and quarters. Quarters we know today as east and west the Phoenicians knew as Asu (sunrise) and Ereb (sunset), labels that live today in the names Asia and Europe. Phoenicians had reliable celestial reference points, such as the little bear constellation and polar star, thus celestrial navigation.

The destruction of the Minoan civilization around 1400 BC and the decline of the Egyptian empire left the Mediterranean open to newcomers, especially to the Phoenicians and to the emerging Greek kingdoms. The Phoenicians had been at sea for some time before the Greeks and were already well established and experienced sailors. The Phoenicians were an empire based on trading. Greeks used a warrior class to expand their territory. These different priorities affected the types of vessels these two maritime powers favored.

Launching of replica of Phoenicia's hull. Courtesy of Phoenicia.org.

However, the area now known as the Levant had been a meeting place of warring empires for millennia. It should not be suprising, therefore, that the vessels used by Phoenicians incorporated features drawn from a variety of sources.[5]

Author and ancient maritime expert, Clive Cussler and his crews have discovered more than sixty ships lost in history. He describes the unique maritime savvy of the Phoenicians circa 900 BC:

The Phoenicians were the finest seamen in the world, adventurous explorers and traders whose maritime empire extended throughout the Mediterranean and beyond the Pillars of Hercules and the Red Sea. Unlike the Greeks and the Egyptians, whose ships hugged the shore and dropped anchor when the sun set, the fearless Phoenicians sailed day and night out of sight of land. With a fair wind from astern, their big trading ships would cover more than a hundred miles a day.

The vessel under the captain's command was a "ship of Tarshish," built specifically for long-range commerce on the open ocean. Unlike the more-tubby short-haul traders, the vessels' lines were long and straight. The deck and hull timbers were hewn from tough Lebanese cedar, and the thick mast was low and strong. The square Egyptian-lined sail, quilted with leather belts for strength, was the most efficient deep water sailing rig in existence. The curved keel and up swept stem and stern presaged

137

THE VOYAGE OF THE
MULEKITES

the Viking ships that would not be built until centuries later.

The secret behind Phoenician mastery of the sea went beyond technology. Organization aboard their ships was legendary. Each crewman knew his place in the well-oiled machinery that was a Phoenician sea venture. Rigging was neatly stowed in an easily accessible room that was the responsibility of the captain's assistant. The lookout man knew the location of each piece of tackle, and constantly tested the ship's rigging to make sure it would work if needed in an emergency.[6]

Since the full extent of the Phoenicians' maritime accomplishments have only come to light in recent decades, Joseph Smith would have had no idea that the Phoenicians had the capacity to reach as far as Peru. Nibley also brought to the attention of students of the Book of Mormon that the Phoencians were colonizing far-off lands at the time of the fall of Jerusalem. He wrote:

> For a long time, the Near East had been getting crowded, the pinch being first felt in Syria and Phoenicia—due perhaps as much to deforestation and over-grazing as to population increase. Of this area Ebers writes: "Their small country could not contain its numerous population; accordingly there sailed out of the Phoenician harbors many a richly laden vessel to search out favorable places of settlement for emigrants bound for the coasts of Africa, Crete, Cyprus and Sicily." Such colonies would continue to enrich the Mother city (hence our word "metropolis") by furnishing her with markets and raw materials.

In the year Lehi left Jerusalem, the Egyptian government sent an expedition consisting largely of Syrian and Phoenician personnel sailing clear around Africa from east to west. Shortly after, the Phoenicians reacted to the challenge by sending Hanno on the same mission of circumnavigation in the opposite direction. In the middle of the sixth century, Scylax reconnoitered the coasts of the Red Sea and the Indian Ocean from the Euphrates to the Indus, while in the west, Carthage "reconnoite[d] the Atlantic Ocean to north and south with mighty fleets." The Phoenicians ended a long phase of fierce mercantile competition in the Mediterranean by burning the great trading city of Tartessus—Isaiah's Tarshish of the proud ships—and closing the whole western Mediterranean and Atlantic areas to all trade but their own in 530 BC.[7]

The "very spirit of the age," writes Paul Herrmann, "seems to have been at work in the Punic voyage into the immense distances of the ocean, announcing the dawn of a new epoch." The ancients always chafed at the limitations of their geographical knowledge (though we are beginning to realize how much greater that knowledge was than we have ever given them credit for), but never until modern times was that knowledge as great as it was in the sixth century.[8]

Nibley notes that in an effort to establish new colonies, the Phoenicians were sailing great distances from their home ports of Tyre and Sidon. In fact, more recent discoveries have provided tangible evidence that an ancient seafaring nation from the Mediterranean Sea traded with far-off Peru. For example, chemical residues from the New World plants of coca and tobacco have been found in the bones of Egyptian mummies as early as 1070 BC.[9] Someone had to have brought those commodities from South America. History suggests it was the Mediterranean's master sailors, the Phoenicians.

After studying the history of migration of plants and linguistic associations, John L. Sorenson of Brigham Young University provided a strong argument for ancient cross-ocean voyages. In 2005 he wrote:

> Over the last four years 98 species of plants have been identified that originated in either the Old World or the New yet were also grown in pre-Columbian times in the opposite hemisphere. That distribution cannot be explained the way cultural parallels have been by inventionist-minded scholars. A plant is an objective fact that demands a physical explanation for the presence of the same species on two sides of an ocean. Yet all purely naturalistic theories fail to account for plants thousands of miles from their natural home. For example, some have supposed that seeds were carried thousands of miles by birds, or evolutionary processes have been claimed as yielding identical species in multiple locations, but these notions are never more than nonempirical speculation. The only rational explanation for multiple plant distributions is that people sailed across the oceans before Columbus, nurturing and transporting plants en route. . . .

What evidence do we consider to be "conclusive" or "decisive"? In some cases it comes from archaeology. For example, in 1966–67 Australian archaeologist Ian Glover excavated in caves on the island of Timor in Indonesia, where he discovered plant remains that included three crops of American origin: *Annon* (custard apple), *Zea* (maize), and *Arachis* (peanut). These dated at the least to AD 1000 and probably well before. The peanuts were duplicated at two sites on the Chinese mainland that date by radiocarbon to as early as 2800 BC.

Proof for one complex of plants involved a particularly wide array of research methods. To the amazement of some scientists and the consternation of others, chemical evidence of tobacco has been found in ancient Egyptian mummies, although tobacco was supposed to be unknown in the Old World prior to Columbus. First, fragments of tobacco were found deep in the abdominal cavity of the 3200-year-old mummy of Pharaoh Ramses II while it was being studied in a European museum. Some skeptics immediately concluded that this had to be due to modern contamination in the museum. This American plant could not possibly have been known in Egypt, they insisted. In 1992 physical scientists in Germany used sophisticated laboratory instrumentation to test nine other Egyptian mummies. They found chemical residues of tobacco, coca (another American plant, the source of cocaine), and the Asian native hashish (the source of marijuana) in the hair, soft tissues, skin, and bones of eight of the mummies. These traces included cotinine, a chemical whose presence means that the tobacco had been consumed and metabolized while the deceased person was alive. (The ninth mummy contained coca and hashish residues but not tobacco.) Dates of the corpses according to historical records from Egypt ranged from 1070 BC to AD 395, indicating that these drugs were continuously available in some Egyptians for no less than 1,450 years. Investigators have since found evidence of the drugs in additional mummies for Egypt.

Equally startling has been the discovery of the same drugs in Peruvian mummies that date back to at least AD 100. Chemical analysis revealed the use of tobacco and cocaine (not surprisingly, since the former was widely used in the Americas and the latter comes from the South American plant *Erythroxylon novagranatense*, commonly known as coca). But hashish was also used in Peru, although it is from Asian *Cannabis sativa*. Furthermore, two species of beetles that infested Egyptian mummies—*Alphitobius Disperinus* and *Stegobium paniceum*—have also been found in mummies in Peru. It is impossible to avoid the conclusion that intentional voyages across an ocean were involved in these transfers.[10]

What Part did Egypt Play in the Mulek Voyage?

The South American–Phoenician connection suggests that the famed Phoenician sailors had established a profitable cross-Atlantic drug trade in coca and tobacco. Probably the wealthy Egyptian nobility financed the trade. Egyptians also likely played an important role in expediting the Mulekite exodus to the promised land. A brief understanding of the politics of Mulek's Jerusalem reveals the possibility that the Egyptians themselves might have arranged for the son of Zedekiah to flee Jerusalem and board a ship to a safe refuge. Richard Wellington writes:

> The Babylonians opened diplomatic relations with Judah, and King Josiah, switching allegiance away from Egypt, attempted to aid their causes by marching his army to Carchemish to try to interrupt the columns of the Egyptian army. Battle was joined and King Josiah was mortally wounded in 609 BC while trying to hold the Megiddo pass. Judah now found herself being swept ever further into a torrent of confusion and political intrigue. Allegiances vacillated between militant extremists who favored insurrection against Babylon and moderates who advocated submission to foreign

rule. Following Josiah's death, the populace placed his second son, Jehoahaz, on the thrown. The Egyptians then swept into Judah, and within three months Jehoahaz was taken in chains to Egypt where he died. In his place, the Egyptians put his unscrupulous brother, Jehoiakim (608–598 BC), as vassal king on the thrown. Regardless, Egyptian influence was short-lived and in 605 BC Assyria collapsed and the Egyptian army was defeated by the Babylonians.

Jehoiakim submitted to the will of the anti-Egyptian party and swore allegiance to Babylon. As long as he remained loyal to Babylon, it seemed the people would remain unharmed. But there were several elements who advocated rebellion. The patriotic party flirted with alliances with surrounding countries with the intention of throwing off the Babylonian yoke. It was now that the prophet Jeremiah spoke out energetically against these foolhardy radicals. Judah's hope of survival lay in submission to Babylon. To attempt to stand against her was courting disaster. Abram Sachar wrote: "He (*Jeremiah*) did not share the popular belief that the Holy City could not be destroyed. It had hardened into a dogma of popular religion."

By speaking out, Jeremiah put his life in danger. He was publicly struck by a temple priest, placed in stocks to be

taunted, and assailed about by a clamoring mob. He would have been executed had these not been fearful of killing a prophet.

But Jeremiah's warnings were to no avail, and after three years Jehoiakim switched allegiances back to Egypt. Nebuchadnezzar ordered contingents in surrounding nations to attack. That winter, as the Babylonian king approached Jerusalem to supervise the siege, King Jehoiakim died and was replaced by his eighteen-year-old son Jehoiachim (598–597 BC). The new king reigned only three months. As the capital city was besieged, he threw himself on the mercy of the Babylonian monarch. He surrendered on March 10, 597 BC when he, the royal family, palace officials, members of the army, "and all the craftsmen and smiths" (2 Kings 24:14) were taken captive to Babylon.

A revealing Babylonian chronicle (the tablets of which are now in the British museum), is a counterpart to the Biblical account and tells us that Nebuchadnezzar, "took the city on the second day of the month of Adduru. He appointed in it a new king of his liking (literally *heart*), took heavy booty from it and brought it into Babylon." The new king was Zedekiah [Mulek's father].

Zedekiah does not appear to have been a righteous ruler because Jeremiah referred to him and his followers as "evil figs" (Jeremiah 24:8). According to the Chronicles, Zedekiah did evil in the site of the Lord and humbled himself not before Jeremiah. During his reign, men and women gave themselves to the worship of the Babylonian goddess of love (Ishtar), as well as to the sun-god. At the same time, worship of the sacred animals of Egypt was carried on in an underground chamber. Lehi must have seen that, as in Israel's past history, wickedness preceded political catastrophe. Ben Sasson wrote: "Zedekiah's first year witnessed extremely difficult conditions in Judah. The new, inexperienced leadership that had replaced the exile court tended to be more militant and surprisingly, even adamantly anti-Babylonian. Zedekiah was playing a dangerous political double-game. The vassal king of Babylonia foolishly found himself flirting with the influence of the pro-Egyptians.[11]

When Nebuchadnezzar learned of Zedekiah's dealings with Egypt, the end came quickly for both Zekediah's reign and the great city of Jerusalem. Nebuchadnezzar had had enough of the two-faced kings of Judah. As Lehi prophesied, the city of Jerusalem and its temple were razed. Zekediah's sons were killed, save Mulek.

Elder James E. Talmage of the Quorum of the Twelve Apostles suggested a possible explanation as to how the son of Zedekiah made his way to the Americas. He wrote, "Mulek was the son of Zedekiah, king of Judah, an infant at the time of his brothers' violent deaths and his father's cruel torture at the hands of the king of Babylon. Eleven years after Lehi's departure from Jerusalem, another colony was led from the city, amongst whom was Mulek. The colony took his name, probably on account of his recognized rights of leadership by virtue of lineage."[12]

The intriguing politics of Lehi's time raises several questions: What deals had the Egyptians made with Zekediah before 586 BC? Had the Pharaoh promised security guarantees to Zekediah and his family if Judah's king switched allegiance to Egypt? Had the Egyptians arranged that if Babylon attacked in retaliation, they would provide the king and his family safe passage to one of Phoenicia's new colonies where they would have refuge until they could be returned one day to the throne of Judah? Did Mulek flee first to Egypt and from there board a Phoenician vessel? Or was he

or others with him already in Egypt as an emissary of his father's new ally at the time Nebuchadnezzer laid seize on Jerusalem? Where was Mulek's party provided passage to the New World? From Egypt or from one of the two Phoenician ports? Did the Pharaoh pay for the passage of his ally's son and court associates so they could board a Phoenician ship that had already been hired by Egyptians to transport their additive drugs from South America to the Nile kingdom? Since the Mulekites first "journeyed in the wilderness" before they "were brought by the hand of the Lord across the great waters" (Omni 1:15–16), a likely scenario could have been that they escaped from Jerusalem at the time of the siege and fled overland to Egypt through the Sinai wilderness. Once in Egypt, the Mulekites perhaps boarded a Phoenician ship contracted by the pharaonic nobles to trade for coca in Peru. As it is in our own day, ancient trade in additive drugs was a lucrative business in which its agents were willing to take risks to reap the rewards. John L. Sorenson writes:

> If we suppose that Phoenicians or other experienced voyagers were involved, we can inquire why such sailors would be willing to sail off into "the unknown." In the first place, as professional seamen,

Phoenicia during her voyage around Africa. Courtesy of Phoencia.org.

they would normally be willing to undertake whatever voyage promised them sufficient compensation. Furthermore, the Phoenicians had confidence in their nautical abilities; where they were told they should sail may not have seemed as "unknown" to them as the term implies to us. Herodotus tells that a few years earlier, dauntingly, Necho II, Egypt's pharaoh in Mulek's day, had sent an expedition of Phoenicians by ship from Ezion-Geber on the Red Sea completely around the continent of Africa.[13]

More Evidence of Ancient Cross-Atlantic Trade

Whoever brought Mulek and his party to the Americas, it is highly likely that their people had a long tradition of voyaging across the Altantic. Numerous speculative claims have been made that ancient sailors from the Mediterranean area reached the shores of the New World. Studying information, sometimes from yet unsubstantiated sources, can help one acquire a concept for the likelihood that Phoenicians were sailing on a somewhat regular basis to the New World. Unfortunately, histories compiled by the Greeks, Romans, Latins, Anglo Saxtons, and Spanish intentually excluded the acquired knowledge, language, literature, science, and mathematics of their foes the Phoenicians, Minoans, Hebrews, Etruscans, Celtics, Arabs, Chinese, and the early peoples of the Americas, as well as many other

ancient civilizations. However, discoveries since World War II in marine environments, archaeological digs on land, and in ancient writings have shed much new light on antiquity and its sailors. Among these insights is the understanding that a trading network was carried on between the so-called Old and New Worlds that can be traced back to the second millennium BC. Among these new claims are:

1. Dick Edgar Grasso believes the two vessels on the center slabs of the Temple of Sechim (roughly 3,000 years old) along the coast of Peru are Phoenician ships.[14]

2. Monoliths near the Temple of Sechim in Peru are believed to show a large oceangoing craft and a sextant.[15]

3. Even more extraordinary are the discoveries made by Bernardo Silva Ramos. This author, president of the Manaus (west Brazil) Geographical Institute, spent over twenty years in the Amazon rain forest, searching for, photographing, and copying 2,800 stone inscriptions. He identified the majority of them as Phoenician and others as Greek.[16]

4. German scholar Lienhardt Delekat (*Phonizier in Amerika*, Bonn 1969) claims that the inscriptions on the

143

Martin Waldseemuller's map, AD 1507.

Paraiba Stone in Brazil were of Canaanite origin and were engraved by Phoenicians. Delekat comes to the conclusion that the passage is written in ancient Tyro-Sidonian, dating to the end of the sixth century BC. His translation reads as follows: "We are children of Canaan, from the city of Sidon. We are a nation of traders. Our ship is beached on this far-off mountainous coast and we want to make a sacrifice to the gods and goddesses. In the 19th year of Irma's reign, we set sail from Ezion-Geber across the Red Sea, with ten ships. We have been sailing now for two years and we have sailed all around this land, both hot and far from the hands of Baal [i.e. cold], and twelve men and three women have arrived here, because ten of the women have died on another coast, because they had sinned. May the gods and goddesses be favorable to us." Looking closely, at the statement, "we have sailed all around this land, both hot and far from the hands of Baal," the words "both hot and far" could refer to Peru from Brazil and "all around this land" and the cold would be they made a voyage around the southern horn of South America.

5. The Los Lunas Inscription, called by ancient Indians of New Mexico, "Cliff of the Strange Writings" is at the base of Mystery Mountain. Some have claimed the strange chiseled characters on volcanic basalt rock were translated as a form of Hebrew writing dating to approximately 1000 BC. The stone preserves an abbreviated form of the Ten Commandments, as written in Exodus 20. The Los Lunas site is located along the Puerco River that flows into the Little Colorado River.

As theoretical to some as these above claims appear, together they suggest a plausible explanation to one of the most intriguing mysteries of the history of the Americas— the Waldseemuller map. The accuracy of this pre-Balboa map confounds scholars. The only plausible answer as to how the map was drawn is that pre-Columbian sailors knew well a sea route from the Mediterranean to Peru. David Alexander explains:

> The only surviving copy of the 500-year-old map that first used the name America goes on permanent display this month at the Library of Congress, but even as it prepares for its début, the 1507 map remains a puzzle for researchers. Why did the mapmaker name the territory America and then change his mind later? How was he able to draw South America so accurately? Why did he put a huge ocean west of America years before European explorers discovered the Pacific?
>
> "That's the kind of conundrum, the question, that is still out there," said John Hebert, chief of the geography and map division of the Library of Congress.
>
> … The map was created by the German monk Martin Waldseemuller. Thirteen years after Christopher Columbus first landed in the Western Hemisphere, the Duke of Lorraine brought Waldseemuller and a group of scholars together at a monastery in Saint-Die in France to create a new map of the world.
>
> The result, published two years later, is stunningly accurate and surprisingly modern.
>
> "The actual shape of South America is correct," said Hebert. "The width of South America at certain key points is correct within 70 miles of accuracy."
>
> Given what Europeans are believed to have known about the world at the time, it should not have been possible for the mapmakers to produce it, he said.
>
> The map gives a reasonably correct depiction of the west coast of South America. But according to history, Vasco Nunez de Balboa did not reach the Pacific by land until 1513, and Ferdinand Magellan did not round the southern tip of the continent until 1520.
>
> "So this is a rather compelling map to say, 'How did they come to that conclusion,'" Hebert said.
>
> The mapmakers say they based it on the 1,300-year-old works of the Egyptian geographer Ptolemy as well as letters Florentine navigator Amerigo Vespucci

Shoreline near Lima, Peru. Photograph by Mylene d'Auriol Stoessel.

wrote describing his voyages to the new world. But Hebert said there must have been something more.[17]

Gavin Menzies cites another South American map mystery in his book *1421*. He writes of the 1513 map by a Turkish admiral that shows the southern tip of South America. Menzies claims the south-west portion of the map was based on a lost map that was aboard Columbus' ship.

A Spanish seaman who had sailed to the Americas with Columbus kept that portion of the map, together with some notes Columbus had written about it. In 1501, the Ottomans captured the ship in which the seaman was serving; he still had the map in his possession. Neither the seaman nor any other who sailed with Columbus could have been the originator of this map because Columbus never sailed south of the equator.

Appreciating the extraordinary value of this captured document, the Ottoman admiral Piri Reis incorporated it into a map known from that day to this as the Piri-Reis map of 1513. This beautiful map can be seen today in the Topkapi Serai Museum high above the Bosphorus in Istanbul. It was based on several different maps, pieced together by the admiral from a number of different sources, and parts of it are unreliable, but the south-western portion based on the map taken from Columbus's seaman is very accurate.[18]

Specific features on the Piri-Reis map clearly suggest that the Turkish admiral had detailed knowledge of Peru. On the land masses where Peru would be placed, the author of the map notes that the "gold mines are endless." Peru, of course, was renowned for the Incas' great gold mines. The map also includes in the same area some mountains indicative of the Andes and animals that some believe represent the Peruvian llama.[19]

While Menzies believes the "only" source of the "lost map" was from a Chinese Treasure fleet,[20] a far more likely source of the information on South America on the lost map would have been from the Mediterranean Sea's own great sailors, the ancient Phoenicians. Another possible explanation for the map's information on the western coast of South America is that it was based on maps made by Arab sailors, perhaps again pointing our investigation back to the navigators who taught Nephi what he knew about sailing. According to Charles Hapgood, who wrote the book *Maps of the Ancient Sea Kings*, the Piri-Reis map was made from twenty ancient source maps, among them eight world maps made during Alexander's period (400 BC to

100 AD) as well as an Arab map.[21] Because the Piri-Reis map has its median passing through Alexandria, we believe that the likely source of its knowledge of Peru came from the Phoenicians.

In summary, while the Waldseemuller and Piri-Reis maps still puzzle and amaze scholars, a growing body of recently discovered artifacts place the Phoenicians along the Pacific Coast of Peru. The idea that the Book of Mormon, printed in 1830, can be interpreted—as this book does—as having the Mulekites traveling to Peru aboard Phoenicians ships is yet additional evidence, if our proposals are correct, that the remarkable account is true history.

The Phoenician Ships in the Days of Mulek

Lebanese website Cedarlands provides this description of a classic Phoenician vessel:

The earliest evidence for Phoenician vessels comes from an Egyptian relief of around 1400 BC at the tomb of Kenamon at Thebes which shows vessels unloading in an Egyptian port. The vessels have much in common with contemporary Egyptian vessels but differ in three significant details. Firstly, the hulls are shorter and were therefore probably more seaworthy. Secondly, there is a wicker fence along the sheerstrake to protect the deck cargo. Thirdly, the Phoenician vessels on the tomb of Kenamon do not have a visible hogging truss which implies that the method of construction was more sound than that of Hatshepsut's vessels and may have included a proper keel.

Another representation of a Phoenician vessel comes from the palace of Sargon at Nineveh and shows a vessel loading timber, and is dated around 700 BC. The vessels on Sargon's tomb are unremarkable symmetrical oared vessels having a less pronounced sickle shape than the first millennium vessels depicted on the tomb of Kenamon. General trade vessels used oars and sails and were round hulled, broad beam with external keel. These vessels could carry much more cargo for a given waterline length. The shape of the hull including an external keel would allow the vessels to track better and also create lateral resistance which would allow the vessel to sail higher to the eye of the wind. [22]

A square sail was originally used to push a Phoenician vessel. A close look at the type, location, and quanity of Phoenician sailing rigs can tell the reader a great deal about how high the vessels could sail into the wind. Square or rectanglular sails were hoisted to the mast top by means of several opposing blocks, which were attached on one end to the masthead and the other ends to various locations on the yard which supported the sail. These blocks had bitter ends (end of the line or rope) leading down to the bottom of the mast where they were made fast. The yard (a spar to support the head of the sail, perpendicular to the mast) and thus the sail could be adjusted leeward (always from the wind) by means of the masthead blocks, thus creating a type of lug rig (square) with the sail. The object of this maneuver was to create apparent wind (wind direction felt on a sailing vessel underway) over the sail, thus horizontal lift, which allows the vessel to point higher into the eye of the wind (into the center of the wind).

On larger vessels, the Phoenicians moved the main mast forward and added another mast which increased, through a slotting effect, the velocity of the apparent wind over the surface of the sails which allowed the vessels to point even higher and increased hull speed. There is evidence on still larger vessels that as many as three masts were incorporated. The sails were made out of flax or cotton and reinforced with leather, which was sewn in laterally. Vertical brailing lines were attached and

The **Phoenicia** *under sail. Courtesy of Phoenicia.org.*

fed through rings attached to the sail at even heights top to bottom. The brailing lines could adjust the sail to form a triangular or pinched fore part of the sails and would change the apparent wind angle, allowing the vessel to head even higher into the wind.

When the vessel's heading was too high in relation to the eye of the wind, stalling occured or when the wind was very light the crew would be ordered to douse the sails and break out the sweeps (long oars) and start rowing. This dual mode of propulsion was very effective and remained in use until modern times.[23]

In the *History and Archaeology of the Ship,*[24] we find some notable discoveries concerning Phoenician hull construction. Excavations along the keel of the first vessel discovered revealed that the original keel must have been about 82 feet (25 meters) in length. The hull was edge-joined using mortise and tenon joints. Hull timbers were fastened to frames with iron nails driven through wooden dowels and clenched over the inner surface. The hull was sheathed with lead over a fabric next to the planks, and the seams were sealed with a white paste.

As a side note regarding the influence of the Phoenicians, the word *bible* itself ultimately derives (through Latin and Greek) from Byblos, the Phoenician city. Because of the city's papyri, Byblos was also the source of the Greek word for book, hence, of the name for the "Bible."

The Voyage of the Mulekites

It is reasonable to believe that if the Phoenicians delivered the Mulekites to Peru, they would have taken the most favorable route from the Mediterranean to Peru. As noted above, there is evidence that the Phoenicians supplied addictive Peruvian drugs to their Egyptian patrons, thus suggesting that to feed their client's addictive habits the Phoenicians would have made somewhat regular voyages to Peru. If this is true, their captains over time would have charted the winds, currents, and landmarks to and from the Old World to Peru. We suggest that the Phoenicians delivered the Mulekites to

149

the New World, used long-known but ever-developing charts, and started their passage by embarking from their harbor at Tyre and then sailed west through the Mediterranean Sea to the Atlantic Ocean and around the southern tip of South America.

The Book of Mormon tells us that the Mulekites originally arrived in the land northward (Helaman 6:10), and the place of their first landing was in the land of desolation (Alma 22:30). It is more than coincidence that when the Spanish arrived in Peru the Incas still called the area around Lima the *land of the people of desolation*.[25] For this reason, our simulation of the Mulek voyage ends at Lima, Peru. However, the land of desolation was not the Mulekites' final place of settlement in the promised land. George thinks the best candidate for the Mulekite settlement of Zarahemla was at Pukara, near Lake Titicaca in southern Peru. A verse in the Book of Mormon suggests that after some time the Mulekites boarded their ships again and sailed south. George thinks that was somewhere in what is today southern Peru. They eventually migrated back to the land northward and finally into the Andes Mountains near Lake Titicaca.

And it [Bountiful] bordered upon the land which they called Desolation, it being so far northward that it came into the land which had been peopled and been destroyed, of whose bones we have spoken, which was discovered by the people of Zarahemla, it being the place of their *first landing*. And they came from there up into the south wilderness. Thus the land on the northward was called Desolation, and the land on the southward was called Bountiful. (Alma 22:30–31, emphasis added).

Hauling colonists from the Mediterranean to Peru and returning with tobacco and coca must have been highly profitable, for the voyage entailed considerable risks. The safest route still required navigating through the sailor's graveyard that would later be called the Strait of Magellan. This passage took ships around South America's Tierra del Fuego and Cape Horn, the world's southern most major cape. To survive the passage, Phoenician captains had to steer their ships through strong winds, large waves, and treacherous currents. It also meant successfully navigating both night and day through the foggy skies and icy waters of the cape passage. Indeed, without the skills of experienced seamen and maritime charts

of the Phoenicians, it would have been nearly impossible for Mulek, the son of a landlocked king, to reach the promised land. Undoubtedly, the most experienced and capable sailors of his day were the Phoenicians and historical records confirm their ability to sail the dangerous waters of southern capes by the time of Mulek. For example, a few years before the Mulekite voyage, a Phoenician fleet successfully navigated around Africa's Cape of Good Hope.[26]

Although the Mulekites' passage to the promised land was substantially shorter than Nephi's passage, it required advanced seamanship skill. The lack of these skills by Nephi and many of his crew is a possible reason why the Lord may have directed Nephi, a novice sailor, to sail eastward on a longer but less dangerous route. The Phoenicians, along with the Omanis, were considered the ancient world's most accomplished sailors. If anyone could survive a passage around the cape of South America in sixth century BC, it would have been the Phoenicians. Even so, these seasoned sailors had to face and conquer gale force winds, towering seas, snow, hail, pounding rains, as well as heavy fog and the occasional iceberg.

Stages of the Mulekite Voyage

Sailing from Lebanon to Peru in an ancient Phoenician ship would have been conducted in roughly five stages of about 15–30 days each.

Stage One

The relatively calm fall-season winds of the Mediterranean Sea would have required much rowing before reaching the Atlantic. Even in the Atlantic, periods of calm would have meant long hours of backbreaking rowing by Phoenician oarsmen. As slow as the going was, Mulek and his court probably felt relief from every stroke of the oars that were taking them further away from the horrors that befell the rest of their family in Jerusalem. In his novel *The Navigator*, Cussler provides this description of sailing aboard a Phoenician ship in the Mediterranean:

> The captain's high station in life entitled him to wear a purple robe dyed with the valuable extract from the murex snail. He preferred to go bare-chested, and wore the cotton kilt of an ordinary crewman. A floppy, conical knit cap covered the close-cropped, wavy black hair.

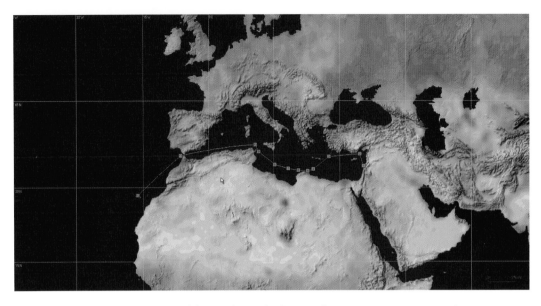

Simulated passage of the Mulekites through the Mediterranean Sea on to the Canary Islands (starting around September 1 and ending on September 21).

Although the voyage was long, it had gone well, thanks to the handpicked Phoenician crew, all seasoned deepwater mariners. The crew included a scattering of Egyptians and Libyans, and others from the countries boarding the Mediterranean. A contingent of Scythian marines provided security.

The captain was not Phoenician by birth, but he was well versed in the sea arts. His command of navigation and seamanship and his cool judgment during bouts of bad weather had quickly gained the crew's respect.

The captain felt something soft brush against his bare leg. Allowing himself a rare smile, he set the wooden box in a receptacle and reached down and picked up the ship's cat. Phoenician cats had their origins in Egypt where the animals were worshipped as gods. Phoenician ships carried cats as trade items and for rat control. The captain stroked the orange-and-yellow-striped cat for a few times, then gently set the purring feline back down on the deck. The ship was approaching the wide mouth of a river.

The captain called out a command to the lookout man.

"Prepare the riggers to drop sail, and alert the oarsmen."

The lookout man relayed the first command to a pair of crewmen, who scrambled like monkeys up the mast to the yardarm. The other sailors tossed lines attached to the lower corners of the sail to the riggers, who used the ropes to reef the big linen square.

Brawny-armed rowers arranged in two ranks of twenty were already at their benches. Unlike the slave rowers on many vessels, the oarsman who powered the ship forward with quick, precise strokes were trained professionals.[27]

Passage Summary Report

Passage Filename: C:\PROGRAM FILES\ VISUAL PASSAGE PLANNER 2\MULEK.PP2

Passage Creation Date: 9/9/2008

Pilot Chart Data Used: Actual dates based on departure specified

Vessel Profile Used: C:\Program Files\ Visual Passage Planner 2\NoName.vp

Minimum Speed Set: 0.50 Knots

Fuel Consumption Set: 0.00 Units/Hour

Currents: ON

Current Values Used: Average All

Wind Values Used: Average All

Waypoint #	Latitude	Longitude Date
1	N33° 58.58'	E35°22.19'
2	N36° 6.78'	E34°31.66'
3	N35° 36.80'	E27°31.69'
4	N33° 22.55'	E23°59.13'
5	N33° 2.80'	E22°45.40'
6	N33° 8.60'	E20°36.10'
7	N33° 28.36'	E18°19.49'
8	N34° 12.49'	E15°14.32'
9	N36° 30.23'	E11°37.67'
10	N37° 47.30'	E10°47.94'
11	N35° 47.97'	W6°20.65'
12	N28° 26.17'	W16°9.75'

General Information	Data
Calculated Great Circle Distance	2953.6 NM
Calculated Rhumbline Distance	2955.1 NM
Actual Distance Traveled due to Beating	3051.7 NM
Elapsed Time to Complete Passage	19.7 Days
Fuel Consumption	0.0 Units
Average Boat Speed	6.5 Knots
Boat Speed Made Good	6.3 Knots

LEG 1 (Stage 1)

Departure Date 1 September

VESSEL PERFORMANCE AND WEATHER CONDITIONS REPORT

Start: N33o 58.58' E35o 22.19' [Lebanon]

End: N36o 6.78 E34o 31.66' [north end of Cyprus island]

Elapsed-time to Complete Leg: 0.7 Days

Calculated Great Circle Distance: 134.7 Nautical Miles [154.6 Miles]

Actual Distance Travel due to Beating: 134.7 Nautical Miles

Average Boat Speed: 7.6 Knots

Boat Speed Made Good: 7.6 Knots

Average Wind Speed: 12.3 Knots

Average Wind Direction from True North: 251.3o

Average Current Drift: 0.0 Knots at **Average Current Set:** 000o

Average Wave Height: 2.3 Feet

Average Sea Temperature: 82.1o F

Average Air Temperature: 77.5o F

Average Percentage Risk of Calms: 4.9%

Average Percentage Risk of Gales: 0.0%

LEG 2

VESSEL PERFORMANCE AND WEATHER CONDITIONS REPORT

Start: N36o 6.78' E34o 31.66' [north end of Cyprus]

End: N35o 36.80' E27o 31.69' [80 Miles from southwest coast of Turkey]

Elapsed-time to Complete Leg: 3.7 Days

Calculated Great Circle Distance: 341.6 Nautical Miles [392.1 Miles]

Actual Distance Travel due to Beating: 426 Nautical Miles

Average Boat Speed: 4.8 Knots

Boat Speed Made Good: 3.8 Knots

Average Wind Speed: 10.6 Knots

Average Wind Direction from True North: 276.4o

Average Current Drift: 0.4 Knots at **Average Current Set:** 149.5o

Average Wave Height: 1.9 Feet

Average Sea Temperature: 80.4o F

Average Air Temperature: 76.2o F

Average Percentage Risk of Calms: 4.3%

Average Percentage Risk of Gales: 0.0%

LEG 3

VESSEL PERFORMANCE AND WEATHER CONDITIONS REPORT

Start: N35o 36.80' E27o 31.69' [80 Miles from Southwest Coast of Turkey]

End: N33o 22.55' E23o 59.13' [coast of Libya]

Elapsed-time to Complete Leg: 1.3 Days

Calculated Great Circle Distance: 220.7 Nautical Miles [253.4 Miles]

Actual Distance Travel due to Beating: 220.7 Nautical Miles

Average Boat Speed: 7.2 Knots

Boat Speed Made Good: 7.2 Knots

Average Wind Speed: 11.2 Knots

Average Wind Direction from True North: 315.0o

Average Current Drift: 0.5 Knots at **Average Current Set:** 187.6o

Average Wave Height: 2.6 Feet

Average Sea Temperature: 76.0o F

Average Air Temperature: 75.7o F

Average Percentage Risk of Calms: 5.0%

Average Percentage Risk of Gales: 0.4%

LEG 4

VESSEL PERFORMANCE AND WEATHER CONDITIONS REPORT

Start: N33o 22.55' E23o 59.13' [coast of Libya]

End: N33o 2.80' E22o 45.40' [coast of Libya]

Elapsed-time to Complete Leg: 0.4 Days

Calculated Great Circle Distance: 64.8 Nautical Miles [73.4 Miles]

Actual Distance Travel due to Beating: 64.8 Nautical Miles

Average Boat Speed: 6.1 Knots

Boat Speed Made Good: 6.1 Knots

Average Wind Speed: 10.4 Knots

Average Wind Direction from True North: 277.1o

Average Current Drift: 0.4 Knots at **Average Current Set:** 180.0o

Average Wave Height: 3.1 Feet

Average Sea Temperature: 75.9o F

Average Air Temperature: 75.9o F

Average Percentage Risk of Calms: 4.0%

Average Percentage Risk of Gales: 1.0%

LEG 5

VESSEL PERFORMANCE AND WEATHER CONDITIONS REPORT

Start: N33o 2.80' E22o 45.40' [coast of Libya]

End: N33o 8.60' E20o 36.10' [coast of Libya]

Elapsed-time to Complete Leg: 0.6 Days

Calculated Great Circle Distance: 108.5 Nautical Miles [124.6 Miles]

Actual Distance Travel due to Beating: 108.5 Nautical Miles

Average Boat Speed: 7.1 Knots

Boat Speed Made Good: 7.1 Knots

Average Wind Speed: 10.0 Knots

Average Wind Direction from True North: 000.0o

Average Current Drift: 0.5 Knots at **Average Current Set:** 170.3o

Average Wave Height: 3.0 Feet

Average Sea Temperature: 76.7o F

Average Air Temperature: 76.4o F

Average Percentage Risk of Calms: 1.6%

Average Percentage Risk of Gales: 0.3%

LEG 6

VESSEL PERFORMANCE AND WEATHER CONDITIONS REPORT

Start: N33o 8.60' E20o 36.10' [coast of Libya]

End: N33o 28.36' E18o 19.49' [coast of Libya]

Elapsed-time to Complete Leg: 0.8 Days

Calculated Great Circle Distance: 115.9 Nautical Miles [133.1 Miles]

Actual Distance Travel due to Beating: 115.9 Nautical Miles

Average Boat Speed: 6.0 Knots

Boat Speed Made Good: 6.0 Knots

Average Wind Speed: 8.7 Knots

Average Wind Direction from True North: 000.0o

Average Current Drift: 0.6 Knots at **Average Current Set:** 135.0o

153

Average Wave Height: 2.6 Feet

Average Sea Temperature: 77.5o F

Average Air Temperature: 77.0o F

Average Percentage Risk of Calms: 2.3%

Average Percentage Risk of Gales: 0.0%

LEG 7

VESSEL PERFORMANCE AND WEATHER CONDITIONS REPORT

Start: N33o 28.36' E18o 19.49'
[200 Miles off coast of Libya]

End: N34o 12.49' E15o 14.32'
[200 Miles off coast of Libya]

Elapsed-time to Complete Leg: 1.2 Days

Calculated Great Circle Distance: 160.0
Nautical Miles [183.7 Miles]

Actual Distance Travel due to Beating:
160.0 Nautical Miles

Average Boat Speed: 5.6 Knots

Boat Speed Made Good: 5.6 Knots

Average Wind Speed: 8.4 Knots

**Average Wind Direction
from True North:** 024.7o

Average Current Drift: 0.5 Knots at
Average Current Set: 234.3o

Average Wave Height: 2.4 Feet

Average Sea Temperature: 77.3o F

Average Air Temperature: 76.9o F

Average Percentage Risk of Calms: 5.7%

Average Percentage Risk of Gales: 0.0%

LEG 8

VESSEL PERFORMANCE AND WEATHER CONDITIONS REPORT

Start: N34o 12.49' E15o 14.32'
[200 Miles off coast of Libya]

End: N36o 30.23' E11o 37.67'
[northeast coast of Tunisia]

Elapsed-time to Complete Leg: 1.6 Days

Calculated Great Circle Distance: 224.0
Nautical Miles [257.0 Miles]

Actual Distance Travel due to Beating:
231.5 Nautical Miles

Average Boat Speed: 5.9 Knots

Boat Speed Made Good: 5.7 Knots

Average Wind Speed: 11.1 Knots

**Average Wind Direction
from True North:** 160.6o

Average Current Drift: 0.4 Knots at
Average Current Set: 135.0o

Average Wave Height: 2.4 Feet

Average Sea Temperature: 76.1o F

Average Air Temperature: 76.0o F

Average Percentage Risk of Calms: 6.9%

Average Percentage Risk of Gales: 0.1%

LEG 9

VESSEL PERFORMANCE AND WEATHER CONDITIONS REPORT

Start: N36o 30.23' E11o 37.67'
[northeast coast of Tunisia]

End: N37o 47.30' E10o 47.94
[north coast of Tunisia]

Elapsed-time to Complete Leg: 0.8 Days

Calculated Great Circle Distance: 86.7
Nautical Miles [95.5 Miles]

Actual Distance Travel due to Beating:
91.7 Nautical Miles

Average Boat Speed: 4.9 Knots

Boat Speed Made Good: 4.6 Knots

Average Wind Speed: 9.8 Knots

**Average Wind Direction
from True North:** 136.6o

Average Current Drift: 0.5 Knots at
Average Current Set: 117.6o

Average Wave Height: 2.7 Feet

Average Sea Temperature: 75.6o F

Average Air Temperature: 75.5o F

Average Percentage Risk of Calms: 5.0%

Average Percentage Risk of Gales: 0.3%

LEG 10

VESSEL PERFORMANCE AND WEATHER CONDITIONS REPORT

Start: N37o 47.30' E10o 47.94'
[north coast of Tunisia]

End: N35o 47.97' E6o 20.65'
[50 Miles south of Cadiz, Spain]

Elapsed-time to Complete Leg: 5.0 Days

Calculated Great Circle Distance: 831.1
Nautical Miles [954 Miles]

Actual Distance Travel due to Beating:
831.2 Nautical Miles

Average Boat Speed: 6.9 Knots

Boat Speed Made Good: 6.9 Knots

Average Wind Speed: 8.4 Knots

Average Wind Direction from True North:
028.0o

Average Current Drift: 0.6 Knots at
Average Current Set: 028.0o

Average Wave Height: 2.8 Feet

Average Sea Temperature: 73.6o F

Average Air Temperature: 74.0o F

Average Percentage Risk of Calms: 8.8%

Average Percentage Risk of Gales: 0.0%

LEG 11

VESSEL PERFORMANCE AND WEATHER CONDITIONS REPORT

Start: N35o 47.97' W6o 20.65'
[50 Miles south of Cadiz, Spain]

End: N28o 26.17 W16o 9.75'
[Canary Islands]

Elapsed-time to Complete Leg: 3.5 Days

Calculated Great Circle Distance: 665.7 Nautical Miles [764.2 Miles]

Actual Distance Travel due to Beating: 665.8 Nautical Miles

Average Boat Speed: 8.0 Knots

Boat Speed Made Good: 8.0 Knots

Average Wind Speed: 9.9 Knots

Average Wind Direction from True North: 0.91.7o

Average Current Drift: 0.4 Knots at
Average Current Set: 205.3o

Average Wave Height: 3.8 Feet

Average Sea Temperature: 71.2o F

Average Air Temperature: 71.8o F

Average Percentage Risk of Calms: 3.5%

Average Percentage Risk of Gales: 0.0%

Summary of Computer Simulation of Mulek's Voyage Passage One

Total days sailing toward the Canary Islands: 19.7 days (20)

Average Boat Speed: 6.5 Knots

Boat Speed Made Good: 6.3 Knots

Total length of voyage: 2,953.6 Nautical Miles [3091 Miles]

Approximate arrival time per the simulation: fourth week of September

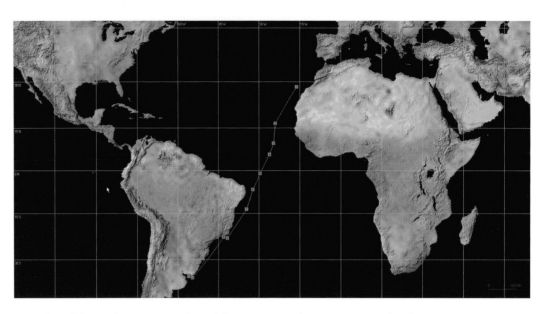

Simulated legs of stage two of Mulekite passage from Canary Islands to Uruguay.

Stage Two

The second stage was from the Canary Islands off Africa to what is today Uruguay. They likely started this stage sometime in October and ended in November, for a duration of nearly three to four weeks, depending on sea and wind conditions. The first days of the journey would have been spent in the relatively short transit between the western tip of Africa and the eastern most cape of South America. Undoubtedly, the Phoenicians would have sailed south along the African shoreline, before striking due south-southwest toward South America. Gavin Menzies describes how sailing ships utilized the winds and currents of this sector of the sea.

North of the equator, the Atlantic is a vast oval-shaped wind and current system rotating clockwise day in, day out, throughout the year. British Admiralty sailing directions advise mariners on how to make use of these winds and **currents:** "From Madeira the best track is to pass just west of, but in sight of, the Cape Verde Archipelago . . . from Cape Verde

155

[tip of west Africa] steer a direct course [for the Caribbean] ... thereafter ... the north equatorial current and south equatorial current converge, forming a broad band of current setting west. Average rates reach 2 knots."[28]

Rather than sailing west to the Caribbean, the Phoenicians would have continued sailing south-southwest toward what is today Brazil. Gavin estimates that by utilizing the currents, the crossing from Africa's Cape Verde to South America's Cape Amazon would have taken approximately three weeks in a medieval Chinese treasure ship freighter.[29] The passage would have taken slightly less time in a Phoenician ship with oarsmen, and even faster if they caught the favorable trade-wind blowing astern.

Oh, I am the wind the seamen love—
I am steady, and strong, and true;
They follow my track by the clouds above,
O've the fathomless tropic blue.

JACK LONDON, "SONG
OF THE TRADE-WIND"[30]

Passage Summary Report

Passage Filename: C:\PROGRAM FILES\ VISUAL PASSAGE PLANNER 2\MULEK2.PP2

Passage Creation Date: 9/10/2008

Pilot Chart Data Used: Actual dates based on departure specified

Vessel Profile Used: C:\Program Files\ Visual Passage Planner 2\NoName.vp

Minimum Speed Set: 0.50 Knots

Fuel Consumption Set: 0.00 Units/Hour

Currents: ON

Current Values Used: Average All

Wind Values Used: Average All

Waypoint #	Latitude	Longitude Date
1	N28° 21.07'	W16°13.06'
2	N16° 29.58'	W24°0.60'
3	N9° 39.39'	W24°33.91'
4	N5° 41.18'	W26°6.50'
5	S1° 4.88'	W29°32.21'
6	S6° 39.57'	W32°8.30'
7	S13° 30.71'	W34°28.67'
8	S23° 19.75'	W41°37.89'
9	S22° 59.83'	W43°6.50'
10	S35° 27.19'	W54°39.20'
11	S35° 1.67'	W56°3.81'

General Information	Data
Calculated Great Circle Distance	4589.3 NM
Calculated Rhumbline Distance	4589.9 NM
Actual Distance Traveled due to Beating	4599.8 NM
Elapsed Time to Complete Passage	22.9 Days
Fuel Consumption	0.0 Units
Average Boat Speed	8.4 Knots
Boat Speed Made Good	8.4 Knots

LEG 1

Departure Date 9 October Passage Two

VESSEL PERFORMANCE AND WEATHER CONDITIONS REPORT

Start: N28o 21.07' W16o 13.06' [Canary Islands]

End: N16o 29.58' W24o 0.60' [954 Miles south southwest of Canary Islands]

Elapsed-time to Complete Leg: 3.5 Days

Calculated Great Circle Distance: 831.8 Nautical Miles [954.0 Miles]

Actual Distance Travel due to Beating: 831.9 Nautical Miles

Average Boat Speed: 9.8 Knots

Boat Speed Made Good: 9.8 Knots

Average Wind Speed: 12.0 Knots

Average Wind Direction from True North: 045.0o

Average Current Drift: 0.5 Knots at **Average Current Set:** 236.5o

Average Wave Height: 4.0 Feet

Average Sea Temperature: 74.8o F

Average Air Temperature: 74.8o F

Average Percentage Risk of Calms: 1.9%

Average Percentage Risk of Gales: 0.1%

LEG 2

VESSEL PERFORMANCE AND WEATHER CONDITIONS REPORT

Southwest of Canary Islands

Start: N16o 29.58' W24o 0.60' [954 Miles south southwest of Canary Islands]

End: N9o 39.39' W24o 33.91' [Azores]

Elapsed-time to Complete Leg: 1.8 Days

Calculated Great Circle Distance: 411.5 Nautical Miles [472.5 Miles]

Actual Distance Travel due to Beating: 411.5 Nautical Miles

Average Boat Speed: 9.5 Knots

Boat Speed Made Good: 9.5 Knots

Average Wind Speed: 10.7 Knots

Average Wind Direction from True North: 0.45.00o

Average Current Drift: 0.5 Knots at
Average Current Set: 252.7o

Average Wave Height: 3.6 Feet

Average Sea Temperature: 80.0o F

Average Air Temperature: 79.9o F

Average Percentage Risk of Calms: 2.6%

Average Percentage Risk of Gales: 0.0%

LEG 3

VESSEL PERFORMANCE AND WEATHER CONDITIONS REPORT

Start: N9o 39.39' W24o 33.91' [Azores]

End: N5o 41.18' W26o 6.50' [800 Miles west of West Africa]

Elapsed-time to Complete Leg: 2.0 Days

Calculated Great Circle Distance: 255.3 Nautical Miles [293.0 Miles]

Actual Distance Travel due to Beating: 263.3 Nautical Miles

Average Boat Speed: 5.4 Knots

Boat Speed Made Good: 5.3 Knots

Average Wind Speed: 8.4 Knots

Average Wind Direction from True North: 137.00o

Average Current Drift: 0.8 Knots at
Average Current Set: 090.00o

Average Wave Height: 3.5 Feet

Average Sea Temperature: 81.50o F

Average Air Temperature: 80.3o F

Average Percentage Risk of Calms: 6.2%

Average Percentage Risk of Gales: 0.0%

LEG 4

VESSEL PERFORMANCE AND WEATHER CONDITIONS REPORT

Start: N5o 41.18' W26o 6.50' [800 Miles west of West Africa]

End: S1o 4.88' W29o 32.21' [500 Miles northeast of east tip of Brazil]

Elapsed-time to Complete Leg: 3.0 Days

Calculated Great Circle Distance: 455.1 Nautical Miles [522.5 Miles]

Actual Distance Travel due to Beating: 457.5 Nautical Miles

Average Boat Speed: 6.4 Knots

Boat Speed Made Good: 6.4 Knots

Average Wind Speed: 10.6 Knots

Average Wind Direction from True North: 142.2o

Average Current Drift: 0.7 Knots at
Average Current Set: 142.2o

Average Wave Height: 4.0 Feet

Average Sea Temperature: 80.4o F

Average Air Temperature: 79.5o F

Average Percentage Risk of Calms: 1.3%

Average Percentage Risk of Gales: 0.0%

LEG 5

VESSEL PERFORMANCE AND WEATHER CONDITIONS REPORT

Start: S1o 4.88' W29o 32.21' [500 Miles northeast of east tip of Brazil]

End: S6o 39.57' W32o 8.30' [175 Miles east off east tip of Brazil]

Elapsed-time to Complete Leg: 2.0 Days

Calculated Great Circle Distance: 369.1 Nautical Miles [423.7 Miles]

Actual Distance Travel due to Beating: 369.1 Nautical Miles

Average Boat Speed: 7.8 Knots

Boat Speed Made Good: 7.8 Knots

Average Wind Speed: 13.5 Knots

Average Wind Direction from True North: 132.8o

Average Current Drift: 0.7 Knots at
Average Current Set: 132.8o

Average Wave Height: 4.6 Feet

Average Sea Temperature: 78.5o F

Average Air Temperature: 78.8o F

Average Percentage Risk of Calms: 0.0%

Average Percentage Risk of Gales: 0.0

LEG 6

VESSEL PERFORMANCE AND WEATHER CONDITIONS REPORT

Start: S6o 39.57' W32o 8.30' [175 Miles east off east tip of Brazil]

End: S13o 30.71' W34o 28.67' [200 Miles off southeast coast of Brazil]

Elapsed-time to Complete Leg: 1.8 Days

Calculated Great Circle Distance: 433.7 Nautical Miles [498.0 Miles]

Actual Distance Travel due to Beating: 433.7 Nautical Miles

Average Boat Speed: 10.1 Knots

Boat Speed Made Good: 10.1 Knots

Average Wind Speed: 11.9 Knots

Average Wind Direction from True North: 093.2o

Average Current Drift: 0.6 Knots at **Average Current Set:** 236.9o

Average Wave Height: 4.4 Feet

Average Sea Temperature: 78.6o F

Average Air Temperature: 78.8o F

Average Percentage Risk of Calms: 0.1%

Average Percentage Risk of Gales: 0.0%

LEG 7

VESSEL PERFORMANCE AND WEATHER CONDITIONS REPORT

Start: S13o 30.71' W34o 28.67' [200 Miles off the southeast coast of Brazil]

End: S23o 19.75' W41o 37.89' [84 Miles east of Rio, Brazil]

Elapsed-time to Complete Leg: 3.2 Days

Calculated Great Circle Distance: 715.7 Nautical Miles [821.6 Miles]

Actual Distance Travel due to Beating: 715.7 Nautical Miles

Average Boat Speed: 9.2 Knots

Boat Speed Made Good: 9.2 Knots

Average Wind Speed: 10.2 Knots

Average Wind Direction from True North: 086.4o

Average Current Drift: 0.6 Knots at **Average Current Set:** 214.1o

Average Wave Height: 4.1 Feet

Average Sea Temperature: 76.0o F

Average Air Temperature: 76.2o F

Average Percentage Risk of Calms: 1.4%

Average Percentage Risk of Gales: 0.0%

LEG 8

VESSEL PERFORMANCE AND WEATHER CONDITIONS REPORT

Start: S23o 19.75' W41o 37.89' [84 Miles east of Rio, Brazil]

End: S22o 59.83' W43o 6.50' [Rio, Brazil]

Elapsed-time to Complete Leg: 0.3 Days

Calculated Great Circle Distance: 83.9 Nautical Miles [96.3 Miles]

Actual Distance Travel due to Beating: 83.9 Nautical Miles

Average Boat Speed: 10.1 Knots

Boat Speed Made Good: 10.1 Knots

Average Wind Speed: 11.5 Knots

Average Wind Direction from True North: 093.9o

Average Current Drift: 0.7 Knots at **Average Current Set:** 254.8o

Average Wave Height: 4.3 Feet

Average Sea Temperature: 70.3o F

Average Air Temperature: 71.1o F

Average Percentage Risk of Calms: 3.9%

Average Percentage Risk of Gales: 0.0

LEG 9

VESSEL PERFORMANCE AND WEATHER CONDITIONS REPORT

Start: S22o 59.83' W43o 6.50' [Rio, Brazil]

End: S35o 27.19' W54o 39.20' [85 Miles east of Montevideo, Uruguay]

Elapsed-time to Complete Leg: 4.8 Days

Calculated Great Circle Distance: 959.6 Nautical Miles [1,148 Miles]

Actual Distance Travel due to Beating: 959.7 Nautical Miles

Average Boat Speed: 8.4 Knots

Boat Speed Made Good: 8.4 Knots

Average Wind Speed: 11.0 Knots

Average Wind Direction from True North: 116.7o

Average Current Drift: 0.7 Knots at **Average Current Set:** 215.7o

Average Wave Height: 4.4 Feet

Average Sea Temperature: 64.6o F

Average Air Temperature: 65.3o F

Average Percentage Risk of Calms: 2.8%

Average Percentage Risk of Gales: 0.9%

LEG 10

VESSEL PERFORMANCE AND WEATHER CONDITIONS REPORT

Start: S35o 27.19' W54o 39.20' [85 Miles east of Montevideo, Uruguay]

End: S35o 1.67' W56o 3.81' [Montevideo, Uruguay]

Elapsed-time to Complete Leg: 0.4 Days

Calculated Great Circle Distance: 73.7 Nautical Miles [84.6 Miles]

Actual Distance Travel due to Beating: 73.7 Nautical Miles

Average Boat Speed: 7.8 Knots

Boat Speed Made Good: 7.8 Knots

Average Wind Speed: 10.6 Knots

Average Wind Direction from True North: 100.6o

Average Current Drift: 3.8 Feet

Average Sea Temperature: 57.2o F

Average Air Temperature: 57.5o F

Average Percentage Risk of Calms: 2.5%

Average Percentage Risk of Gales: 1.5%

Summary of Computer Simulation of Mulek's Voyage Passage Two

Total Days sailing toward the Canary Islands: 22.9 days (23)

Average Boat Speed: 8.4 Knots

Boat Speed Made Good: 8.4 Knots

Total length of voyage: 4,589.3 Nautical Miles [5268.5 Miles]

Approximate arrival time per the simulation: first week of November

Stage Three

This stage was a southerly passage along the entire Atlantic coast of today's Argentina. Eventually, the Phoenician captain would have locked onto the shoreline of the Patagonia mainland and the island of Staten Land. There was no need

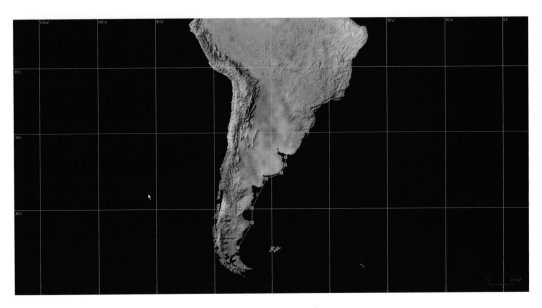

Simulated Mulekite passage from Uruguay to southern Argentina.

for the Phoenicians to row in these waters because the trade-winds grew stronger and waves became more intense as the boats continued southward. Indeed, these waters would have provided ideal sailing conditions, a predecessor to the rough waters that were ahead of them. Jack London wrote of such pleasant days at sea:

> At last, after three days of variable winds, we caught the northeast trades. I came on deck, after a good night's rest in spite of my poor knee, to find the *Ghost* foaming along, wing and wing and with every sail drawing except the jibs, with a fresh breeze astern. Oh, the wonder of the great trade-wind! All day we sailed, and all night, and the next day, and the next, day after day, the wind always astern and blowing steadily and strong. The schooner sailed herself. There was no pulling and hauling on sheets and tackle, no shifting of topsails, no work at all for the sailors to do except to steer. At night, when the sun went down, the sheets were slackened; in the morning, when they yielded up the damp of the dew and relaxed, they were pulled tight again—and that was all.[31]

As time went on, the Mulekites must have realized more clearly than ever that their

159

land of refuge would be far from their homeland, and the probability of returning a risky lost dream. During this stage of their passage, whale sightings would have been common.

Passage Summary Report

Passage Filename: C:\PROGRAM FILES\ VISUAL PASSAGE PLANNER 2\MULEK3.PP2

Passage Creation Date: 9/10/2008

Pilot Chart Data Used: Actual dates based on departure specified

Vessel Profile Used: C:\Program Files\ Visual Passage Planner 2\NoName.vp

Minimum Speed Set: 0.50 Knots

Fuel Consumption Set: 0.00 Units/Hour

Currents: ON

Current Values Used: Average All

Wind Values Used: Average All

Waypoint #	Latitude	Longitude Date
1	S35° 15.27'	W56°22.43'
2	S36°51.72'	W56°27.58'
3	S38°22.13'	W57°26.77'
4	S39°29.54'	W61°23.51'
5	S44°50.42'	W65°9.69'
6	S47°24.22'	W65°7.58'
7	S51°28.53'	W68°49.92'

Leg #	Beating (Apparent wind 0° to 45°)	Tight Reaching (Apparent wind 45° to 112.5°)	Broad Reaching (Apparent wind 112.6° to 157.5°)	Running (Apparent wind 157.6 to 180)
1	0% at 0 Knots	45% at 12.9 Knots	55% at 9.8 Knots	0% at 0 Knots
2	0% at 0 Knots	0% at 0 Knots	0% at 0 Knots	100% at 10.0 Knots
3	0% at 0 Knots	0% at 0 Knots	73% at 10.6 Knots	27% at 9.0 Knots
4	9% at 4.3 Knots	55% at 13.3 Knots	36% at 9.5 Knots	0% at 0 Knots
5	54% at 12.9 Knots	0% at 0 Knots	0% at 0 Knots	46% at 8.6 Knots
6	55% at 34.0 Knots	33% at 15.7 Knots	12% at 12.8 Knots	0% at 0 Knots

General Information	Data
Calculated Great Circle Distance	1194.0 NM
Calculated Rhumbline Distance	1194.1 NM
Actual Distance Traveled due to Beating	1204.7 NM
Elapsed Time to Complete Passage	7.8 Days
Fuel Consumption	0.0 Units
Average Boat Speed	6.5 Knots
Boat Speed Made Good	6.4 Knots

LEG 1

Departure Date 1 December
Passage Three

VESSEL PERFORMANCE AND WEATHER CONDITIONS REPORT

Start: S35° 15.27' W56° 22.43' [east coast of Argentina]

End: S36° 51.72' W56° 27.58' [east coast of Argentina]

Elapsed-time to Complete Leg: 0.5 Days

Calculated Great Circle Distance: 96.5 Nautical Miles [110.8 Miles]

Actual Distance Travel due to Beating: 96.5 Nautical Miles

Apparent Wind Angle Information:

Numbers indicate percent of leg sailed at that column's relative wind angle. Relative wind angle given is the direction from which the wind comes. (See table above.)

Average Boat Speed: 8.8 Knots

Boat Speed Made Good: 8.8 Knots

Average Wind Speed: 11.2 Knots

Average Wind Direction from True North: 065.2°

Average Current Drift: 0.4 Knots at
Average Current Set: 315.0°

Average Wave Height: 4.9 Feet

Average Sea Temperature: 67.3° F

Average Air Temperature: 68.6° F

Average Percentage Risk of Calms: 4.6%

Average Percentage Risk of Gales: 4.6%

LEG 2

VESSEL PERFORMANCE AND WEATHER CONDITIONS REPORT

Start: S36° 51.72' W56° 27.58' [east coast of Argentina]

End: S38° 22.13' W57° 26.77' [east coast of Argentina]

Elapsed-time to Complete Leg: 0.6 Days

Calculated Great Circle Distance: 101.8 Nautical Miles [116.8 Miles]

Actual Distance Travel due to Beating: 101.8 Nautical Miles

Average Boat Speed: 7.2 Knots

Boat Speed Made Good: 7.2 Knots

Average Wind Speed: 10.0 Knots

Average Wind Direction from True North: 045.0°

Average Current Drift: 0.2 Knots at
Average Current Set: 181.1°

Average Wave Height: 4.6 Feet

Average Sea Temperature: 64.5° F

Average Air Temperature: 66.3°F

Average Percentage Risk of Calms: 1.3%

Average Percentage Risk of Gales: 1.1%

LEG 3

VESSEL PERFORMANCE AND WEATHER CONDITIONS REPORT

Start: S38° 22.13' W57° 26.77' [east coast of Argentina]

End: S39° 29.54' W61° 23.51' [east coast of Argentina]

Elapsed-time to Complete Leg: 1.0 Days

Calculated Great Circle Distance: 196.1 Nautical Miles [359.3 Miles]

Actual Distance Travel due to Beating: 196.1 Nautical Miles

Average Boat Speed: 8.0 Knots

Boat Speed Made Good: 8.0 Knots

Average Wind Speed: 10.2 Knots

Average Wind Direction from True North: 064.0°

Average Current Drift: 0.2 Knots at
Average Current Set: 106.7°

Average Wave Height: 4.7 Feet

Average Sea Temperature: 63.1° F

Average Air Temperature: 64.5° F

Average Percentage Risk of Calms: 1.4%

Average Percentage Risk of Gales: 0.2%

LEG 4

VESSEL PERFORMANCE AND WEATHER CONDITIONS REPORT

Start: S39° 29.54' W61° 23.51' [east coast of Argentina]

End: S44° 50.42 W65° 9.69' [east coast of Argentina]

Elapsed-time to Complete Leg: 2.1 Days

Calculated Great Circle Distance: 361.9 Nautical Miles [415.5 Miles]

Actual Distance Travel due to Beating: 362.5 Nautical Miles

Average Boat Speed: 7.2 Knots

Boat Speed Made Good: 7.2 Knots

Average Wind Speed: 11.1 Knots

Average Wind Direction from True North: 173.9°

Average Current Drift: 0.0 Knots at
Average Current Set: 000°

Average Wave Height: 4.6 Feet

Average Sea Temperature: 59.5° F

Average Air Temperature: 63.4° F

Average Percentage Risk of Calms: 4.8%

Average Percentage Risk of Gales: 0.3%

LEG 5

VESSEL PERFORMANCE AND WEATHER CONDITIONS REPORT

Start: S44° 50.42 W65° 9.69' [east coast of Argentina]

End: S47° 24.22 W65° 7.58' [east coast of Argentina]

Elapsed-time to Complete Leg: 1.2 Days

Calculated Great Circle Distance: 153.8 Nautical Miles [176.6 Miles]

Actual Distance Travel due to Beating: 157.7 Nautical Miles

Average Boat Speed: 5.5 Knots

Boat Speed Made Good: 5.4 Knots

Average Wind Speed: 11.0 Knots

Average Wind Direction from True North: 079.8°

Average Current Drift: 0.7 Knots at
Average Current Set: 315.0°

Average Wave Height: 4.1 Feet

Average Sea Temperature: 57.3° F

Average Air Temperature: 60.9° F

Average Percentage Risk of Calms: 8.7%

Average Percentage Risk of Gales: 0.0%

LEG 6

VESSEL PERFORMANCE AND WEATHER CONDITIONS REPORT

Start: S47° 24.22' W65° 7.58' [east coast of Argentina]

End: S51° 28.53' W68° 49.92' [Reo Gallegos, Argentina]

Elapsed-time to Complete Leg: 2.4 Days

Calculated Great Circle Distance: 183.8 Nautical Miles [325.8 Miles]

Actual Distance Travel due to Beating: 290.0 Nautical Miles

Average Boat Speed: 5.0 Knots

Boat Speed Made Good: 4.9 Knots

Average Wind Speed: 25.4 Knots

Average Wind Direction from True North: 224.9°

Average Current Drift: 0.2 Knots at **Average Current Set:** 260.3°

Average Wave Height: 4.9 Feet

Average Sea Temperature: 51.1° F

Average Air Temperature: 53.5° F

Average Percentage Risk of Calms: 0.0%

Average Percentage Risk of Gales: 0.0%

Summary of Computer Simulation of Mulek's Voyage Passage Three

Total days sailing toward Reo Gallegos, Argentina: 7.8 days (8)

Average Boat Speed: 6.5 Knots

Boat Speed Made Good: 6.4 Knots

Total length of voyage: 1,194.0 Nautical Miles [1370.7 Miles]

Approximate arrival time per the simulation: second week of December

Simulated leg of stage four of Mulekites' dangerous journey through what would later be known as the Strait of Magellan.

Stage Four

The fourth segment of the voyage took the Mulekites from the southern end of Argentina to the waters of the Pacific Ocean. This was by far the most dangerous and unpredictable stage of the voyage. Starting in the Atlantic, their cape passage took the Mulekite ship to the inside lee shore islands of Chile. We believe that by design, the Phoenicians would have sailed around the cape during the warmest months in the Southern Hemisphere and by taking the Strait of Magellan they avoided the more dangerous waters of the Antarctica Ocean. The passage was safer, but slower, and required much rowing during calms to navigate safely during the days of thick fog that is common in the pass.

Even during periods of calm winds, sailing around the cape through the Strait of Magellan is a perilous experience. Thick fog is common, and although the winds are calmer, large ocean swells continue to drive ships toward the rocky pinnacles that form the shoreline of the cape. Phoenicians would have lowered their sails

162

and carefully rowed through the pea-soup fog. As haunting as that must have been, the experienced Phoenicians realized that eventually the weather in the cape would turn against them. Although it was nearly summer in the south, Dana made this entry in his long on the 9 November 1834:

Between five and six—the sun was then nearly three hours high—the cry of "All starbowlines ahoy!" summoned our watch on deck; and immediately all hands were called. A true specimen of Cape Horn was coming upon us. A great cloud of a dark slate-color was driving on us from the south-west; and we did our best to take in sail, (for the light sails had been set during the first part of the day,) before we were in the midst of it. We had got the light sails furled, the courses hauled up, and the topsail reef-tackles hauled out, and were just mounting the fore-rigging, when the storm struck us. In an instant the sea, which had been comparatively quiet, was running higher and higher; and it became almost as dark as night. The hail and sleet were harder than I had yet felt them; seeming almost to *pin us down* to the rigging. We were longer taking in ropes and riggings covered with snow and sleet, and we ourselves cold and nearly blinded with the violence of the storm. By the time we had got down upon deck again, the little brig was plunging madly into a tremendous head sea, which at every drive rushed in through the bow-ports and over the bows, and buried all the forward part of the vessel. At this instant the chief mate, who was standing on the top of the windlass, at the foot of the spenser mast, called out, "Lay out there and furl the jib!" This was no agreeable or safe duty, yet it must be done. An old Swede (the best sailor on board), who belonged on the forecastle, sprang out upon the bow-sprit. Another one must go: I was near the mate, and sprang forward, threw the downhaul over the windlass and jumped between the knight-heads out upon the bowsprit. The crew stood abaft [toward or at the stern] the windlass and hauled the jib down, while we got out upon the weather side of the jib-boom, our feet on the foot-ropes, holding on by the spar, the great jib flying off to leeward and *slatting* so as almost to throw us off of the boom. For some time we could do nothing but hold on, and the vessel diving into two huge seas, one after the other, plunged us twice into the water up to our chins. We hardly knew whether we were on or off; when coming up, dripping from the water, we were raised high into the air. John (that was the sailor's name) thought the boom would go, every moment, and called out to the mate to keep the vessel off, and haul down the staysail; but the fury of the wind and the breaking of the seas against the bows defied every attempt to make ourselves heard, and we were obliged to do the best we could in our situation. Fortunately, no other seas so heavy struck her, and we succeeded in furling the jib "after a fashion"; and, coming in over the staysail nettings, were not a little pleased to find that all was snug, and the watch gone below; for we were soaked through, and it was very cold. The weather continued nearly the same through the night.

Monday, Nov. 10th. During a part of this day we hove to, but the rest of the

time were driving on, under close-reef sails, with a heavy sea, a strong gale, and frequent squalls of hail and snow.

Tuesday, Nov. 11ᵗʰ. The same.

Wednesday. The same.

Thursday. The same.[32]

The fact that the Mulekites could make a passage around the horn of South American in an ancient ship, attests to the great sailing skills of the Phoenicians. Again, it is likely they made their passage around the cape during the summer season because a winter passage would have seemed nearly impossible. Conrad remembers sailing with a cook who had an unfortunate experience rounding Cape Horn during the winter. The old cook aboard Conrad's Alaskan fishing boat had sailed as a young lad around South America on a square-rigger. The teenager was caught aloft in the high rigging tops in the process of reefing sails during an ice storm. While trying to hang on for his life, the young lad's hands became frozen to a steel yardarm. He would have died up there had the captain not gone aloft and chopped his hands off with a hatchet.

Conrad himself experienced similar cold weather sailing conditions while working on a crab vessel in Alaska 1963 through 1967. The crew fished for Alaskan king crab and halibut in the Shumagin Islands and Aleutian Islands, which are located in the Gulf of Alaska and the Bering Sea. During those years, Conrad experienced class 1, 2, and 3 hurricane-strength winds in addition to ice storms and giant rogue waves. Crab fishing in Alaska is "living on the edge" and requires endurance to cold, hard work, and a lack of sleep beyond what most people would think is possible. One such trip started at Sand Point on Popof Island in the Shumagin Islands. Conrad relates:

> After off-loading our last load of crab, we brought on new stores of food, bait, and fuel for a two-week trip to return to our crab pots in the Gulf of Alaska on a long shelf at a depth of about 100 fathom

And now there came both mist and snow
And it grew wondrous cold:
And ice, mast-high, came floating by,
As green as emerald.

THE RIME OF THE ANCIENT MARINER, SAMUEL TAYLOR COLERIDGE

(600 feet) near Wazinski Island. The trip began in very cold weather with little or no wind, which resulted in moon-colored ice-fog of silver puffs floating at different levels on the surface of the water. Tending crab pots for the first few days began in an easy maneuver, but warning signs began with no wind, white sky, and white water. These signs are sure tell-tales of powerful wind to come. We continued to pull pots in hopes to get to the last pot and empty and bait it before we ran for cover behind some island or shore where the seas would be diminished. Fishing went on a regular basis till 65 knots of wind. We were at that point when the captain yelled, "Rogue wave!" A wall of water fifty feet above the main deck of the vessel hit us with the speed and force of a freight train. I only had time to grab with one hand a strut at the pot puller. But I still got washed up and over the side, hanging on for dear life, knowing that if I let go it would be the end of life on this side of the veil.

I managed somehow to scramble back on deck and headed for cover in the wheelhouse when I heard the captain yelling that the other deckhand was missing and he could hear him yelling for help. I climbed to the top of the wheelhouse to see if my crewmate could be spotted. The wind at that time had reached hurricane force and the vessel was awash with seas that were threatening to swallow everything. At this desperate moment, I saw the other crewmate wedged back aft under the elevated walkway behind the pilothouse. He was pinned there, along with king crabs biting him and being half-drowned from seawater that was freezing solid to every surface. I yelled to the captain that I had located the other crewmate who was unable to free himself and that I was heading down for the rescue.

The rescue took some time and effort, but was managed before loss of life. The captain then headed for safety on the south side of Pavlof Volcano, which was erupting lava, ash, boulders, rocks the size of baseballs, and lightning bolts. We set anchor near shore in Volcano Bay in 125 knots of freezing, screaming wind that was coming straight over the volcano from the Bering Sea. The crew tried to get something to eat and we went to our bunks for a restless few hours of sleep. When we awoke the next morning, the storm had abated, but the vessel was so frozen no one could get out on deck. We were forced to chop one of the doors loose with an ax. Our auxiliary power generator was out and it was so cold that the battery banks were frozen. The result was that we had no way to start the generator

to get some heat in the vessel. Power also was needed to start the air compressor in order to charge air banks to start the old "Washington," three-cylinder main engine. The inside of the vessel was freezing because it was a wooden vessel built in the 1920s. If we didn't get things started soon, freezing to death was looking at us. The angel of death must had been in Hawaii that day because another vessel in the middle of that killer storm anchored near us. We had not shown any smoke from our vessel, so they came over to see if we needed help. Jumper wires were used to get our generator going, and our fishing vessel came back to life.

Regardless of the season of the year in which the Phoenicians transited the Horn, the days spent sailing around the cape would have been a hair-raising and miserable experience for their Mulekite passengers. It is even more daunting to think of their conditions if the Phoenicians had been unaware of the Strait of Magellan. This would have meant a full swing into the Antarctic Ocean's violent seas, brutal winds, and a watery forest of icebergs.

Passage Summary Report

Passage Filename: C:\PROGRAM FILES\ VISUAL PASSAGE PLANNER 2\MULEK DRAKE PASSAGE.PP2

Passage Creation Date: 1/29/2009

Pilot Chart Data Used: Actual dates based on departure specified

Vessel Profile Used: C:\Program Files\ Visual Passage Planner 2\Hagoth.VP

Minimum Speed Set: 0.50 Knots

Fuel Consumption Set: 0.00 Units/Hour

Currents: ON

Current Values Used: Average All

Wind Values Used: Average All

Waypoint #	Latitude	Longitude Date
1	S51°35.62'	W68°58.95'
2	S52°25.03'	W68°14.14'
3	S52°26.66'	W69°29.72'
4	S52°38.86'	W69°47.11'
5	S52°45.34'	W70°31.25'
6	S54°0.73'	W71°0.68'
7	S53°21.92'	W72°59.73'
8	S52°53.02'	W73°55.25'
9	S52°38.45'	W73°43.21'

General Information	Data
Calculated Great Circle Distance	364.6 NM
Calculated Rhumbline Distance	364.6 NM
Actual Distance Traveled due to Beating	371.4 NM
Elapsed Time to Complete Passage	6.3 Days
Fuel Consumption	0.0 Units
Average Boat Speed	2.5 Knots
Boat Speed Made Good	2.4 Knots

LEG 1:

Departure Date 12 December
Passage Four

VESSEL PERFORMANCE AND WEATHER
CONDITIONS REPORT

Start: S51o 35.62' W68o 58.95'
[Reo Gallegos, Argentina]

End: S52o 25.03' W68o 14.14'
[east entrance Strait of Magellan]

Elapsed-time to Complete Leg: 0.3 Days

Calculated Great Circle Distance: 56.6
Nautical Miles [65 Miles]

**Actual Distance Travel due to
Beating:** 56.6 Nautical Miles

Average Boat Speed: 8.3 Knots

Boat Speed Made Good: 8.3 Knots

Average Wind Speed: 22.0 Knots

**Average Wind Direction
from True North:** 292.7o

Average Current Drift: 0.0 Knots at
Average Current Set: 000o

Average Wave Height: 5.0 Feet

Average Sea Temperature: 48.7o F

Average Air Temperature: 50.3o F

Average Percentage Risk of Calms: 0.0%

Average Percentage Risk of Gales: 0.0%

LEG 2

VESSEL PERFORMANCE AND WEATHER
CONDITIONS REPORT

Start: S52° 25.03' W68° 14.14'
[Strait of Magellan]

End: S52° 26.66' W69° 29.72'
[Strait of Magellan]

Elapsed-time to Complete Leg: 0.7 Days

Calculated Great Circle Distance: 46.1
Nautical Miles [53 Miles]

Actual Distance Travel due to Beating:
46.1 Nautical Miles

Average Boat Speed: 2.8 Knots

Boat Speed Made Good: 2.8 Knots

Average Wind Speed: 18.7 Knots

Average Wind Direction from True North:
283.9°

Average Current Drift: 0.0 Knots at
Average Current Set: 000°

Average Wave Height: 5.0 Feet

Average Sea Temperature: 48.2° F

Average Air Temperature: 49.7° F

Average Percentage Risk of Calms: 0.0%

Average Percentage Risk of Gales: 0.0%

LEG 3

VESSEL PERFORMANCE AND WEATHER
CONDITIONS REPORT

Start: S52° 26.66' W69° 29.72'
[Strait of Magellan]

End: S52° 38.86' W69° 47.11'
[Strait of Magellan]

Elapsed-time to Complete Leg: 0.1 Days

Calculated Great Circle Distance: 16.1
Nautical Miles [18.5 Miles]

**Actual Distance Travel due to
Beating:** 16.1 Nautical Miles

Average Boat Speed: 8.0 Knots

Boat Speed Made Good: 8.0 Knots

Average Wind Speed: 24.0 Knots

**Average Wind Direction
from True North:** 045.0°

Average Current Drift: 0.0 Knots at
Average Current Set: 000°

Average Wave Height: 5.3 Feet

Average Sea Temperature: 48.0° F

Average Air Temperature: 49.0° F

Average Percentage Risk of Calms: 0.0%

Average Percentage Risk of Gales: 0.0%

LEG 4

VESSEL PERFORMANCE AND WEATHER
CONDITIONS REPORT

Start: S52° 38.86' W69° 47.11'
[Strait of Magellan]

End: S52° 45.34' W70° 31.25'
[Strait of Magellan]

Elapsed-time to Complete Leg: 0.6 Days

Calculated Great Circle Distance: 27.5
Nautical Miles [31.6 Miles]

Actual Distance Travel due to
Beating: 30.9 Nautical Miles

Average Boat Speed: 2.2 Knots

Boat Speed Made Good: 1.9 Knots

Average Wind Speed: 19.5 Knots

Average Wind Direction
from True North: 256.0°

Average Current Drift: 0.0 Knots at
Average Current Set: 000°

Average Wave Height: 1.9 Feet

Average Sea Temperature: 46.9° F

Average Air Temperature: 48.1° F

Average Percentage Risk of Calms: 3.8%

Average Percentage Risk of Gales: 8.4%

LEG 5

VESSEL PERFORMANCE AND WEATHER CONDITIONS REPORT

Start: S52° 45.34 W70° 31.25'
[Strait of Magellan]

End: S54° 0.73 W71° 0.68'
[Strait of Magellan]

Elapsed-time to Complete Leg: 0.7 Days

Calculated Great Circle Distance: 77.4
Nautical Miles [88.9 Miles]

Actual Distance Travel due to
Beating: 77.4 Nautical Miles

Average Boat Speed: 4.6 Knots

Boat Speed Made Good: 4.6 Knots

Average Wind Speed: 19.1 Knots

Average Wind Direction
from True North: 270.0°

Average Current Drift: 0.0 Knots at
Average Current Set: 000°

Average Wave Height: 1.6 Feet

Average Sea Temperature: 46.9° F

Average Air Temperature: 48.0° F

Average Percentage Risk of Calms: 4.0%

Average Percentage Risk of Gales: 9.0%

LEG 6

VESSEL PERFORMANCE AND WEATHER CONDITIONS REPORT

Start: S54° 0.73' W71° 0.68'
[Strait of Magellan]

End: S53° 21.92' W72° 59.73'
[Strait of Magellan]

Elapsed-time to Complete Leg: 2.1 Days

Calculated Great Circle Distance: 80.5
Nautical Miles [92.4 Miles]

Actual Distance Travel due to
Beating: 83.8 Nautical Miles

Average Boat Speed: 1.7 Knots

Boat Speed Made Good: 1.6 Knots

Average Wind Speed: 19.1 Knots

Average Wind Direction
from True North: 270.0°

Average Current Drift: 0.0 Knots at
Average Current Set: 000°

Average Wave Height: 1.6 Feet

Average Sea Temperature: 46.9° F

Average Air Temperature: 48° F

Average Percentage Risk of Calms: 4.0%

Average Percentage Risk of Gales: 9.0% °

LEG 7

VESSEL PERFORMANCE AND WEATHER CONDITIONS REPORT

Start: S53° 21.92' W72° 59.73'
[Strait of Magellan]

End: S52° 53.02' W73° 55.25'
[west end of Strait of Magellan]

Elapsed-time to Complete Leg: 1.8 Days

Calculated Great Circle Distance: 44.1
Nautical Miles [50.6 Miles]

Actual Distance Travel due to
Beating: 44.2 Nautical Miles

Average Boat Speed: 1.0 Knots

Boat Speed Made Good: 1.0 Knots

Average Wind Speed: 19.2 Knots

Average Wind Direction
from True North: 19.2°

Average Current Drift: 0.9 Knots at
Average Current Set: 135.0°

Average Wave Height: 1.8 Feet

Average Sea Temperature: 46.8° F

Average Air Temperature: 48° F

Average Percentage Risk of Calms: 4.0%

Average Percentage Risk of Gales: 9.0%

LEG 8

VESSEL PERFORMANCE AND WEATHER CONDITIONS REPORT

Start: S52° 53.02' W73° 55.25'
[west end of Strait of Magellan]

End: S52° 38.45' W73° 43.21'
[south end of Lee Islands, Chile]

Elapsed-time to Complete Leg: 0.1 Days

Calculated Great Circle Distance: 16.3
Nautical Miles [18.7 Miles]

Actual Distance Travel due to
Beating: 16.3 Nautical Miles

Average Boat Speed: 7.8 Knots

Boat Speed Made Good: 7.8 Knots

Average Wind Speed: 19.1 Knots

Average Wind Direction
from True North: 270.0°

Average Current Drift: 0.0 Knots at
Average Current Set: 000°

Average Wave Height: 1.6 Feet

Average Sea Temperature: 46.9° F

Average Air Temperature: 48.0° F

Average Percentage Risk of Calms: 4.0%

Average Percentage Risk of Gales: 9.0%

Summary of Computer Simulation of Mulek's Voyage Passage Four

Total days sailing toward the Lee
Islands, west coast Chile: 6.3 days (7)

Average Boat Speed: 2.5 Knots

Boat Speed Made Good: 2.4 Knots

Total length of voyage: 364.6 Nautical
Miles [418.5 Miles]

Approximate arrival time per the simulation: fourth week of December

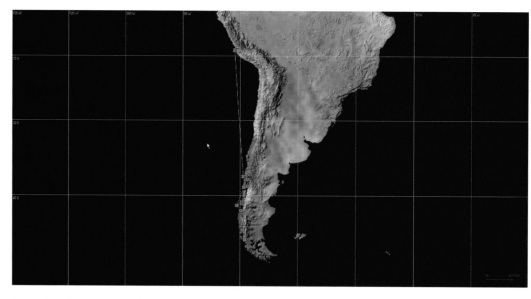

Simulated legs of Mulekite passage along western coast of South America to Peru.

Stage Five

Fortunately, the final segment of their voyage returned the Phoenicians and their passengers to fair sailing conditions. Their passage northward along the Pacific coast of South America would have been a welcome relief. The Humboldt Current and the southwest winds would have meant a speedily northward voyage to Peru and a safe harbor.

Passage Summary Report

Passage Filename: C:\PROGRAM FILES\
VISUAL PASSAGE PLANNER 2\MULEK 4.PP2

Passage Creation Date: 3/16/2009

Pilot Chart Data Used: Actual dates
based on departure specified

Vessel Profile Used: C:\Program Files\
Visual Passage Planner 2\Hagoth.VP

Minimum Speed Set: 0.50 Knots

Fuel Consumption Set: 0.00 Units/Hour

Currents: ON

Current Values Used: Average All

Wind Values Used: Average All

Waypoint #	Latitude	Longitude Date
1	S52°23.00'	W73°42.89'
2	S50°50.02'	W74°22.30'
3	S50°11.60'	W74°44.63'
4	S49°49.65'	W74°20.98'
5	S47°40.65'	W74°45.94'
6	S46°45.34'	W75°50.30'
7	S43°28.92'	W74°1.28'
8	S43°18.43'	W73°8.74'
9	S42°3.11'	W73°0.86'
10	S41°30.79'	W74°10.48'
11	S13°37.06'	W76°29.70'

General Information	Data
Calculated Great Circle Distance	2429.7 NM
Calculated Rhumbline Distance	2429.7 NM
Actual Distance Traveled due to Beating	2445.4 NM
Elapsed Time to Complete Passage	23.8 Days
Fuel Consumption	0.0 Units
Average Boat Speed	4.3 Knots
Boat Speed Made Good	4.3 Knots

LEG 1

Departure Date 20 December Passage Five

VESSEL PERFORMANCE AND WEATHER CONDITIONS REPORT

Start: S52° 23.00' W73° 42.89' [south end of Lee Islands, Chile]

End: S50° 50.02' W74° 22.30' [inside Lee Islands, Chile]

Elapsed-time to Complete Leg: 1.3 Days

Calculated Great Circle Distance: 96.1 Nautical Miles [110.3 Miles]

Actual Distance Travel due to Beating: 96.5 Nautical Miles

Average Boat Speed: 3.0 Knots

Boat Speed Made Good: 3.0 Knots

Average Wind Speed: 13.6 Knots

Average Wind Direction from True North: 278.0°

Average Current Drift: 0.7 Knots at **Average Current Set:** 161.8°

Average Wave Height: 7.2 Feet

Average Sea Temperature: 46.2° F

Average Air Temperature: 45.7° F

Average Percentage Risk of Calms: 2.9%

Average Percentage Risk of Gales: 5.9%

LEG 2:

VESSEL PERFORMANCE AND WEATHER CONDITIONS REPORT

Start: S50° 50.02' W74° 22.30' [inside Lee Islands, Chile]

End: S50° 11.60' W74° 44.63' [inside Lee Islands, Chile]

Elapsed-time to Complete Leg: 1.0 Days

Calculated Great Circle Distance: 41.0 Nautical Miles [47.0 Miles]

Actual Distance Travel due to Beating: 43.7 Nautical Miles

Average Boat Speed: 1.9 Knots

Boat Speed Made Good: 1.8 Knots

Average Wind Speed: 11.5 Knots

Average Wind Direction from True North: 315°

Average Current Drift: 0.2 Knots at **Average Current Set:** 225.0°

Average Wave Height: 7.7 Feet

Average Sea Temperature: 47.4° F

Average Air Temperature: 46.8° F

Average Percentage Risk of Calms: 11.0%

Average Percentage Risk of Gales: 0.0%

LEG 3

VESSEL PERFORMANCE AND WEATHER CONDITIONS REPORT

Start: S50° 11.60' W74° 44.63' [inside Lee Islands, Chile]

End: S49° 49.65' W74° 20.98' [inside Lee Islands, Chile]

Elapsed-time to Complete Leg: 0.2 Days

Calculated Great Circle Distance: 26.7 Nautical Miles [30.7 Miles]

Actual Distance Travel due to Beating: 27.7 Nautical Miles

Average Boat Speed: 4.5 Knots

Boat Speed Made Good: 4.5 Knots

Average Wind Speed: 11.9 Knots

**Average Wind Direction
from True North:** 315.0°

Average Current Drift: 0.3 Knots at
Average Current Set: 225.0°

Average Wave Height: 5.5 Feet

Average Sea Temperature: 47.8° F

Average Air Temperature: 48.1° F

Average Percentage Risk of Calms: 7.3%

Average Percentage Risk of Gales: 5.0%

LEG 4

VESSEL PERFORMANCE AND WEATHER CONDITIONS REPORT

Start: S49° 49.65' W74° 20.98'
[inside Lee Islands, Chile]

End: S47° 40.65' W74° 45.94'
[inside Lee Islands, Chile]

Elapsed-time to Complete Leg: 3.1 Days

Calculated Great Circle Distance:
130.1 Nautical Miles [149.4 Miles]

**Actual Distance Travel due to
Beating:** 131.1 Nautical Miles

Average Boat Speed: 1.7 Knots

Boat Speed Made Good: 1.7 Knots

Average Wind Speed: 12.8 Knots

**Average Wind Direction
from True North:** 315.0°

Average Current Drift: 0.4 Knots at
Average Current Set: 180.0°

Average Wave Height: 3.5 Feet

Average Sea Temperature: 48.6° F

Average Air Temperature: 49.8° F

Average Percentage Risk of Calms: 2.5%

Average Percentage Risk of Gales: 9.3%

LEG 5

VESSEL PERFORMANCE AND WEATHER CONDITIONS REPORT

Start: S47° 40.65' W74° 45.94'
[inside Lee Islands, Chile]

End: S46° 45.34' W75° 50.30'
[Lee Shore, Chile]

Elapsed-time to Complete Leg: 1.5 Days

Calculated Great Circle Distance: 70.5
Nautical Miles [80.9 Miles]

**Actual Distance Travel due to
Beating:** 74.7 Nautical Miles

Average Boat Speed: 2.1 Knots

Boat Speed Made Good: 2.0 Knots

Average Wind Speed: 15.6 Knots

**Average Wind Direction
from True North:** 284.0°

Average Current Drift: 0.3 Knots at
Average Current Set: 128.6°

Average Wave Height: 7.8 Feet

Average Sea Temperature: 50.7° F

Average Air Temperature: 50.1° F

Average Percentage Risk of Calms: 0.2%

Average Percentage Risk of Gales: 3.9%

LEG 6

VESSEL PERFORMANCE AND WEATHER CONDITIONS REPORT

Start: S46° 45.34' W75° 50.30'
[Lee Shore, Chile]

End: S43° 28.92' W74° 1.28'
[Lee Shore, Chile]

Elapsed-time to Complete Leg: 1.5 Days

Calculated Great Circle Distance:
210.9 Nautical Miles [242.1 Miles]

**Actual Distance Travel due to
Beating:** 210.9 Nautical Miles

Average Boat Speed: 6.0 Knots

Boat Speed Made Good: 6.0 Knots

Average Wind Speed: 13.7 Knots

**Average Wind Direction
from True North:** 261.6°

Average Current Drift: 0.3 Knots at
Average Current Set: 135.0°

Average Wave Height: 7.1 Feet

Average Sea Temperature: 52.1° F

Average Air Temperature: 51.8° F

Average Percentage Risk of Calms: 0.5%

Average Percentage Risk of Gales: 1.8%

LEG 7

VESSEL PERFORMANCE AND WEATHER CONDITIONS REPORT

Start: S43° 28.92' W74° 1.28'
[Lee Shore, Chile]

End: S43° 18.43' W73° 8.74'
[Lee Shore, Chile]

Elapsed-time to Complete Leg: 0.3 Days

Calculated Great Circle Distance:
39.6 Nautical Miles [45.5 Miles]

**Actual Distance Travel due to
Beating:** 39.6 Nautical Miles

Average Boat Speed: 5.1 Knots

Boat Speed Made Good: 5.1 Knots

Average Wind Speed: 9.0 Knots

**Average Wind Direction
from True North:** 270.0°

Average Current Drift: 0.3 Knots at
Average Current Set: 270.0°

Average Wave Height: 6.6 Feet

Average Sea Temperature: 53.3° F

Average Air Temperature: 53.1° F

Average Percentage Risk of Calms: 0.0%

Average Percentage Risk of Gales: 0.0%

LEG 8

VESSEL PERFORMANCE AND WEATHER CONDITIONS REPORT

Start: S43° 18.43' W73° 8.74'
[Lee Shore, Chile]

End: S42° 3.11' W73° 0.86'
[Lee Shore, Chile]

Elapsed-time to Complete Leg: 0.6 Days

Calculated Great Circle Distance: 75.5
Nautical Miles [86.7 Miles]

Actual Distance Travel due to
Beating: 75.5 Nautical Miles

Average Boat Speed: 5.7 Knots

Boat Speed Made Good: 5.7 Knots

Average Wind Speed: 10.3 Knots

Average Wind Direction
from True North: 239.1°

Average Current Drift: 0.3 Knots at
Average Current Set: 270.0°

Average Wave Height: 6.8 Feet

Average Sea Temperature: 53.7° F

Average Air Temperature: 53.5° F

Average Percentage Risk of Calms: 2.1%

Average Percentage Risk of Gales: 1.4%

LEG 9

VESSEL PERFORMANCE AND WEATHER CONDITIONS REPORT

Start: S42° 3.11' W73° 0.86'
[Lee Shore, Chile]

End: S41° 30.79' W74° 10.48'
[Lee Shore, Chile]

Elapsed-time to Complete Leg: 0.7 Days

Calculated Great Circle Distance: 61.1
Nautical Miles [70.1 Miles]

Actual Distance Travel due to
Beating: 61.1 Nautical Miles

Average Boat Speed: 3.5 Knots

Boat Speed Made Good: 3.5 Knots

Average Wind Speed: 10.8 Knots

Average Wind Direction
from True North: 225.0°

Average Current Drift: 0.8 Knots at
Average Current Set: 045.0°

Average Wave Height: 6.8 Feet

Average Sea Temperature: 54.0° F

Average Air Temperature: 53.8° F

Average Percentage Risk of Calms: 3.1%

Average Percentage Risk of Gales: 1.9%

LEG 10

VESSEL PERFORMANCE AND WEATHER CONDITIONS REPORT

Start: S41° 30.79' W74° 10.48' [Lee
Shore, Chile]

End: S13° 37.06' W76° 29.70' [Peru]

Elapsed-time to Complete Leg: 10.9 Days

Calculated Great Circle Distance:

1,678.1 Nautical Miles [1,926.5 Miles]

Actual Distance Travel due to
Beating: 1678.1 Nautical Miles

Average Boat Speed: 6.4 Knots

Boat Speed Made Good: 6.4 Knots

Average Wind Speed: 11.5 Knots

Average Wind Direction
from True North: 184.1°

Average Current Drift: 0.6 Knots at
Average Current Set: 230.8°

Average Wave Height: 5.0 Feet

Average Sea Temperature: 60.5° F

Average Air Temperature: 61.4° F

Average Percentage Risk of Calms: 1.6%

Average Percentage Risk of Gales: 1.0%

Summary of Computer Simulation of Mulek's Voyage Passage Five

Total days sailing toward Peru: 21.1
days (21)

Average Boat Speed: 4.8 Knots

Boat Speed Made Good: 4.8 Knots

Total length of voyage: 2,429.7
Nautical Miles [2,789.3 Miles]

Approximate arrival time per the
simulation: second week of January

Tree of Life, along the shoreline of Peru, believed to be a marker for ships returning to Peru; however, the origin is still unknown. Photograph by Mylene d'Auriol Stoessel.

At last the Phoenicians could drop off their passengers, trade for drugs for their Egyptian patrons, make repairs on their ship, and return to the Mediterranean. Cussler describes such a Phoenician journey home:

> While the captain wrote in his log, the crew celebrated late into the night. They were astir well before dawn, and the sun was just peeking over the trees as they cast off the mooring lines. Powered by the ranks of oarsmen and the wind, the ship moved swiftly out into the bay, the rowers putting their backs into their work. Like every other man on board, they were impatient to return home.[33]

Notes

1. George Potter, *Nephi in the Promised Land* (Springville, Utah: CFI, 2009), 12, 13.

2. *Collected Works of Hugh Nibley*, vol. 6, 46.

3. Ibid., vol. 8, 542.

4. John L. Sorenson, "When Lehi's Party Arrived in the Land, Did They Find Others?" *Journal of Book of Mormon Studies* 1, (Fall 1992): 13.

5. "Trade and Ships," Pheonician Enterprising, accessed Sept. 2009, http://phoenicia.org/trade.html

6. Clive Cussler, with Paul Kemprecos, *The Navigator* (New York: Berkley Books, 2008), 3–4.

7. *Collected Works of Hugh Nibley*, vol.6, 40–41.

8. Ibid., 44.

9. John L. Sorenson, "Ancient Voyages Across the Ocean to America: From 'Impossible' to 'Certain,'" *Journal of Book of Mormon Studies* 14, no. 1 (2005): 4, 5.

10. Ibid., 2, 3, 5.

11. Potter and Wellington, *Lehi in the Wilderness*, 17, 18.

12. James E. Talmage, *Articles of Faith* (Salt Lake City: Deseret Book, 1984), 262.

CHAPTER FIVE

13. John L. Sorenson, "The Mulekites," BYU Studies, 30, no. 3 (1990): 9.

14. Dick Grasso, *La Representatación de America en mapas romanas de tiempos de Cristo* (Buenos Aires, 1970).

15. Julio C. Tello, *Arqueologia del valle de Casma* (Lima, 1956).

16. Bernardo de Azevedo da Silva Ramos, *Inscricoes e tradicoes da America pre-historica, especialmente do* (Brasil, Rio de Janeiro: Imrrenta, 1930).

17. David Alexander, "Map that named America is a puzzle for researchers", Reuters, Dec. 3, 2007), 1, http://www.reuters.com/article/newsOne/idUSN0332239320071203.

18. Gavin Menzies, *1421, The Year China Discovered the World* (New York: Bantam Books, 2003), 139–40.

19. No author stated, "Nabataeans in Antarctica," *Nabataen Travel and Trade, Nabataea.net* (Nabataea.net, April 1, 2009), 2.

20. Menzies, *1421*, 140.

21. No author stated, "Nabataeans in Antarctica," 1–2.

22. Cederland website, "Phoenician Vessels," http://www.oocities/capitolhill/parliament/2587/ships.html, accessed 8 June 2007.

23. Ibid.

24. John Illsley, "History and Archaeology of the Ship, Lecture Notes," web article, 1999.

25. William Sullivan, *The Secret of the Incas* (New York: Three Rivers Press, 1996), 226.

26. John M. Lundquist and Stephen D. Ricks, eds., "By Study and Also by Faith: Essays in Honor of Hugh W. Nibley on the Occasion of His Eightieth Birthday," 27 March 1990, 2 vols., 1:72.

27. Clive Cussler, *The Navigator* (Putnam Adult, 2007), 2–4.

28. Menzies, *1421*, 281.

29. Ibid., 145.

30. Jack London, *The Works of Jack London*, 261.

31. Ibid., 259.

32. Dana, *Two Years Before the Mast*, 70–71.

33. Cussler, *The Navigator*, 11.

Kauai's Na Pali coastline

Raise your sail one foot, and you get ten feet of wind.

CHINESE PROVERB

HAGOTH'S AND OTHER NEPHITE VOYAGES

THE NEPHITE homeland in the first century BC was a place of great fear. The Lamanite wars were driving the Nephites toward the sea. The great city of Zarahemla had fallen to the Lamanites. Wicked people prevailed while the righteous were persecuted. During these precarious days, "an exceedingly curious man" man named Hagoth built a very large ship (Alma 63:5). So fine was the vessel and so difficult was life in the promised land in his time that it seems Hagoth had no shortage of volunteers willing to sail away with him. "Behold, there were many of

A bay in Hawaii

CHAPTER SIX

the Nephites who did enter therein and did sail forth with much provisions, and also many women and children; and they took their course northward" (Alma 63:6).

A year later, Hagoth returned and built other ships. With his enlarged fleet, he took many more colonists northward from Peru (Alma 63:7). However, Hagoth was not the only shipbuilder at the time. Another ship was built that perhaps followed Hagoth's instructions for traveling north (Alma 63:8).

So, where did all these immigrants go? Did they go to some upper areas of the northern end of South America? To the area of Panama? To Central America? To Mexico? Where might they have gone? Could they have gone to several locales?

In 1851, while serving a mission in Hawaii, Elder George Q. Cannon began teaching the Hawaiians that their Polynesian ancestors included people from the Book of Mormon. Later, Brother Cannon became a counselor in the First Presidency. In a letter written to the Hawaiian king Kamehameha V, President Brigham Young outlined the same information that has been affirmed by other Church leaders: among the Polynesians' ancestors

were the people of Hagoth. President Joseph F. Smith said, "I would like to say to you brethren and sisters . . . you are some of Hagoth's people, and there is NO PERHAPS about it!"[1] President Heber J. Grant again endorsed this doctrine in the dedication prayer of the Hawaii Temple, saying that there were descendants of Lehi in Hawaii.[2]

Jerry K. Loveland has studied extensively the Hagoth-Polynesian topic. He writes that although "we have not . . . found irrefutable evidence in the histories and/or genealogies of the Polynesians to suggest that they had a tradition of Hagoth's voyages,"[3] he concluded that:

"Our question here . . . is whether we can find any tradition that suggests an affinity with the Hagoth account in the Book of Mormon, any event that occurred 1,600 years before the first Europeans entered the Pacific to note and record any Polynesian traditions. The answer here is yes, but [it is confusing]. . . . In 1920, [Craig] Handy recorded a Marquesan tradition of a great double-canoe, the Kaahua, which sailed from Hivaoa east to Tafiti. (The Polynesian word Tafiti or Tahiti designates a foreign place.) Some explorers left the vessel there while others returned. Handy's informant insisted

that the [return] voyage was in the direction of the rising sun, that is, toward South America, not southwest toward the island of Tahiti.

"The most striking Polynesian account of a Hagoth-like voyage is that of Hawaii Loa, or Hawaii-nui. (He is called Hawaii Loa or Ke Kowa I Hawaii in the Fornander story and Hawaii-nui in the Kepelino version.) More tradition has it that Hawaii Loa and Hagoth are the same person, and LDS temple records show them as being the same. The Hawaii Loa story is a part of the Kumuhonua legends referred to above."[4]

In the Hawaii Loa story, a great fisherman and navigator went on long voyages, including a voyage to a westward land and returned with some white men.[5] Although the Kumuhonua legends, which were recorded in 1886 are possibly true, the origins of the legends are considered "discredited."[6]

All the same, Bruce S. Sutton uses the Hawaii Loa legend to suggest that Book of Mormon people were the first to colonize Hawaii. While all other Polynesian genealogies begin with the demigods Wakea and Papa, the Hawaiian pedigree begins with Hawaii Loa and at a later period includes

Wakea and Papa.[7] The implication here is that Book of Mormon people first colonized Hawaii, which was later colonized by waves of Polynesians from the far-off islands of the Eastern Polynesia.

So, although we cannot confirm Hagoth's voyage to Hawaii using Polynesian oral tradition, we can be certain that Peruvians had the ability to sail to and from Hawaii. Indeed, the original pre-Book of Mormon people of South America may have arrived in the Americas by ship! Recent discoveries in Chile suggest that humans have lived there for more than thirty thousand years, an age that preceded the opening of the land bridge between Asia and North America. The new discoveries prompted Charles Mann to say in his book *1491*: "Perhaps the first people traveled [to Chile] by boat, and didn't need the land bridge."[8] The Spanish chronicler Cabello Valboa (a great-nephew of Vasco Nuñez Balboa, who discovered the Pacific for the Europeans), wrote that according to the legends of the Incas, in primordial times, the Peruvians were invaded by people from the sea in a fleet of balsas.[9] The first encounter by the Spanish with the Incas was at sea, when they saw a large Inca balsas ship (probably a catamaran). The Inca ship was three hundred miles from

its home port in Peru and was in route to trade with an island in the Pacific.[10]

It is clear the Peruvians maintained a significant seafaring culture from the time of the Nephites to the arrival of the Spanish. In his book *Voices from the Dust*, David G. Calderwood indicates not only the amazing level of Peruvian maritime skills but also relates how the Incas were possibly duplicating Hagoth's feat:

> In Peru, Martín de Murúa wrote that in the late 1400s, the Lord Inca Tupa Inca Yupanqui [also spelled Topa Inca Yupanqui], father of Inca Huayna Cápac, finished the great fortress at Sacsahuamán near Cuzco, which his father Pachacuti Inca Yupanqui had begun many years earlier. After this project was finished, according to several elderly Indians who served as informants for Murúa, Tupa Inca Yupanqui went north overland to the mouth of the Guayas River [the modern city of Guayaquil, Ecuador, is located at the mouth of the Guayas River] and embarked by raft or barge and sailed into the Pacific Ocean for more than one year. Murúa's informants, Tupa Inca Yupanqui claimed to have reached some islands which he called *Hahua Chumpi* and *Niña Chumpi* …

> Manuel Ballasteros Gambrois, who edited and annotated the 1987 edition of

Murúa's book, wrote that in Quechua *Chumpi* means a belt or a ring and *Nina* means fire. Ballasteros suggests that Tupa Inca Yupanqui may have discovered some islands surrounded by fire or where there was an active volcano. The similarity in the sounds between *Hahua* or Hawa and Hawaii cannot be overlooked nor considered mere coincidence, especially when coupled with the description of a ring of fire, possibly in reference to a volcano. Captain Cook did not discover the Sandwich Islands (Hawaiian Islands) until 1778, many years after Murúa wrote his manuscript in 1611; consequently, Murúa could not have known the name. From Murúa's description, it is possible that Tupa Inca Yupanqui reached the Hawaiian Islands.

The chronicler Pedro Sarmiento de Gamboa provided a similar description of the voyage of Lord Inca Tupa Inca Yupanqui into the Pacific. Sarmiento wrote that all along the coast of Peru, the natives believed that there were many islands in the Mar del Sur. Sarmiento wrote that, while Tupa Inca Yupanaqui was conquering the coast of Peru and Ecuador, some strangers arrived on the coast near Tumbez by large sail-powered rafts. They reportedly told the Lord Inca that they came from some islands called *Auachumbi* and *Niñachumbe*.

The natives reported that Tupa Inca Yupanqui built a large number of rafts and sailed toward the west with a 20,000-man army. Tupa Inca Yupanqui found the two Islands and he returned bringing with him a few people from those islands who were described as black.[11]

The ability of ancient Peruvians to sail to Polynesia was first demonstrated by Thor Heyerdahl in 1947. His balsa raft *Kon-Tiki* sailed from Lima to the Tuamotu Islands. In 1999, American explorer Phil Buck replicated Heyerdahl's feat. His pre-Columbian type of reed ship, the *Viracocha*, reached Easter Island from Chile. Heyerdahl's successful experiment, the *Kon-Tiki* voyage, led Heyerdahl to postulate that the Polynesian islands could have been colonized in part from South America.

Besides oral traditions, linguistic evidence points to South American contact with Hawaii. John L. Sorenson says:

> The name for sweet potato among Chibchan speakers of Colombia and Panama precisely matches the Hawaiian name for the plant. Kare H. Rensche's linguistic study of names for sweet potato resulted in his proposing "that the sweet potato reached Polynesia at least

twice: once via a northern route through Hawaii under the guise of kuara/kuala, and once via a southern route as kumara, with Easter Island as its point of entry."[12]

Historian Peter Marsh believes the sweet potato is direct evidence for migrations from Peru to Polynesia:

> The Kumara or sweet potato (Iqomoea Batatas) is a South American plant. In the Kechua dialect of north Peru, the name for sweet potato is Kumar. As the general name of the plant is Kumara throughout the Pacific, the tuber must have been obtained from an area that used the name Kumar.

> A small but tasty pineapple as well as tasteless paw paw (both South American plants) are found among ruins in the Marquesas. Incidentally, skulls found in burial mounds as seen by Thor Heyerdahl in the Marquesas were distinctly Caucasian, suggesting their origins were from South America. . . .

> The totora reed of Lake Titicaca [Peru/Bolivia] is used for raft building; this same reed is also found growing in abundance in the crater lake Rano Raraku on Rapa Nui [Easter Island]. There is a legend that the God Ure brought it there. Is it mere coincidence that Maoris also make their canoes out of the Totora tree?

Or is it so named because of its importance as a boat building material?[13]

Thus, in concluding this review of data, it is apparent that South American sailors reached Hawaii and the Easter Islands in ancient times. The fact that Hagoth and others built exceedingly large sailing ships capable of reaching Hawaii indicates that they came from a culture that had an advanced seafaring lore. Obviously, the Nephites had become technically advanced as shipbuilders and seaman, otherwise there would have been no Hagoth. Such skills took generations to develop and are known to have been mastered at that level by only one group of ancient people in the New World, the Peruvians. Earlier in this book we discussed at length that the ship the Lehites sailed in could not have been a raft. Does this information that large rafts with small parties sailed the Pacific undercut the conclusion? Not in the least. For the Lord's purposes, Nephi needed a ship with quarters under a deck for a great deal of seeds and storage, for their numerous younger children, for his elderly parents, for the brass plates, and for much, much more that required a ship large enough to provide the most safety, security, and convenience for its time as was possible.

The Book of Mormon tells us that as the Nephite civilization developed, they built ships large enough to transport timbers from the land of Bountiful to the land northward (see Helaman 3:10).[14] So extensive was the Nephite shipping industry that a note is written by Mormon of the Book of Mormon to explain that his record does not include a "hundredth part of the proceedings of this people . . . and their shipping and their building of ships" (Helaman 3:14). In other words, there must have been significant oceangoing shipbuilding on the part of the Nephites.

Anthropologist Jocelyn Linnekin has discovered parallels between Hawaii and Peru that could be seen as background evidence that an ancient Peruvian, possibly Hagoth, brought a Nephite culture to the islands. She writes:

> In an analysis of Andean gender, ideologist Silverblatt (1987) has used the phrase "gender parallelism." This term aptly describes Hawaiian gender relations as well. The structural and ideological similarities between Hawaii and the Inca are striking. Both were politically hierarchical societies with a pronounced degree of "gender segregation" (Silverblatt 1987:64). In both societies high-ranking women controlled material resources

of their own and exercised considerable independent authority, albeit in spheres parallel to those of men. Both Hawaii and Inca Peruvians are ethnographic footnotes for the institutions of "royal incest." Among the Inca, too, the sexual division of the cosmos is portrayed.[15]

Hagoth and Other Nephite Voyages to Hawaii

Using images on pre-Inca ceramics and also of traditional Polynesian craft designs, the famous Andean explorer Gene Savoy constructed a replica of an ancient Peruvian vessel. To the degree that it would have matched the design of Hagoth's, we can only speculate. Savoy completed his replica in 1997 and named it the *Feathered Serpent III*. The 73-foot double-hulled canoe was made from strong Peruvian mahogany. To form the catamaran, Savoy lashed the hulls together using rope. After a 42-day voyage with no motor, Savoy and his crew of seven completed their passage from Callao (Lima, Peru) to Radio Bay at Hilo, Hawaii. Savoy's voyage showed that pre-Columbian Peruvians had the technology to sail to Hawaii and beyond.[16] Since the Book of Mormon tells us that Hagoth's ship was exceedingly large, we will use Gene Savoy's replica as the prototype for

Hagoth's ship in our computer simulation that will be presented later.

Savoy started his voyage to Hawaii from the Callao, the port at Lima. As previously noted, Lima was the area the Incas called the *land of the people of desolation*. The land of desolation was the place where the Mulekites landed. However, it was *near* desolation but not *at* desolation that Hagoth built his ships and embarked on his journeys to Hawaii. The Book of Mormon tells us that this "exceedingly curious" seaman launched his ships from the west sea (Pacific) of the land of Bountiful on its northern borders by desolation, by the narrow neck of land (Alma 63:5). University of Utah anthropologist Richard Hauck, in his book *Deciphering the Geography of the Book of Mormon*, identifies the narrow neck of land as an important transportation corridor in a narrow valley leading from the Pacific into the mountains.[17] In other words, the narrow neck of land mentioned in the Book of Mormon need not be an isthmus, as is commonly believed. Rather, the narrow neck of land ran from the west sea to the east. Nowhere in the Book of Mormon does it say that the narrow neck of land ran between two seas. The "east" in ancient Peru meant the Andes Mountains. In his

179

book *Nephi in the Promised Land*, George Potter proposes that the Lurin Valley, some fifteen miles south of Lima (land of desolation), is the important transportation corridor that formed the narrow neck that the Nephites had to protect in order to keep the Lamanites from attacking the land northward from all sides. Through this narrow Lurin Valley ran the Inca's main highway from their capital in Cuzco to the area they called desolation. Joining this main highway at the mouth of the Lurin valley was the Inca's coastal highway. The Lurin Valley meets all the attributes of the Book of Mormon's narrow neck of land and it is also just south of the what appears to be the Book of Mormon's land of desolation.

An important characteristic of the Lurin Valley is that it is forested with large trees from which ships could be constructed. Another key element of the Hagoth story is the need for a protected harbor, and one is found near the Lurin Valley. Hagoth would have needed a harbor to fabricate his ships and launch them safely into the sea. In Peru, this would require a harbor that provided shelter from the strong southern swells that pound South America's western shoreline. Just ten miles from the Lurin Valley is found the Bay of Santa Maria. To

this day, the bay provides a safe harbor for fishing boats and pleasure vessels alike. We suggest that the Bay of Santa Maria is a qualified candidate for where Hagoth embarked for Hawaii. It will be our starting point for our simulation of Hagoth's voyages to the islands of the Pacific.

From Hawaii to Polynesia

Now we come to another important fact that needs discussion. While Hagoth helped colonized Hawaii, it is likely that descendants of his colony also spread Lehi's seed deep into Polynesia. The prevailing theory among many scientists is that the bulk of Polynesian ancestry came from waves after wave of migration from southern Asia. However, we know that the people of eastern Polynesia have within their blood the DNA of father Lehi. At the

Ocean-voyaging canoe leaving Hawaii. Drawing by Jose Flores.

dedication of the New Zealand Temple, President David O. McKay prayed, "We express gratitude that to these fertile lands, thou didst guide descendants of Father Lehi, and hast enabled them to prosper . . ."[18] The *Encyclopedia of Mormonism* says of the Polynesians:

> While some non-LDS scientists have insisted on their Western Hemisphere origins, the prevailing scientific opinion from anthropological, archaeological, and linguistic evidence argues a west-to-east migratory movement from Southeast Asia that began as early as 1200 BC.

> What seems clear from the long-standing debate is that considerable interaction was maintained over the centuries from many directions. The island peoples had both the vessels and the skill to sail with or against ocean currents. It would be as difficult to say that no group could have migrated from east to west as to argue that opposite in absolute terms. Church leaders, who have attested to Polynesians roots in the Nephite peoples, have not elaborated on the likelihood of other migrating groups in the Pacific or of social mixing and intermarriage.[19]

Despite attempts by some scholars, including Thor Heyerdahl, to show that the islands of the east Pacific were primarily colonized by Native Americans, their theories for the most part have fallen out of favor. Even so, Heyerdahl and his *Kon-Tiki* showed that small parties of South American sailors could have settled among the people of eastern Polynesia. And while such interactions took place between tribes of the mainland of South America and the islanders of the Pacific, the foundational culture of Polynesia existed long before Nephi's ship entered the Pacific Ocean.

Patrick Vinton Kirch writes, "The discovery of Lapita [culture] and the tracing of continuous archaeological sequences within Western Polynesia that begin with Lapita and emerge as typical Polynesian in their material culture, totally altered these older migrationist theories. Kenneth Emory, originally schooled in the migrationist paradigm, later in his career grasped the significance of the new archaeological finds from Fiji, Tonga, and Samoa when he wrote that the origins of the Polynesians would be found 'in a western archipelago in the Polynesian area about 1500 BC.'"[20] Recent DNA maps have supported the archaeological record that, for the most part, the Polynesians bloodlines are from Southeast Asia and that the Polynesian islands, with the exception of Hawaii, were populated well before Hagoth set sail from Peru.

In this context, it is important to remember that President Joseph F. Smith said to the Polynesians, "You are some [not all] of Hagoth's people." While scientific evidence points to western origins of the Polynesians, it does not exclude the real likelihood that from time to time small groups, such as Hagoth's, settled alongside and intermarried with native Polynesian people. In such a fashion, Lehi's seed would have spread throughout all of central and eastern Polynesia. For example, Peruvians have fished the Pacific Ocean for thousands of years. Even during the last decade, fishermen from Peru have been blown out to sea and ended up drifting to islands in eastern Polynesia. Gene Savoy showed that replicas of Peruvian ships could sail to Hawaii and Thor Heyerdahl showed that balsa rafts could have drifted to Easter Island (Rapa Nui). From Hawaii and Easter Island, it is likely that Lehi's seed would have been spread throughout the Pacific Islands by Polynesian sailors who visited the islands on trading missions. It should be remembered that in prior ages a customary trading commodity was unmarried daughters. It is also true that a common way of preservinghomogeneous cultures between distant tribes or a common means of solidifying bonds between tribes was to exchange brides and grooms.

Polynesian voyaging canoes were large enough to carry trading goods, including to trade brides and skilled servants. The Hawaiian proverb, *He po'e ho'opiha wa'a,* translates to "Canoe fillers," meaning useless people or riders in the canoe who did not help the crew. Another proverb from the islands, *Ha'alele koa wa'a i koa kanaka,* translated to "The koa canoe departed, leaving the warriors behind." This was said when the voyaging canoe departed and left people behind.[21] Over the ages, certainly some of the "canoe fillers" could have been descendants of Hagoth from Hawaii or other Peruvians via Easter Island. For example, Thor Heyerdahl was convinced that Peruvian stonemasons practiced their trade on Rapa Nui (Easter Island). And scientists have wondered how the native South America sweet potato became a food staple throughout Polynesia. Perhaps better questions would be: *Who were the women who carried the sweet potato with them and who cooked it for their families? Or who are the descendants of these stone-carving South Americans?*

Catamaran-voyaging canoes allowed small parties to sail between distant islands. Drawing by Jose Flores.

What is often unappreciated is that DNA markers mask the introduction of small groups of people into a greater population, and as such have little meaning when it comes to the broad standards for membership in the house of Israel. According to Scott Woodward, director of the Sorenson Molecular Genealogy Foundation, when a small group of people intermarry into a much larger population, their DNA marker could disappear completely even though millions of people have descended from the small group.[22] British geneticist Steve Jones illustrated this fact by showing how the famous Yemenite Jews, who strongly discouraged intermarrying, had over time lost all of their Hebrew DNA markers and had taken on the DNA of the greater Arab population.[23]

On the other hand, it would seem quite naïve to believe that the Polynesians who sailed great distances between the Pacific Islands were not partially descendants of people from the American continents that were to their east. Certainly, islanders would have ventured to the Americas and sailors from the promised land would have ventured to islands of the Pacific. In combination, these sailors of the Pacific spread the seed of Lehi across the world's largest ocean. Here is an excerpt from a letter written by the First Presidency to the Saints of the New Zealand Mission in response to their request that an Apostle attend a New Zealand Mission conference. The letter is written in such a manner as to suggest that it was read from the pulpit.

February 6, 1911

To the Officers and Members of The Church of Jesus Christ of Latter-day Saints of the New Zealand Mission, in General Conference assembled:

[This excerpt is several pages into the letter:]

But here, beloved brethren and sisters, let us pause a moment and raise the question in our own minds, why you, in common with others of your race inhabiting the isles of the sea, were to be more greatly blessed and favored of the Lord than the rest of the remnant of the house of Israel inhabiting this our land of America? Was it because of any desire on the part of our Heavenly Father to bestow blessings upon you, upon your brethren and sisters of Samoa, Hawaii, Tahiti and other places, over and above those of your brothers and sisters, also of the house of Israel, living on the American continent?

No, it was simply because your forefathers, who were first moved upon to occupy the isles of the sea, and who did so under the immediate overruling hand of the God of your fathers, were better than the rest of their brethren who occupied this continent, [and] because they were more obedient and more faithful, the Lord in His superior wisdom, directed their course away from this continent to their island homes, that they might be separated from their more wicked, disobedient brethren, that they might not be left to be preyed upon and destroyed by the more wicked part of the house of Israel [...].

This, dear brethren and sisters, is the key to your preservation as a nation, also to the preservation of your brothers and sisters of the other isles of the sea before mentioned, and this is the secret of the overruling hand of providence which has been over you all from that time until you received the gospel through the preaching of the elders [...].

And we repeat, the reason that you of the isles of the sea have been more highly favored and blessed of the Lord than those of your brethren of this continent is because of the worthiness of your forefathers who were led away and separated from their brethren of this continent, and because of the blessing of the Lord which has attended you, their children, from that time to the present.[24]

The remarkable sailing legacy of the eastern Polynesians began when the first settlers landed in Samoa and Tonga aboard voyaging canoes. Aboard these vessels they carried plants, animals, and the language of their place of origins. These original colonizers of the islands of the eastern Pacific established in Samoa and Tonga the *cradle of Polynesia*. From this cultural birthplace, bold sailors eventually boarded canoes and explored northward as far as Hawaii, eastward to the Rapa Nui, and southwest to New Zealand. This process of discovering the distant islands of the Pacific took the Polynesians over two thousand years. To their credit, these brave sailors had colonized the vast Pacific long before the Europeans began their Age of Exploration.[25]

183

The Polynesians' command of the entire Pacific is illustrated by a story Conrad tells. For four years, Conrad crabbed and fished in the waters of the Shumagin Islands and Aleutian Islands that are located in the Gulf of Alaska and the Bering Sea. During these years, Conrad met a man he called Grandfather Gilbert. The elderly man had come asking for work one day. During the interview, Conrad found out that the man was sixty-eight years old but had never worked for wages. Grandfather Gilbert had been a fisherman and trapper his entire life. At the time, he was out of food and heating oil and was hoping he could work through the winter until he could go gill-netting salmon. It was standard policy in Alaska to put the needy to work. During the winter months, Conrad and Grandfather Gilbert became friends and shared many stories. At the time, Conrad had been reading and studying about Polynesians and their trade route that started in Hawaii, thence to Japan, then to Alaska via Aleutian and Shumagan Islands, then to south eastern Alaska, then down the outside of Vancouver Island and on to Washington/Oregon/California coasts and finally back to Hawaii.

A discussion came up between Conrad and Grandfather Gilbert if there were any knowledge of these Polynesian voyages that had been handed down from early times. Grandfather Gilbert said that when his great-great-grandfather was a young boy of eight, which he estimated to be at about the year 1800, a Polynesian twin-hulled vessel of about eighty feet long with two inverted sails arrived late in the season and decided to winter in the Shumagan Islands on Popof Island. All the Hawaiians wore fur seal-skin cloths, parkas, boots, and gloves that were constructed to be water tight. The vessel was full of trade goods, food, salt, spices, fresh water stored in containers, and much fishing gear. As a confirmation of Grandfather Gilbert's information, Conrad learned from the Aleuts that Hawaiians had been trading in the Aleutian and Shumagin Islands on their way back to Hawaii for as long as history could be remembered.

John L. Sorenson has studied the distribution of plants across the Pacific and believes that such botanical evidence proves ancient sailors were trading throughout the Pacific. He writes:

> Methods of research familiar to botanists who study the distribution of plants were also involved in our study. For example, turmeric, *Curuma longa*, was originally Asiatic (it had names in Sanskrit, Chinese, Hebrew, and Arabic), and from there it spread eastward throughout many Pacific islands. So when we learn that turmeric was also grown by native people in the remote Amazon River drainage of eastern Peru, the conclusion seems inescapable—it was carried to South America, presumably from the islands, on some prehistoric voyage.
>
> Other evidence from distributions concerns that of the bottle gourd, *Lagenario siceraria*. Some have proposed that it was capable of drifting across an ocean, although scientists are uncertain whether seeds would still grow after a months-long float to some American beach. But the gourd was absent from western Polynesia, although it does appear in the islands of eastern Polynesia. Obviously, the gourd did not drift from island to island all the way across the Pacific to Peru or else the species would have grown in western Polynesia as well. Yet it appeared in an archaeological site on the coast of Peru almost 5,000 years ago. The only scenario that makes sense of these facts has Asian mariners carrying gourds in their vessels from Asia or the western Pacific to western South America thousands of years ago. Later voyages could have carried the plant to eastern Polynesia, but not farther west,

from the mainland aboard vessels like the *Kon-Tiki* raft.[26]

Ancient trading between the Pacific islands is not speculation. Hard archaeological evidence backs the Polynesian oral traditions, botanical evidences, and linguistic clues. While conducting research for Hawaii's Bishop Museum, anthropologist Kenneth Emory discovered several basalt-stone adzes in Tuamotus in central Polynesia. Volcanic rock does not exist naturally on the coral atolls of the Tuamotus. Chemical analysis by the University of Queensland in Australia indicates that the basalt rock of the Tuamotus' adzes originated in Hawaii, nearly 2,500 miles away:

> This innovative multi-discipline research by the University of Queensland researchers has provided the first physical confirmation of the remarkable voyages from Hawai'i to central Polynesia that are documented in the oral histories.
>
> By confirming the extent of ancient inter-island trade within East Polynesia, they have also resolved a fundamental and long-standing archaeological problem concerning migration and cultural exchange within East Polynesia, the last region on Earth settled by humans during prehistory. This uninterrupted

travel between Hawai'i and the Tuamotus represents the longest documented voyage in world prehistory.[27]

As noted in the previous chapter, linguist Karl H. Rensch believes that the South America sweet potato reached Polynesia at least twice: once via Hawaii and again by way of the Easter Islands. The oral traditions of Peru, Easter Island (Rapa Nui), and Hawaii confirm that trade interactions existed between the ancient islanders and the native people of the Americas. In additon, replica ships constructed by Thor Heyerdahl, Gene Savoy, and Phil Buck have demonstrated that Peruvian sailors possessed the technology to reach Hawaii and Easter Island. It would be naïve to suggest that descendants of Lehi did not sail aboard Polynesian voyaging canoes. Not only would they be among the Polynesian crews, they certainly intermarried among peoples of the Pacific islands.

The Polynesian Voyaging Canoes

Surprisingly, the exact nature of the ocean-voyaging canoes used by the ancient Polynesians to explore and trade is not known. Original designs have been lost with time. As Herb Kawainui Kane notes, "Ships are as mortal as their makers."[28]

Except for fragments of ancient canoes that have been found in New Zealand and petroglyphs of ships on Easter Island, no model is available from which to reconstruct an "ancient" Polynesian canoe.[29] The drawings in this chapter by Jose Flores are research-based on *Hokelea*, the replica ocean-voyaging canoe that Kane designed for the Polynesian Voyaging Society. The hulls of the *Hokelea* were most constructed of fiberglass whereas traditional voyaging canoes were constructed of wood. To obtain the same amount of flotation from wood for a similar number of crew and passengers estimated for *Hokelea*, the wooden hulls would need to have been considerably larger. Also, in order to have the same freeboard (the distance between the waterline and the deck) the hulls would have been greater in size. If Hagoth's ships were voyaging canoes, we are postulating that the design of *Hokelea* accurately reflects in a general way ships of that period for Hagoth's exodus from Peru.

Also, we are postulating that the sailing rig of *Hokelea* is accurate for Hagoth's period, which it very well may not be. For example, because the voyage from Peru to Hawaii is pretty much off wind, Hagoth's rig could well have been a square rig.

185

Describing his effort to rediscover the elements of ancient Polynesian ships, Kane reports:

> What were the design features of the ancient double-hulled voyaging canoes (*vaka taurua*)? Applying the "age-distribution" method, we assume that similarities in hull shape, sail shape, and construction techniques which were widely distributed when Europeans arrived must have been carried outward from the centers of cultural diffusion during ancient eras of exploration and settlement, and may be accepted as features of the ancient canoes. By limiting the design of a voyaging canoe to these features, a performance-accurate replication of the ancient canoe is possible. Such features formed the design vocabulary of the replica *Hokule'a*.
>
> Kenneth Emory and I went through all designs of canoes recorded in early drawings and in other evidence and sifted out those features from hull design to sail plan which by their wide distribution may be taken to be most ancient. These I applied to the conceptual design. From my own experience with the Pacific swell and in consultation with more experienced sailors, I arrived at a waterline length of 55 to 60 feet as one that could handle the swells yet recover easily in the troughs, and Emory found that this

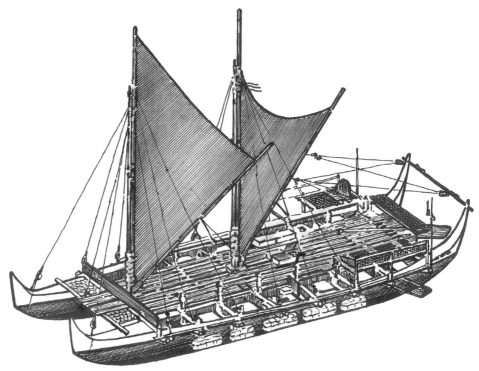

Pen and ink drawing by Jose Flores of ocean-voyaging catamaran, based on conceptual drawing by the Polynesian Voyaging Society of Hawaii.

could be taken as an average for the length of canoes used in the 18th and 19th centuries for long distance voyaging in the Tuamotus and Tahitian islands. Canoes of far greater length would put great stress on the lashings. The double-ended *ndura* of Fiji and *kalia* of Tonga were of greater length, but these carried a smaller hull to windward involving less stress on the lashing than two hulls of equal length, and were generally used on shorter voyages, which means during periods of predictable weathers.[30]

Based on his research, Kane and his associates built a replica of an ancient Polynesian voyaging canoe that was Christened the *Hokule'a*. Aboard ships like these, the descendants of Lehi could have sailed between the distanced islands of the Pacific.

How Did the Polynesians Steer Their Large Voyaging Canoes?

The Polynesian multi-hulled canoes had no conventional rudders. Instead, a steering paddle was used in the manner of a rudder. When sailing downwind, the paddle was used to make long sweeping turns. Otherwise, the paddle was held against the lee side of the hull allowing the pressure of the water against the paddle to help hold it in place and to steer the vessel. The paddle was only employed in the water when needed.[31]

On long stretches, paddles were probably not needed. The canoes' sails could be set to steer the vessels on the desired course. Kane explains:

> The aftersail is eased out slightly more than the foresail. As the canoe rounds up into the wind, the aftersail luffs and loses power. Pressure on the foresail now causes the vessel to turn off the wind a few degrees. The aftersail is again presented to the wind; it fills, and the vessel begins another slight turn to windward. Sailing slightly into the wind and off the wind, the canoe will steer itself on a close reach for hours.

In light or moderate winds the double canoe will come about (turn into and through the eye of the wind) without stalling if the crew backs the foresail, harnessing the wind to push the bows over. In a strong breeze, however, it's difficult to come about without sailing. Then it is better to jibe (make the turn with the wind astern) by luffing the aftersail until the foresail powers the vessel well off the wind, then close-hauling both sails as the stern passes through the eye of the wind. Here, the blades of the steering paddle are held at full depth to grip the stern in the water. A double hulled vessel is slow to turn because its two hulls give it twice the waterline length of a sailboat of the same length.[32]

Weathering Pacific Storms

The Polynesian voyaging canoes were subject to fast-rising storms that if not managed quickly and exactly could doom the vessel. Riding out such storms required great skill. As storms approached, the sails and spars had to be lowered. Even deck shelters were jettisoned to save the canoes from capsizing in the wind. To keep the ship facing the wind, sea anchors (strong baskets) were let out on long lines of rope. If the situation became desperate,

Polynesians had one last but remarkable procedure—they deliberately swamped the canoe. They filled the hulls with water and rode out the storms riding inside the water-filled hulls. The logs from which the hulls were formed provided sufficient floatation to keep the canoe and its crew from sinking. This allowed those of the crew to keep their heads and shoulders above the water. With the canoe mostly underwater, it held its position to the storm. When the storm subsided, the crew bailed out the hulls, raised the sails, and continued their voyage.[33]

The Wayfinders: How Did Polynesians Navigate between Small Distant Islands?

Undoubtedly the most amazing feat of Polynesian sailors was their ability to successfully navigate the massive waters of the Pacific Ocean and return to their own tiny islands. Without this ability to sail between Pacific islands, the seed of Lehi would never have spread from Hawaii and Easter Island to the far distant isles of New Zealand, Fiji, Samoa, Tonga, Tahiti, Micronesia, and so on. How did they accomplish these amazing voyages without navigating instruments?

The answer lies in the Polynesian ability to carefully observe nature's signals. The most important of these skills was the ability to develop a mental construct of the sky or what is known as a star map. The Hawaiians knew the houses of the stars; that is, the places where the stars ascended from the ocean and fall back into the sea. Having memories of the star houses, Polynesian navigators could use them to read the flight path of birds and determine the direction of the waves. Altogether, the ancient sailors could determine the direction they were traveling.[34]

The heavens were not the only compass nature provided these remarkable sailors. They could also read the position of the

sun and even read the path of the sun upon the water when the sun first rose above the sea. The width and color of the sun's path on the water helped the Polynesian navigators determine the exact position of the sun when it rose. From the position of the sun, the navigator could memorize the direction of the wind and the direction of the wind-generated swells. At sunset, the same information would be determined based on the position of 220 stars. Of these stars, the most important were those of the steady Southern Cross, the southern hemisphere's version of the North Star.[35]

But what did the Polynesian sailors do when the sky was cloudy and the sun and stars failed to reveal the ship's position and direction? It was then that these sailors read the ocean itself. They used the predetermined direction of the swells to fix a course to sail. Dennis Kawaharada of the Polynesian Voyaging Society explains:

> During midday and on cloudy nights when celestial bodies are not available at the horizon as direction clues, the navigator uses the winds and swells to hold a course. However, the direction of wind and swells cannot be determined independently; their direction can only be determined by reference to celestial bodies such as the rising or setting sun.

Swells are waves that have traveled beyond the wind systems or storms that have generated them, or waves that persist after the generating storm has died away. Swells are more regular and stable in their direction than waves. ("Waves," as opposed to "swells," are generated by local, contemporary winds.) Sometimes swells can be felt better than they can be seen, having flattened out after traveling long distances. In the Pacific, the northeast trade winds generated a northeast swell; the southeast tradewinds created a southeast swell, and so on. Storms in the South Pacific during the Hawaiian summer generate a south swell; storms in the north Pacific during the Hawaiian winter generate a north swell.

Swells move in a straight line from one house of the star compass to a house of the same name on the opposite side of the horizon, 180° away. Thus, a swell from the direction of Manu Ko'olau (NE) will pass under the canoe and head in the direction of Manu Kona (SE). A swell from 'Aina Malanai (ESE) will pass under the canoe and head in the direction of 'Aina Ho'olua (WNW).

The navigator can orient the canoe to these swells. For example, if the canoe is

heading SE Manu with a swell coming from the SE Manu, the person steering keeps the canoe heading directly into the swell, which lifts the bow, and passes beneath, then lifts the stern. If the canoe is traveling SW, a SE swell would roll the canoe from side to side, lifting first the port hull, then starboard hull as it passes beneath.[36]

Seamarks

A host of other natural phenomena helped the Polynesian navigators find their way between the islands. Among these were the spotting of porpoises, swarms of fish, flocks of birds, groups of driftwood, and the conditions of waves. For example, a red spotted ray or a tan shark making lazy movements indicated to the experienced navigator that they had reached a part of the ocean where these creatures lived. There were hundreds of such traditional seamarks that were used by the Polynesians, each providing a piece of information useful to the sailors. One seamark, called "the swarming of beasts," was a place in the ocean where sharks assembled in large numbers. Once the sharks were spotted, the navigator knew he was one-day's sail downwind of land.[37]

Signs of Landfall

Land-based seabirds were especially helpful to ancient Polynesians. In the mornings they fly out from their islands to feed. As night falls, they fly back to the islands to rest. The direction of their flight is direct, thus allowing the navigator to following their course to the island. However, seabirds were not the only sign that the canoe was close to an island. Drifting land vegetation, cloud formations that are common to islands, the glow of sunlight or moonlight off the white sands of a beach or reef, and the refracting pattern of the waves off an island were important indicators that they were near landfall.[39]

In Summary: Sailing Skills Transferred the Blood of Lehi to the Islands

How Lehi's seed spread throughout Polynesia is no mystery—Polynesian traders made routine voyages between the islands. We know this because of the

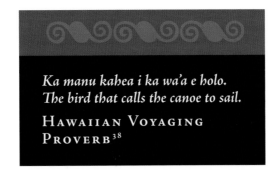

Ka manu kahea i ka wa'a e holo.
The bird that calls the canoe to sail.
HAWAIIAN VOYAGING PROVERB[38]

uniformity of the Polynesian culture within the dispersed islands. From Fiji to Easter Island and from New Zealand to Hawaii, the Polynesians considered each other as brothers. Linguistically and culturally, they were connected, and in such a manner homogeneously that it could only have been because of constant connections.

In addition, the Book of Mormon tells us that the Nephites were skilled shipbuilders and experienced seaman. Inca oral traditions suggest that South America seaman traded with far-off islands, perhaps as far as Hawaii. Thor Heyerdahl believed the oral traditions of Easter Island clearly indicated that fair-skinned traders from South America visited the remote islands. Backing up his claim, Heyerdahl and later Phil Buck used ancient Andean technology to construct balsa and reed ships and sailed them successfully from South America to Polynesia. Gene Savoy showed that ancient Peruvian shipbuilding technology could reach Hawaii by building his replica ship the *Feathered Servant III*. It is clear that many occasional contacts were made between the descendants of the Book of Mormon peoples and the Polynesians, and over the millennia there likely would have been hundreds of spreading colonizations in many directions. From these regular

189

contacts, the remarkable sailing skills of the Polynesians transferred the seed of Lehi throughout the Polynesian Pacific.

Hagoth's Voyages to Hawaii

We return to Hagoth and his northward journeys. It is important to know that in all of the Americas, the only course to Hawaii that would begin with a northward leg is South America. To reach Hawaii from Peru, one would sail northward on the Humboldt Current before making a westward turn for the islands. While sailing north from Peru would have provided favorable trade winds, Hagoth's voyages were far from easy. Indeed, his achievement stands as a witness to the Nephites' sailing capabilities. While sailing the *Banyan* to the South Pacific, Jody Lemmon crossed from Panama to the Galapagos Islands, thus cutting straight through the course the simulator predicts Hagoth would have sailed to reach Hawaii. Jody reports:

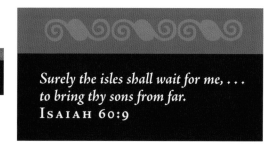

Surely the isles shall wait for me, . . . to bring thy sons from far.
Isaiah 60:9

Date: Sat. 25 Apr 2009
Subject: Re: The big blue

Well, we are really under way now. We have been sailing at 6-8 knots for the past 20 hours in 15–18 knots of wind.

We are on a beam reach, but for most of the day we have been wing and wing. The wind has gradually switched from west to east. We are aiming for a little island owned by Colombia called Isla Matapalo. The sailing directions say to go a bit south east of the island and then turn for the Galapagos. This will give us a better sailing angle once we get into the southwest trade winds. We are really flying, the swell is about 3 feet and as I write this the ocean is beginning to get a bit rough. It has been smooth all day, but as the night begins to rear its ugly head the ocean appears to be responding in kind. We put a good deep reef in the main about an hour ago, that settled things out a bit, but we are now getting into the open ocean, the rolling begins!!!

Jody

Jody's experience illustrates that sailing from Peru to Hawaii provides favorable winds and currents; however, the passage has its challenges. Jody complained of the oceans swells. We note that after sailing from Peru to Hawaii, these Pacific Ocean's swells broke Gene Savoy's *Feathered Serpent II* in half shortly after it continued

westward after Hawaii. In comparison, Hagoth's stout ship made one round trip to Hawaii from Peru and hopefully made it to Hawaii a second time.

8:00 pm April 28th
2 43.00 W
082 42.00 N

We are now 200 hundred miles off Ecuador. Our main objective for the past 4 days has been to take advantage of the coastal Northerly winds and sail as far South as we can before the Southerly trade winds begin. This morning that finally happened to our disbelief. Sailing has been our agenda and we have stuck to our guns since leaving Panama's famed Punta Mala.

Although we have suffered greatly, first with too much wind and then with too little, today we broke down. After sailing at around 3 knots for most of the day the wind died to a mere 5 knots. The batteries meanwhile were getting low and a decision needed to be made; either we start up the little gas powered generator or fire up the big boy diesel engine. Well, I opted for the diesel so we have been listening to the motor for the past 4 hours. At least we are making water and giving the batteries a much needed charge, to our consternation of course, what with the racket and all.

Anyway, back to our day before the interruption of the combustion engine. Last night was peaceful, due to no sail changes being affected.

Jody

Passage Summary Report

Passage Filename: C:HAGOTHCDFL.PP2

Passage Creation Date: 1/26/2008

Pilot Chart Data Used: Actual dates based on departure specified, (1 January)

Vessel Profile Used: C:Hagoth.VP

Minimum Speed Set: 0.50 Knots

Fuel Consumption Set: 0.00 Units/Hour

Currents: ON

Current Values Used: Average All

Wind Values Used: Average All

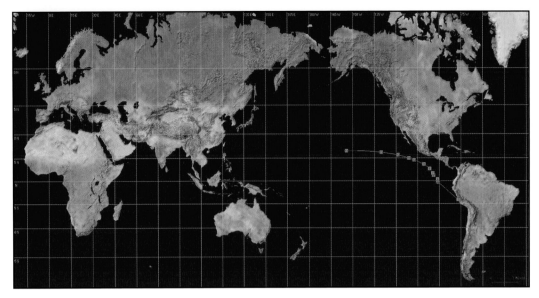

Waypoint #	Latitude	Longitude Date
1	S12°24.37'	W76°46.43'
2	S0°56.72'	W90°34.43'
3	S0°13.44'	W90°55.60'
4	N1°0.99'	W90°59.43'
5	N3°21.10'	W93°25.21'
6	N3°31.67'	W93°46.91'
7	N5°4.08'	W94°22.22'
8	N7°59.37'	W96°31.08'
9	N10°55.87'	W100°33.92'
10	N13°40.64'	W107°19.79'
11	N14°54.31'	W110°49.20'
12	N16°56.81'	W118°34.80'
13	N18°38.22'	W130°6.98'
14	N19°39.93'	W154°16.42'

The simulator plots the best course from Peru to Hawaii is by first sailing north from Peru (see Alma 63:7) and then west.

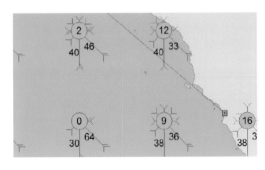

LEG 1

Departure Date 1 January

VESSEL PERFORMANCE AND WEATHER CONDITIONS REPORT

Start: S12° 24.37' W76° 46.43' [Santa Maria Bay, Peru]

End: S0° 56.72' W90° 34.43' [Galapogos Islands]

Elapsed-time to Complete Leg: 8.8 Days

Calculated Great Circle Distance: 1070.9 Nautical Miles [1294.4 Miles]

Actual Distance Travel due to Beating: 1070.9 Nautical Miles

Average Boat Speed: 5.1 Knots

Boat Speed Made Good: 5.1 Knots

Average Wind Speed: 8.3 Knots

Average Wind Direction from True North: 144.0°

Average Current Drift: 0.4 Knots at
Average Current Set: 273.4°

Average Wave Height: 3 Feet

Average Sea Temperature: 73.2° F

Average Air Temperature: 74.1° F

Average Percentage Risk of Calms: 3.1%

Average Percentage Risk of Gales: 0%

191

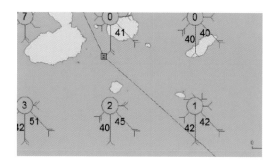

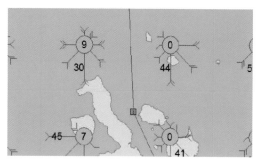

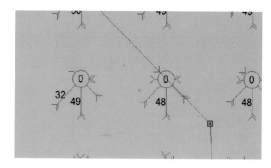

LEG 2

VESSEL PERFORMANCE AND WEATHER CONDITIONS REPORT

Start: S0° 56.72′ W90° 34.43′ [Galapogos Islands]

End: S0° 13.44′ W90° 55.60′ [Galapogos Islands]

Elapsed-time to Complete Leg: 0.3 Days

Calculated Great Circle Distance: 48.2 Nautical Miles [55.3 Miles]

Actual Distance Travel due to Beating: 48.2 Nautical Miles

Average Boat Speed: 5.8 Knots

Boat Speed Made Good: 5.8 Knots

Average Wind Speed: 7.3 Knots

Average Wind Direction from True North: 135.0°

Average Current Drift: 0.8 Knots at **Average Current Set:** 270.0°

Average Wave Height: 2.3 feet

Average Sea Temperature: 78.4° F

Average Air Temperature: 78.7° F

Average Percentage Risk of Calms: 0.0%

Average Percentage Risk of Gales: 0.0%

LEG 3

VESSEL PERFORMANCE AND WEATHER CONDITIONS REPORT

Start: S0° 13.44′ W90° 55.60′ [Galapogos Islands]

End: N1° 0.99′ W90° 59 43′ [Galapogos Islands]

Elapsed-time to Complete Leg: 0.6 Days

Calculated Great Circle Distance: 74.5 Nautical Miles [85.5 Miles]

Actual Distance Travel due to Beating: 74.5 Nautical Miles

Average Boat Speed: 5.3 Knots

Boat Speed Made Good: 5.3 Knots

Average Wind Speed: 8.7 Knots

Average Wind Direction from True North: 172.7°

Average Current Drift: 0.3 Knots at **Average Current Set:** 270.5°

Average Wave Height: 3.1Feet

Average Sea Temperature: 79.2° F

Average Air Temperature: 78.0° F

Average Percentage Risk of Calms: 0.0%

Average Percentage Risk of Gales: 0.0%

LEG 4

VESSEL PERFORMANCE AND WEATHER CONDITIONS REPORT

Start: N1° 0.99′ W90° 59.43′ [631 Miles west of Equador]

End: N3 21.10 W93 25.21′ [1150 Miles west of Colombia]

Elapsed-time to Complete Leg: 1.2 Days

Calculated Great Circle Distance: 202.1 Nautical Miles [232 Miles]

Actual Distance Travel due to Beating: 202.1 Nautical Miles

Average Boat Speed: 7.0 Knots

Boat Speed Made Good: 7.0 Knots

Average Wind Speed: 11.3 Knots

Average Wind Direction from True North: 180°

Average Current Drift: 0.0 Knots at **Average Current Set:** 000°

Average Wave Height: 3.4 Feet

Average Sea Temperature: 79.5° F

Average Air Temperature: 77.8° F

Average Percentage Risk of Calms: 0.7%

Average Percentage Risk of Gales: 0.0%

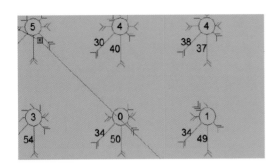

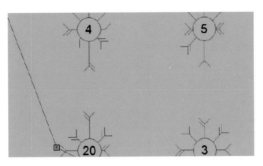

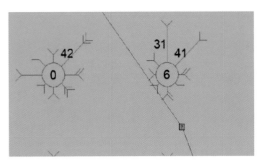

LEG 5

VESSEL PERFORMANCE AND WEATHER CONDITIONS REPORT

Start: N°3 21.10′ W93° 25.21′ [1150 Miles west of Colombia]

End: N3° 31.67′ W93° 46.91′ [1150 Miles west of Colombia]

Elapsed-time to Complete Leg: 0.1 Days

Calculated Great Circle Distance: 24 Nautical Miles

Actual Distance Travel due to Beating: 24 Nautical Miles

Average Boat Speed: 7.4 Knots

Boat Speed Made Good: 7.4 Knots

Average Wind Speed: 11.3 Knots

Average Wind Direction from True North: 180°

Average Current Drift: 0.0 Knots at **Average Current Set:** 000°

Average Wave Height: 3.4 Feet

Average Sea Temperature: 79.4° F

Average Air Temperature: 78.2° F

Average Percentage Risk of Calms: 0.5%

Average Percentage Risk of Gales: 0.0%

LEG 6

VESSEL PERFORMANCE AND WEATHER CONDITIONS REPORT

Start: N3° 31.67′ W93° 46.91′ [1150 Miles west of Colombia]

End: N5° 4.08′ W94° 22.22′ [1205 Miles west of Colombia]

Elapsed-time to Complete Leg: 0.6 Days

Calculated Great Circle Distance: 98.9 Nautical Miles [113.5 Miles]

Actual Distance Travel due to Beating: 98.9 Nautical Miles

Average Boat Speed: 6.7 Knots

Boat Speed Made Good: 6.6 Knots

Average Wind Speed: 11.0 Knots

Average Wind Direction from True North: 137.5°

Average Current Drift: 0.9 Knots at **Average Current Set:** 151.9°

Average Wave Height: 3.5 Feet

Average Sea Temperature: 79.7° F

Average Air Temperature: 78.9° F

Average Percentage Risk of Calms: 1.2%

Average Percentage Risk of Gales: 0.0%

LEG 7

VESSEL PERFORMANCE AND WEATHER CONDITIONS REPORT

Start: N°5 4.08′ W94° 22.22′ [1205 Miles west of Colombia]

End: N7° 59.37′ W96° 31.08′ [861 Miles west of Central America]

Elapsed-time to Complete Leg: 1.8 Days

Calculated Great Circle Distance: 217 Nautical Miles [249 Miles]

Actual Distance Travel due to Beating: 217 Nautical Miles

Average Boat Speed: 5.0 Knots

Boat Speed Made Good: 5.0 Knots

Average Wind Speed: 11.0 Knots

Average Wind Direction from True North: 052.5°

Average Current Drift: 0.7 Knots at **Average Current Set:** 233.6°

Average Wave Height: 3.9 Feet

Average Sea Temperature: 79.7° F

Average Air Temperature: 79.3° F

Average Percentage Risk of Calms: 0.0%

Average Percentage Risk of Gales: 1.6%

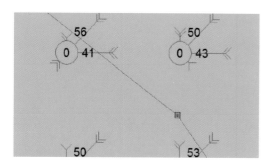

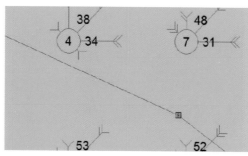

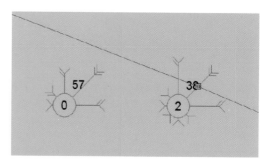

LEG 8

VESSEL PERFORMANCE AND WEATHER
CONDITIONS REPORT

Start: N7° 59.37' W96° 31.08'
[861 Miles west of Central America]

End: N10° 55.87' W100° 33.92'
[1033 Miles west of Central America]

Elapsed-time to Complete Leg: 1.9 Days

Calculated Great Circle Distance: 297.5
Nautical Miles [341.5 Miles]

**Actual Distance Travel due to
Beating:** 297.5 Nautical Miles

Average Boat Speed: 6.5 Knots

Boat Speed Made Good: 6.5 Knots

Average Wind Speed: 12.1 Knots

**Average Wind Direction
from True North:** 045.0°

Average Current Drift: 0.8 Knots at
Average Current Set: 294.5°

Average Wave Height: 4.3 Feet

Average Sea Temperature: 80.5° F

Average Air Temperature: 79.8° F

Average Percentage Risk of Calms: 0.8%

Average Percentage Risk of Gales: 0.0%

LEG 9

VESSEL PERFORMANCE AND WEATHER
CONDITIONS REPORT

Start: N10° 55.87' W100° 33.92'
[1033 Miles west of Central America]

End: N13° 40.64' W107° 19.79'
[400 Miles southwest of Mexico]

Elapsed-time to Complete Leg: 3.3 Days

Calculated Great Circle Distance: 429.4
Nautical Miles [493 Miles]

**Actual Distance Travel due to
Beating:** 429.4 Nautical Miles

Average Boat Speed: 5.4 Knots

Boat Speed Made Good: 5.4 Knots

Average Wind Speed: 9.6 Knots

**Average Wind Direction
from True North:** 045.0°

Average Current Drift: 0.9 Knots at
Average Current Set: 210.9°

Average Wave Height: 3.2 Feet

Average Sea Temperature: 81.7° F

Average Air Temperature: 80.7° F

Average Percentage Risk of Calms: 4.6%

Average Percentage Risk of Gales: 0.0%

LEG 10

VESSEL PERFORMANCE AND WEATHER
CONDITIONS REPORT

Start: N13° 40.64' W107° 19.79'
[459 Miles southwest of Mexico]

End: N14° 54.31' W110° 49.20'
[603 Miles southwest of Mexico]

Elapsed-time to Complete Leg: 1.3 Days

Calculated Great Circle Distance: 215.9
Nautical Miles [247.9 Miles]

**Actual Distance Travel due to
Beating:** 215.6 Nautical Miles

Average Boat Speed: 6.7 Knots

Boat Speed Made Good: 6.7 Knots

Average Wind Speed: 11.3 Knots

**Average Wind Direction
from True North:** 045.0°

Average Current Drift: 0.4 Knots at
Average Current Set: 273.6°

Average Wave Height: 3.6 Feet

Average Sea Temperature: 80.7° F

Average Air Temperature: 78.4° F

Average Percentage Risk of Calms: 1.7%

Average Percentage Risk of Gales: 0.0%

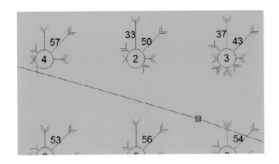 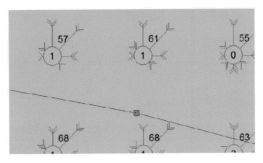 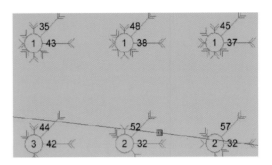

LEG 11

VESSEL PERFORMANCE AND WEATHER CONDITIONS REPORT

Start: N14° 54.31' W110° 49.20' [603 Miles southwest of Mexico]

End: N16° 56.81' W118° 34.80' [2,526 Miles east of Hilo, Hawaii]

Elapsed-time to Complete Leg: 2.7 Days

Calculated Great Circle Distance: 464.1 Nautical Miles [533 Miles]

Actual Distance Travel due to Beating: 464.1 Nautical Miles

Average Boat Speed: 7.3 Knots

Boat Speed Made Good: 7.3 Knots

Average Wind Speed: 13.2 Knots

Average Wind Direction from True North: 045.0°

Average Current Drift: 0.3 Knots at **Average Current Set:** 209.9°

Average Wave Height: 4.3 Feet

Average Sea Temperature: 77.3° F

Average Air Temperature: 75.0° F

Average Percentage Risk of Calms: 0.7%

Average Percentage Risk of Gales: 0.1%

LEG 12

VESSEL PERFORMANCE AND WEATHER CONDITIONS REPORT

Start: N16° 56.81' W118° 34.80' [2,526 Miles east of Hilo, Hawaii]

End: N18° 38.22' W130° 6.98' [1,572.8 Miles east of Hilo, Hawaii]

Elapsed-time to Complete Leg: 3.6 Days

Calculated Great Circle Distance: 666.7 Nautical Miles [776.4 Miles]

Actual Distance Travel due to Beating: 666.7 Nautical Miles

Average Boat Speed: 7.7 Knots

Boat Speed Made Good: 7.7 Knots

Average Wind Speed: 14.8 Knots

Average Wind Direction from True North: 045.0°

Average Current Drift: 0.4 Knots at **Average Current Set:** 224.3°

Average Wave Height: 5.3 feet

Average Sea Temperature: 72.9° F

Average Air Temperature: 70.8° F

Average Percentage Risk of Calms: 0.0%

Average Percentage Risk of Gales: 0.3%

LEG 13

VESSEL PERFORMANCE AND WEATHER CONDITIONS REPORT

Start: N18° 38.22' W130° 6.98' [1,572.8 Miles east of Hilo, Hawaii]

End: N19° 39.93' W154° 16.42' [Hilo, Hawaii]

Elapsed-time to Complete Leg: 7.4 Days

Calculated Great Circle Distance: 1,369.5 Nautical Miles [1,572.8 Miles]

Actual Distance Travel due to Beating: 1,369.5 Nautical Miles

Average Boat Speed: 7.7 Knots

Boat Speed Made Good: 7.7 Knots

Average Wind Speed: 15.2 Knots

Average Wind Direction from True North: 072.3°

Average Current Drift: 0.5 Knots at **Average Current Set:** 262.0°

Average Wave Height: 6.5 Feet

Average Sea Temperature: 73.2° F

Average Air Temperature: 71.6° F

Average Percentage Risk of Calms: 0.9%

Average Percentage Risk of Gales: 0.4%

195

Summary of Computer Simulation of
Hagoth's Voyage

Total days sailing toward the Hawaian Islands from Peru: 29.4 days (30)

Average Boat Speed: 7.4 Knots

Boat Speed Made Good: 7.3 Knots

Total length of voyage: 5,178.8 Nautical Miles [5945.3 Miles]

Approximate arrival time Hilo, Hawaii, per simulation: last day of January

Apparent Wind Angle Information:

Numbers indicate percent of leg sailed at that column's relative wind angle. Relative wind angle given is the direction from which the wind comes. (See table below.)

Leg #	Beating (Apparent wind 0° to 45°)	Tight Reaching (Apparent wind 45° to 112.5°)	Broad Reaching (Apparent wind 112.6° to 157.5°)	Running (Apparent wind 157.6 to 180)
1	0% at 0 Knots	0% at 0 Knots	18% at 6.5 Knots	82% at 8.7 Knots
2	0% at 0 Knots	0% at 0 Knots	0% at 0 Knots	100% at 7.3 Knots
3	0% at 0 Knots	0% at 0 Knots	15% at 7.3 Knots	85% at 9.0 Knots
4	0% at 0 Knots	0% at 0 Knots	100% at 8.5 Knots	0% at 0 Knots
5	0% at 0 Knots	0% at 0 Knots	100% at 11.3 Knots	0% at 0 Knots
6	0% at 0 Knots	8% at 8.9 Knots	67% at 11.2 Knots	25% at 11.3 Knots
7	0% at 0 Knots	82% at 10.8 Knots	18% at 12.0 Knots	0% at 0 Knots
8	0% at 0 Knots	100% at 12.1 Knots	0% at 0 Knots	0% at 0 Knots
9	0% at 0 Knots	59% at 9.3 Knots	41% at 10.0 Knots	0% at 0 Knots
10	0% at 0 Knots	0% at 0 Knots	100% at 11.3 Knots	0% at 0 Knots
11	0% at 0 Knots	0% at 0 Knots	100% at 13.2 Knots	0% at 0 Knots
12	0% at 0 Knots	0% at 0 Knots	100% at 14.8 Knots	0% at 0 Knots
13	0% at 0 Knots	0% at 0 Knots	19% at 15.9 Knots	81% at 14.5 Knots

Notes

1. W. A. Cole and E. W. Jensen, *Israel in the Pacific* (Salt Lake City, 1961), 388.

2. Heber J. Grant, *Improvement Era*, 23 Feb. 1920: 283. See *Encyclopedia of Mormonism*, vol. 3, *Polynesians*.

3. Jerry K. Loveland, "Hagoth and the Polynesian Tradition," *BYU Studies* 17, no. 1 (Autumn 1976): 73.

4. Ibid., 70.

5. Ibid., 71.

6. Ibid., 72.

7. Bruce S. Sutton, *Lehi, Father of Polynesia* (Orem, Utah: Hawaiki Publishing, 2001), 96.

8. Charles Mann, *1491: New Revelations of the Americans Before Columbus* (New York: Knopf, 2005), 18.

9. Gary Urton, *The Legendary Past, Inca Myths* (Austin: University of Texas Press, 1999), 59.

10. Mann, *1491*, 93.

11. David G. Calderwood, *Voices From the Dust* (Austin, Texas: Historical Publications, 2005), 371–73.

12. Sorenson, "Ancient Voyages Across the Ocean to America," 4.

13. Peter Marsh, "Plants and Animals," see http://users.on.net/~mkfenn/page7.htm, 4.

14. The land Bountiful was Nasca, Peru, and the land northward was Norte Chico, Peru. See Potter, *Nephi in the Land of Promise*.

15. Jocelyn Linnekin, *Sacred Queens and Women of Consequence: Rank, Gender, and Colonialism* (University of Michigan Press, 1990), 232.

16. Gene Savoy, http://genesavoy.org.

17. F. Richard Hauck, *Deciphering the Geography of the Book of Mormon* (Salt Lake City: Deseret Book, 1988), 12.

18. David O. McKay, *Church News*, 10 May 1959, 2, 6.

19. "Polynesians," *Encyclopedia of Mormonism*, vol. 3.

20. Patrick Vinton Kirch, *On the Road of the Winds* (Berkeley: University of California Press, 2002), 208–209.

21. Pukui, *'Olelo No'eau*, 1–2.

22. Michael De Gotte, "Hebrew DNA found in South America?" *Deseret News*, 12 May 2008, http://www.deseretnews.com/article/1,5143,700225191,00.html.

23. Steve Jones, *In the Blood, God, Genes, and Destiny* (London: Harper Collins, 1996), 156–57.

24. First Presidency Letterpress, Copybooks CR 1/20 Vol. 47, Reel #42.

25. Herb Hawainui Kane, "In Search of the Ancient Polynesian Voyaging Canoe," Polynesian Voyaging Society, 2 October 2007, 1.

26. Sorenson, "Ancient Voyages Across the Ocean to America."

27. Bishop Museum, "Unraveling the Mystery: The Hawaii and Tuamotus Connection," http://www.bishopmuseum.org/media/2007/pr07093.html, accessed 3 March 2008.

28. Ibid.

29. Ibid.

30. Kane, "In Search of the Ancient Polynesian," 1–2.

31. Ibid., 4.

32. Ibid.

33. Ibid., 5.

34. Dennis Kawaharada, "Wayfinding, or Non-Instrument Navigation," Polynesian Voyaging Society, http://www.pvs-hawaii.com/navigation/summary.htm, accessed 10 Feb. 2007.

35. Ibid.

36. Ibid.

37. Ibid.

38. Pukui, *'Olelo No'eau*, 1.

39. Ibid., 7.

While writing this book, Jody Lemmon and his crew have sailed the *Banyan* from Long Beach, Callifornia, to New Zealand. His email logs have added significantly to our appreciation of the challenges overcome by the voyagers of the Book of Mormon. When we requested Jody's authorization to share with readers of this book his reports to his parents, he readily gave his approval. While in Samoa he was most fortunate, for the *Banyan* was one of the ships that survived the tsunami that devastated Pago Pago, Samoa, on 29 September 2009. Here is Jody's report.

September 29, 2009 Earthquake/Tsunami report from American Samoa

Tuesday morning (Sep. 29) I awoke after a fitful sleep at 5 a.m. I, then, made my way, in the dark, down to the phone station as a flock of giant fruit bats glided past me through the morning haze. I needed to make a call regarding parts that we needed shipped to Samoa to fix our broken head stay. (There is a 3 hour time difference with California.) As I returned to the boat a massive earthquake hit us. We were docked alongside a large cement wharf with 7 other sailboats. The earthquake lasted around 1 1/2 minutes and before it ended everyone was up and out of their boats. We all exchanged comments on the magnitude of the

earthquake and how long it lasted. After about 10 minutes everyone returned to their boats to start their day.

I went below to get another hour of sleep and as I stepped down one of our crew members, Emily, was coming up. She was coming up to do yoga on the dock. This is her normal morning onshore routine and luckily this early morning ritual gave us a slight warning to what happened next. A few minutes later, from below deck, I heard a heavy creaking and groaning. Then, we heard Emily yelling at us to get up topside. I jumped up on deck and all I could see was water rushing out and huge dripping pilings next to my head. I looked up 15 feet and saw Emily's shoes and heard her screaming at us to escape. Luckily, Matt had left his sharp knife by the companionway and I immediately began slashing the dock lines that weren't already broken by the strain. I fired up the engine. Meanwhile, the boys were frantically pushing the boat away from the concrete pilings with their soon bloodied hands and yelling for Emily to run. The water was sucking out so much that all the sailboats around us were hitting bottom and leaning over on their sides. Somehow Banyan was in water just a little deeper.

Emily was trying to climb back aboard the boat. As the boat sunk lower and lower the mast and the rigging leaned over and pushed against the cement dock where Emily was attempting to climb down. She was pressed hard against a giant fender tire and our wire rigging. After barely squeezing out she fell onto the deck of our boat. Amidst the panic she told me later that she then decided to climb back onto the tire and then the dock and make a run for it.

I was unaware of what was going on due to our canopy blocking my view. I decided to quickly fire up the engine and slash the last line attached to our stern. I gunned the engine full throttle and headed out into the harbor. We made it about 15 feet away from the dock when I realized Emily wasn't on board. The next instant the water switched directions and came flooding back toward us. We went from almost dry land into a surge of water 30–40 feet high. I shoved the throttle to full and we actually traveled up the face of the oncoming tsunami wave. Luckily, the face was only a 45 or so degree angle. We were able to actually motor up and over it. The feeling was surreal. I must have put the throttle to full just has the surge hit us. The boat remained 15–20 feet from the dock and we miraculously held our ground against the incoming flow.

From our vantage point we saw Emily wade through the rushing water to a light post on the dock. She clung to this post as the water began to rise ever higher. The other six boats on the dock hadn't slashed their lines quickly enough, so as the water rose they all began to bunch up and smash against each other as they got crushed under the dock. The catamaran, directly in front of us, got one of her hulls stuck under the dock and was crushed as the water rose. Within seconds her bow snapped and the boat sprung into the air with a violent rush. Our eyes were glued to Emily as she clung to the light pole. Soon the water had risen above her head and she disappeared from our view. Mike and I frantically attempted to launch the dinghy in hopes of trying to save her. As soon as we launched the dinghy, with the motor attached, the force of the tsunamis surge hit us and the dingy instantly flipped over. At this time a sailboat on the other side of the dock broke free and was thrown up onto the dock. The water had risen more than 30 feet and this 45-foot sail boat was soon sliding along the cement dock toward Emily clinging to her pole. Somehow, the captain fired up his engine, cut his lines, and was able to motor off the dock narrowly avoiding the light pole. Soon the water sucked back out to sea and we could see Emily running from the light pole to the edge of the dock. We all frantically yelled at her to run to high ground. She then took off toward the dock gate and the side of the mountain. When a second surge hit us she actually struggled through waist deep water to make it to the end of the dock. From the safety of our boat we peered through the binoculars and could see that she had made it to safety. It would be hours before we were finally able to find her again and to learn that she had run straight up the side of the jungle covered hill. It was a barefoot hike of more than 300 vertical feet. After reaching the summit she found a tree and climbed it to get a bird's eye view of the whole bay.

By this time the few sailboats that hadn't been damaged too badly made their way out to where we were circling around in deep water. We, then, heard frantic yelling coming from the boat that had been tied up directly behind us. I jumped in the dinghy and went over to see if I could help. The woman was hysterical. She told me her husband had fallen off the boat while attempting to cut the dock lines. She actually witnessed him getting sucked into the water and carried away. We later learned from Emily that, from her vantage point on high ground, she could see huge whirlpools sucking docks and containers under water. I quickly went around the distraught woman's boat and cleaned up her lines to avoid getting them sucked into the propeller.

The next 3–4 hours were spent motoring around looking for Emily and the woman's husband. After everything had subsided Mike jumped into the dinghy and I gave him a ride to shore in hopes of finding Emily somewhere. As we approached the dock we realized that our bicycle and generator were hanging by their chain cable off the side of the dock. We pulled them both dripping onto the dock. Mike jumped on the bike and set off through the disaster zone to look for Emily.

Later Mike told us that he had gone to the head of the bay. He found a friend of ours whose boat was wrecked. His boat was stranded high up on a grassy bluff. Mike helped him unload his valuables as looters were instantly ransacking stores, shops, and boats. It was total anarchy. When he turned around to continue his search for Emily, he realized his bike had been stolen.

He, then, returned on foot through the streets where gangs of teenagers were running rampant looting and bashing everything with sticks that they all carried. Somehow Mike followed a trail of people who had seen the white "palangi girl." He eventually found her at the top of the mountain still perched in a tree. We were completely relieved to hear the radio report from him stating that she was high, dry, and uninjured.

I hope to have more reports on the aftermath once I get a chance. We are all pretty shaken, but so thankful to have escaped with no injuries. Our Banyan suffered no damage at all and we only received minor scrapes and cuts. Just today we finally fixed our headstay in a "jury rig" fashion with a chain extension. Under the circumstances that is the best repair that we can do and it will be fine. We are going to use some jib sails we salvaged (in place of our damaged self furling jib—damage not from tsunami, but done previously to arriving in Samoa) off a wrecked boat that we helped the owner unload. Everyone wants to leave this place.

Jody

CHAPTER SEVEN

I will make a man more precious than fine gold;
even a man than the golden wedge of Ophir.
2 NEPHI 23:12

OPHIR, THE JAREDITES' HARBOR

O N   A   SABBATH   DAY   in 1996, George was reading in Ether, fourteenth book in the Book of Mormon. The saga of the Jaredites had always interested him, but that day a light seemed to turn on as he read, "The Lord commanded them [Jaredites] that they should go forth into the wilderness, yea, into that quarter where there never had man been." *A quarter? Where no one had ever been!* He immediately knew the probable route the Jaredites traveled through the wilderness. He realized that the Jaredite exodus likely was through the most hellish place on earth, the famous *Empty Quarter* of the Arabian wilderness. With this insight, George's studies led to an even more interesting possibility—that the Book of Mormon's brother of Jared may have been none other than the Biblical seaman named Ophir.

To explore this possibility for identifying the Jaredite trail and harbor where the Jaredites built their barges, George and Richard Wellington retraced most of the Jaredite trail through eastern Arabia, including a deep penetration into the famed Empty Quarter.[1]

Exploring the dunes of the Arabian Empty Quarter, a sand desert the size of Utah.

Prior models about the Jaredites, for the most part, seem to be based on supposition. For example, a common idea is that the Jaredites crossed Asia and embarked for the promised land from the Pacific shoreline of China:

> The Jaredites carried on the warring ways of the steppes of Asia "upon this north country" (Ether 1, 3-6). Issuing forth from the well-known dispersion center of the great migrations in western Asia, they accepted all volunteers in a mass migration (Ether 1:41–42). Moving across central Asia they crossed shallow seas in barges (Ether 2:5–6). Such great inland seas were left over from the last ice age (CWHN 5:183–85, 194–96). Reaching the "great sea" (possibly the Pacific), they built ships with covered decks and peaked ends, "after the manner of Noah's ark" (Ether 6:7), closely resembling the prehistoric "magur boats" of Mesopotamia.[2]

J. M. Sjodahl summarizes a popular version formulated by George Reynolds:

> According to this theory, which however Mr. Reynolds characterizes as a supposition merely, the Jaredites went in a northerly direction from the Valley of Nimrod as far as the Caspian Sea, which they crossed; then, turning eastward,

they journeyed along the Central Asia plateau; thence to the Pacific seaboard, most probably on the coast of China . . . all that is actually revealed is that their journey was a long one, beyond the limits of the then inhabited world.[3]

A deeper look, however, into the Bible, the Book of Mormon, geography of Arabia, and that which is known about the ancient world of Mesopotamia reveals enough evidence to establish an improved proposal for the Jaredites.

The Arabian Trail of the Jaredites

The position of this book is this: The Jaredites were instructed to go north to the Valley of Nimrod, where they would be met by the Lord. From the valley of Nimrod, the Lord led them south into the Arabian wilderness (desert) where they

Map of the Jaredite Trail.

eventually took the Dakakah Trail through the Empty Quarter. The most likely place on the southern Arabian coast where they could build ships was the inlet harbor of Khor Rori, the same place where Nephi built his sailing ship, the site that for generations would be an important harbor.

Support for an Arabian Trail for the Jaredites

1. THE JAREDITES CROSSED THE WILDERNESS, A QUARTER WHERE NO MAN HAD EVER BEEN

The Book of Ether indicates that from the Valley of Nimrod the Jaredites were led directly into a wilderness or desert (Ether 2:5). The Tower of Babel is believed to have been within the city walls of ancient Babylonia[4] (near today's Baghdad). The Valley of Nimrod was north of Babel, probably near the ruins of Nineveh that was settled by Nimrod the hunter (Ether 2:1).[5] The ruins of Nineveh are approximately 250–300 miles north of the ruins Baghdad. From the valley of Nimrod, "the Lord commanded them that they should go forth into the wilderness." The Book of Mormon does not state which direction, whether north, south, east, or west, that the Jaredites took from Nimrod to

reach the wilderness. However, linguist Hugh Nibley explains: "What is meant by 'wilderness'? That word has in the Book of Mormon the same connotation as in the Bible, and usually refers to desert country . . . in the Bible 'wilderness' almost always means desert."[6] The great desert proximate to ancient Nineveh is Arabia to the south and is land that has since antiquity been known as both a geographic and political wilderness.[7]

2. THE *AR RUB KHALI*, THE EMPTY QUARTER

The Book of Mormon specifically says, "The Lord commanded them [the Jaredites] that they should go forth into the wilderness, yea, into *that quarter where there never had man been*" (Ether 2:5, emphasis added). This clue is meaningless to most Westerners, but for anyone living in the Near East, where the Jaredites started their saga, it is a clear reference to southern Arabia. To an Arab, crossing the quarter *where no man had ever been* is as descriptive as telling an American that the Utah Pioneers crossed the Rocky Mountains. Arab mythology holds that God created the world, and that two quarters are where people lived, and that one quarter was the sea, and one quarter was

the desert where no man ever lived. To this day, the great sand desert of southern Arabia is called the *Ar Rub Khali* or *Empty Quarter*. Being larger than the state of Utah, the Empty Quarter of Arabia is the largest sand desert in the world, and there is still no archaeological evidence that man has ever dwelt therein.[8]

3. THE JAREDITES CROSSED *MANY WATERS* (ETHER 6:7)

If one travels south of ruins of Nineveh to Arabia, he will eventually enter the Empty Quarter. There is only one known route through the Empty Quarter, the Dakakah Trail. The Dakakah trail is not a trail in the traditional sense—that is, there are no worn tracks in the sand. It is a series of distant watering holes, that if found, can support a passage through the Empty Quarter. The trail ends at the Salalah Coastal Plain on the Indian Ocean in Oman, the place where most LDS scholars believe Nephi built his ship. In other words, the only trail across the Empty Quarter leads straight to the body of water that Nephi called *Irreantum*, meaning "many waters." Thus, the term "many waters" can be seen as a possible Book of Mormon place-name that identified a particular location—the waters off southern Arabia. It would also

Photograph of Empty Quarter in Arabia.

be true that if the Jaredites embarked from Khor Rori into the Arabian Sea, they would have had to cross many bodies of water (seas and oceans) to reach the New World. This would not have been the case if the Jaredites departed from the shores of the Pacific or the Atlantic.

4. THE LORD LED THEM IN A CLOUD

The Lord "did go before" the Jaredites "in a cloud, and gave directions whither they should travel" (Ether 2:5–6). The Lord led Moses and the children of Israel into Arabia (Midian)[9] in a cloud and a pillar of fire (Exodus 13:21). The Lord guided Lehi and his family through Arabia by giving them the Liahona (1 Nephi 16:10). What all three of these events have in common is that the Lord led them into a wilderness. We know that in the cases of Moses[10] and Lehi that the wilderness was Arabia. The reason the Lord had to guide them is simple for those who know and travel about Arabia: it is easy, and extremely dangerous, to become disoriented in the wasteland deserts of Arabia. At the same time, it is nearly always fatal if one gets lost and misses the watering holes, a fact that is never truer than in the Empty Quarter where summer temperatures can climb to 145 degrees F. It must

be remembered that the Jaredites traveled in an uninhabited place. There was no one to stop and ask directions to the next well or village.

The Arabs have a name for wide deserts where one can become disorientated, lose his way, and perish, and that name is *taymā*. In the early part of the last century, the crossing of the Empty Quarter was considered as great a challenge as climbing Mount Everest. The first successful Westerner to accomplish the feat was Bertram Thomas. Thomas needed guides from the Murri tribe, the only people who knew how to find the watering holes of the ancient Dakakah Trail.

There is one more reason the Lord needed to guide the Jaredites through the Empty Quarter, a route through a vast land of towering sand dunes. The dunes in the Empty Quarter can tower as high as 700–800 feet. Even with his guides, Thomas found it difficult to navigate the dunes. He wrote: "Our camels, wretched beasts, climbed arduously up to knife-edge summits and slithered knee-deep down precipitous slopes. Here and there, we turned back for very fear, and tried a better way."[11]

One indication that the Jaredites crossed a great desert is that the Lord had them take into the wilderness large stocks of provisions (Ether 2:1–3). Andrew Taylor writes of Bertram Thomas's difficulties in crossing the Empty Quarter:

> The Dakakah had been composed mainly of sweeping red landscapes of hard sand, with dunes running in all directions, but after they left Suwahib, the colours became more muted, and the terrain softer—"a wide expanse of pale sands in the mood of an ocean calm"—with occasional scrub of nadh bushes. Here, the climate had been less kind: the Murri tribesmen could remember grazing their animals across this region, but now, after four waterless years, Thomas found nothing but "a hungry void, and an abode of death to whoever should loiter there." It was a grim reason for yet more checking of supplies and calculations.[12]

Why else would the Lord need to guide the Jaredites if it were not for the dangers of the trek? Arabist Taylor says:

> All travelers kept to the side of the great wastes of the Empty Quarter.

205

Travelling into the sands, they were well aware, would mean death just as certainly as swimming out into the ocean. There was no hope of survival, nothing to sustain life—and just as important, no reason to make the journey. The Empty Quarter, they all knew, was just that—empty, barren, and hostile. It was best left alone.[13]

5. MARITIME RESOURCES NEEDED TO BUILD A SHIP

The Jaredites needed the same tangible resources to build their barges as Nephi needed to fabricate his ship: strong straight hardwoods, cotton or other fabric for sails, cordage for rope, and so on. As we noted in chapter one, these materials would have been available in several locations in the Old World, but in Arabia probably only in Oman at the inlet known as Khor Rori. The Rori had an excellent moorage in its natural harbor in the Jaredite period and was later used as the exporting harbor for the important frankincense trade.

Ships require large timbers for structural support. The leading marine archaeologists believe that the shipbuilders of Salalah used imported timbers from India.[14] We have no specific documentation that Khor Rori was trading for shipbuilding timbers as far back as 2500 BC.[15] However, there are written records that timbers were exported from White India to Mesopotamia as early as 2520 BC,[16] which suggests that other seafaring ports in the region were doing likewise. Khor Rori is believed to have been an active harbor since 3000 BC. The Jaredites built eight barges for two extended families, their friends and their families. In or on these barges they also carried water and food provisions for what became a 344-day voyage (Ether 3:1; 6:11). The Jaredite barges had to be large, yet we know they were only the length of a tree (Ether 2:17). Fortunately, the best wood for building a ship comes from the tall straight teak tree.

Mount Samban, Oman.

In India, a teak tree can grow straight up to a height of 150 feet.

6. A Mountain of Exceeding Height

The brother of Jared met the Lord on a mountain he described as being of "exceeding height" (Ether 3:1). The great mountain noted by the brother of Jared would have been located near the seashore where they built their ships because the brother of Jared carried sixteen stones up the mountain. Rising above Khor Rori stands Mount Samban, which reaches a height of nearly six thousand feet. It is the tallest mountain in all of southern Oman. Mount Samban is a mountain of religious importance. Not only is it possibly the mountain where the Lord appeared to the brother of Jared, it was probably the mountain where the Lord spoke as well to Nephi,[17] and is one of the few mountains that is mentioned in the Bible[18] (Genesis 10:30).

7. White Clear Stones

The brother of Jared melted out of a rock sixteen stones that were "white and clear, even as transparent glass" (Ether 3:1). Arabia is famous for its clear quartz, so transparent that it is cut into semi-precious stones called the "Diamonds of the Sultans" (also known as Desert Diamonds and Qaysumah Diamonds). These clear stones are found throughout Arabia and are mined in the Empty Quarter.[19] On the western side of the Empty Quarter, just south of the town Bishah, is found on the old Frankincense Trail a two-thousand-foot-tall pure white mountain formed entirely of quartz.[20] Veins of quartz are also found in the mountains of southern Oman.[21] Today, Oman exports silicon quartz sand for the production of semi-conductors.[22] Besides quartz, Oman mines other ophiolites (plagioclase crystals that form augites) and gems. The plagiogranites of Oman are dominated by quartz, plagioclase, albite, muscovite, and epilote.[23]

At the request of the brother of Jared, the Lord touched the stones causing the "stones to shine in darkness" (Ether 3:6; 6:3). One interesting gem of southern Arabia is the "Oman Magic Perfume Gemstone," which soaks up liquids. If the gem is soaked in perfume, the gemstone remains fragrant for years.[24] If the Creator can make gems that retain fragrances and quartz sand that can be used for computer chips which can process and store millions of pieces of information, then why not a miracle of having these stones retain light?

8. Honeybees

Honeybees were not native to much of the ancient world. The earliest Biblical record of honey is when Jacob (Israel) instructed his sons to take a gift of honey to the Egyptian (Joseph) to try to win the release of his two sons (Genesis 43:11). Yet hundreds of years earlier, the Book of Mormon records that the Jaredites took honeybees with them from Nimrod to the seashore where they built their ships. Here the Book of Mormon is much in harmony with what is known about the history of Babel (Sumeria). As early as the twenty-first century BC, the cuneiform writings of Sumeria and Babylonia mention honeybees.[25]

However, what did the Jaredites do with their honeybees when they left for the promised land? When the Spanish conquered Mexico and Central America, they found that native populations of Mexico and Central America were beekeepers.[26] Yet, the New World bees probably were not the bees of the Jaredites, rather they probably were bees unique to the Americas.[27] The European honey bee that Native Americans called "white man's flies" were not introduced in the Americas until 1638.[28] It is likely that the Jaredite

207

honeybee was the warm climate dwarf bee *Apis florea*. The range of these small wild bees is the warm climates of southeast Asia. The bees of Mesopotamia could have been native or could have been brought there via India, which had bees at that time and traded with Sumeria.[29]

The wild Apis Florea bees provide an intriguing aspect of the Jaredite trail. When the Jaredites left for the New World, they left their swarms of honeybees with their other brothers at Ophir where in time some of the bees would have gone wild. We can speculate on this for three reasons: (1) there is no specific reference in the Book of Mormon that the Jaredites took their bees aboard their ships (Ether 6:4); (2) since the Jaredites sailed in somewhat air tight barges, it would have made sense to leave the bees behind; and (3) Old World bees were not found in the New World.

The most suitable place for the Jaredites to build their barges was the inlet of Khor Rori where Nephi later constructed his ship. Nephi wrote that "we did come to the land which we called Bountiful, because of its much fruit and also *wild honey*, and all these things *were prepared of the Lord* that we might not perish" (1 Nephi 17:5, emphasis add). Nephi may have realized

or learned that the Lord had prepared Bountiful with *wild*, not domesticated, honey. To this day, honey in Oman is still gathered mostly as wild honey, and the bees are still considered wild, being only "somewhat managed."[30] Local residents have shown us where wild honey is still harvested at Khor Rori. Further, with the exception of Oman where Khor Rori is found, honeybees are not native to Arabia, an area the size of Europe.[31] How did these wild honey bees originally come to Oman? Did they fly across the Persian Gulf? Or were they left with the other brothers as one of the ways the area was prepared for Nephi's party? (1 Nephi 17:5).

9. The Jaredites Were "A Very Large Race of Men, a Very Large People"[32]

Our first indication that the Jaredites were a physically large people is found in the Book of Mosiah wherein King Limhi tells Ammon of his search for the land of Zarahemla. Regarding this scouting expedition, the text says: "And they were lost in the wilderness for a space of many days, yet they were diligent, and found not the land of Zarahemla but . . . discovered a land which was covered with bones of men, and of beasts, and was also covered with ruins

of buildings of every kind, having discovered a land which had been peopled with a people who were as numerous as the host of Israel. And for a testimony that the things that they had said are true they have brought twenty-four plates which are filled with engravings, and they are of pure gold. And behold, also, they have brought breastplates, which are large, and they are of brass and of copper, and are perfectly sound" (Mosiah 8:8–10).

A second reference to the physical largeness of the Jaredites is in the Book of Ether wherein Moroni is recounting the end of the Jaredites. He says, "And when the night came there were thirty and two of the people of Shiz, and twenty and seven of the people of Coriantumr. And it came to pass that they ate and slept, and prepared for death on the morrow. And they were large and mighty men as to the strength of men" (Ether 15:25–26).

Perhaps as a result of these references, the author of an article in the Mormon *Evening and Morning Star* wrote of the Jaredites, "They were a very large race of men."[33]

The large stature of the Jaredites gives another specific clue in seeking to identify the place where the Jaredites built their ships: Khor Rori had a very large people living there for at least a short period of time around 2500 BC. The ruling tribe that lived in the Salalah plain during that time was the Adites. According to local tradition, the Adites were giants.[34]

10. ARABIA IS THE TRADITIONAL LAND FOR PREPARATION

The Jaredites left Babel bound for a promised land. However, they did not seem overly righteous at the time. The brother of Jared was their spiritual leader, yet at one point he had not prayed for a long period of time (Ether 2:15) and the Lord chastised the Jaredites because of their sinning (Ether 2:15). It seems that a preparatory period was necessary before they would be worthy and seen to be obedient (Ether 2:8). An established place for preparing for a promised land has been Arabia. Before entering their promised land, the children of Israel had to wander in the wilderness of northern Arabia for forty years.[35] The Lehites spent eight years in the Arabian desert before building their ship to sail to the New World. The great explorer Sir Richard Burton wrote of his time in Arabia:

Cave above Khor Rori where Ali Al-Shahri collected wild honey as a boy.

It was a desert peopled only with echoes—a place of death for what little there is to die in it—a wilderness where, to use my companion's phrase, there is nothing but He, *La siwa hu*—ie, where there is none but Allah.[36]

President David O McKay noted a special significance of this desert peninsula:

After a few days of fiery disputations in the synagogues, Saul concluded to leave Damascus and go into retirement; so, bidding his new friends good-bye, he went into Arabia in the mountains near the Red Sea. Here he received instruction in the School of Solitude.

"O sacred solitude! divine retreat!

Choice of the prudent! envy of the great!

By thy Pure stream, or in thy waving shade,

We court fair wisdom."

Like Moses, Elijah, John the Baptist, and even the Savior Himself, Paul now sought to be alone with God, and to learn how to get his spirit in communion with the Holy Spirit.

How long he remained there, we do not know. All he says about this journey is: "I went into Arabia, and returned again to Damascus."[37]

11. Metal Plates

The Jaredites possessed a technology that was very rare in the ancient world. They knew how to refine metal and to hammer it into gold plates (Mosiah 8:9; 21:27). It is not surprising, then, that archaeologists have discovered the Peruvians who lived along Peru's northern coast, who we think were the Jaredites, were making gold plates as early as 1900 BC.[38]

Artifacts excavated at the Khor Rori include a small bronze plaque.[39] As noted in chapter one, in the early 1950s the American archaeologist Wendell Phillips discovered at Khor Rori seven bronze plates with text on them. In 2007, another bronze plate with writing on it was discovered at Khor Rori and is now on exhibit at the Land of the Frankincense Museum in Salalah, Oman.

The Brother of Jared Was the Biblical Ophir

Why is the Biblical character Ophir another clue for understanding where the Jaredites built their barges? The answer lies in that Ophir was the brother of Jerah. Jerah fled Mesopotamia with Ophir and his other brothers at the time of the confounding of the languages. The family of Jerah initially migrated to southern Arabia[40] (Genesis 10:26–30). The leader of the family was Jerah,[41] who George thinks is none other than the family leader named Jared in the Book of Mormon.

Reverend Charles Forster, a preacher in the Cathedral of Christ, Canterbury, provides these variant spellings for Jerah—*Jarah* (Arabia Felicis), *Jarach, Jare* (St. Jerome), and *Jerhä* by modern Arabs.[42] *Smith's Bible Dictionary* (London, 1863, 1:964) states that "Jared" is the Jered of 1 Chronicles 1:2. According to Smith and Sjodahl's commentary on the Book of Ether, some early Bible translations spelled Jerah, "Jared."[43] Even more impressive are the parallel stories in the books of Genesis and Ether, which make it probable that Jerah of the Bible and Jared of the Book of Mormon are the same person (Genesis 10:25–30; 11:1–9).[44] One element of those parallel accounts is that the brother (Ophir) of Jerah as noted in the Bible and the brother of Jared of the Book of Mormon (who is named Moriancumer according the Prophet Joseph Smith[45]) each had a harbor named after him (1 Kings 10:11, 22; Ether 2:13). Indeed, these two accounts are the only in scripture of a harbor being named after the same person who is a prophet. It would appear that Biblical Ophir and Book of Mormon Moriancumer were the same person.

The brother of Jared's name was revealed to the Prophet Joseph Smith in Kirtland, Ohio, while the Saints were headquartered there. George Reynolds wrote, "While residing in Kirtland, Elder Reynolds Cahoon had a son born to him. One day when President Joseph Smith was passing his door he called the Prophet and

the land of Dhofar, with its port at Khor Rori, was the Biblical land of Sephar[47] where the man Ophir settled (1 Genesis 10:29–30). Local Khor Rori historian Ali Al-Shahri, who has been invited to make presentations at Brigham Young University, is a member of the Shahri tribe. As noted earlier, he has published a book that traces his own genealogy to the man Ophir. His family still owns land surrounding the harbor of Khor Rori, and he claims that Khor Rori is the Biblical port of Ophir[48] and is the property of his tribe. His book of his family's genealogy traces the family roots to the man Ophir and includes a map indicating that the Ophir tribal lands includes Khor Rori.[49] If true, then the port Khor Rori is not only the place where Nephi built his ship, but it is also the port where Solomon's ships of Tarshish were sent to bring back gold, peacocks, and other riches from Ophir (1 Kings 10:11–22). It is generally accepted by Biblical scholars that King Solomon's Tarshish was probably a port on the Indian Ocean (see LDS Bible Dictionary). It has also been claimed by historians that Ophir is the original name for Khor Rori.[50] Indeed, growing evidence indicates the Jaredites and the Nephites built their ships at the same harbor in

Driving the dunes in the Empty Quarter of Arabia.

asked him to name the baby. Joseph did so and gave the boy the name Mahonri Moriancumer. When he had finished the blessing, he laid the child on the bed, and turning to Elder Cahoon he said, the name *I have given your son is the name of the Brother of Jared; the Lord has just shown (or revealed) it to me.*[46]

The LDS Bible Dictionary states that Ophir was probably a port in southern Arabia. Indeed, many scholars believe that the port of Khor Rori, where we say Nephi built and launched his ship, was the ancient port of Ophir. The Reverend Charles Forster, for example, sustains the traditional argument that

211

southern Arabia. Further, since the Book of Mormon does not tell us that all of the Jaredites and their friends left in their eight barges, and since it appears the Lord had to command the Jaredites after a long stay at Khor Rori to get to work building their transoceanic barges, some of the Jared party likely did not favor the idea of sailing for an unknown destination and stayed behind to become Ali Al-Shahri's ancestors.

The implications here are powerful. First, Biblical Jerah appears to be the same person as the Book of Mormon Jared. Second, the brother of Jared in the Book of Mormon appears to have been Biblical Ophir who had a harbor named after him—perhaps so named because it was the place from which he and his important family and associates built ships and departed from Arabia. Like the city and harbor location that they named Ophir and which was named after the brother of Biblical Jerah/Jared, the Book of Mormon Jaredites also named the land where they had built their barges and sailed away after the brother of Jared. They called that area Moriancumer (Ether 2:13). The question is, why would the same man, the brother of Jared, be called by two names, Ophir and Moriancumer?

Ali Al-Shahri discusses with George his tribe's geneaology.

At first this might seem confusing that the brother of Jared was named Ophir in the Bible but was not called by that name in the Book of Mormon. Moroni's abbreviated version of the Book of Ether was included in the "sacred" Nephite record. The original Jaredite plates were probably written entirely in the New World and may not have referred to the brother of Jared as Ophir or Moriancumer. To understand why, we need to remember that something special happened to the brother of Jared (Ophir) just before he left the Old World for the promised land. The brother of Jared may have been given a new or sacred name when he saw the Lord through the veil (Ether 3:13). Under similar circumstances, new names were given to Abram (Abraham), Jacob (Israel), Saul (Paul), and other prophets. In other words, it maybe that the man Ophir, who went up the mountain with sixteen stones, came down the mountain as Moriancumer (see "Tall Mountain" on page 59).

The Jaredites called the land where they built their ships next to the sea *Moriancumer* (Ether 2:13, emphasis added). Tribes in the Near East have the tradition of naming mountains, wadis, and other geographical features after people who are important to them. Lehi was no exception in his naming the valley they camped in after his son Lemuel and the river that flowed by their tents after another son, Laman. For this reason, we think it possible that the tribal name of the Jaredites may have been "Moriancumer" after the great prophet.[51] Note these facts: the two mountain ranges just to the west of the Khor Rori are called the Marrah mountains and the Qamar mountains, the latter sometimes spelled Camar or Comar. These mountains run parallel to the Indian Ocean and follow each other. It is common to see on maps of southern Arabia the two names written side by side, the Marrah Camar[52] mountains. Of course, Latin spellings of Arabic words change over time, and it is also true that Arabic is a vocalized language where

vowels are not written. By removing the vowels we have *Mrncmr* (Moriancumer, the land where the Jaredites built their ships) or *Mrrcmr* (Marrah Camar, the two mountain ranges immediately to the west of the Salalah coastal plain).

There is one more linguistic clue that points to the Jaredites having sailed from southern Arabia. Nibley notes: "The name Kish, which is both an Old World and a Jaredite name. Now this name—Kish, Kash, Kush—is according to Hrozny, the most widespread proper name in the ancient world."[53] Kish or Kush (Cush) was the grandson of Noah, and the father of Nimrod. According to the LDS Biblical Dictionary, Cush's descendants established the Kingdom of Cush in southern Arabia.[54]

In partial summary, we think it is quite defensible to suggest that there was a small colony of people at Khor Rori when the Jaredites arrived. This was only five generations after the Flood. Those people already at Khor Rori likely were not sophisticated in many things, yet they were already trading with India for teak wood and cotton. The immigrating Jaredites brought with them language and technical arts from Mesopotamia and quickly organized the

people and took control of southern Oman. The names they gave to the lands and geographic features survived. As Reverend Forster pointed out, Jerad is considered the father of all the tribes of southern Arabia. After a period, the Lord chastened the brother of Jared for not praying. They were at the place where they built barges for four years and perhaps were thinking it was an isolated place where their language would not be corrupted and didn't see the need to move on. When two (Jerah and Ophir) of the thirteen sons of Joktan (Genesis 10:25–30) left for the promised land, some of Jerah's and Ophir's own families as well as their brothers' families stayed behind, continuing to maintain the place where Ophir had built the barges. Salalah is a very pleasant place to live; the climate and coastline remind one of southern California. We can assume many families remained because of the fact that Ali Ali-Shahri's tribal genealogy is traced back to Ophir. As religious history shows, some people hear the calling and respond, while others stay put. Further, the fact that Khor Rori was once named Ophir is documented in Ali's book published by the Ministry of Culture of the Sultan of Oman.

213

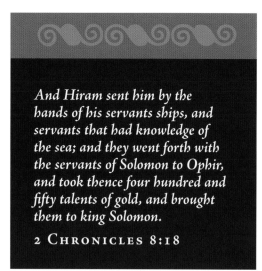

And Hiram sent him by the hands of his servants ships, and servants that had knowledge of the sea; and they went forth with the servants of Solomon to Ophir, and took thence four hundred and fifty talents of gold, and brought them to king Solomon.

2 CHRONICLES 8:18

Notes

1. B. H. Roberts, *New Witnesses for God*, vol. 3, 170; Hugh W. Nibley, *The Collected Works of Hugh Nibley*, vol. 5; "Book of Mormon Near Eastern Background," *Encyclopedia of Mormonism*, vol. 1.

2. "Book of Mormon Near Eastern Background," *Encyclopedia of Mormonism*, vol. 1.

3. J. M. Sjodahl, *An Introduction to the Study of the Book of Mormon* (Salt Lake City: Deseret News Press, 1927), 410.

4. "Tower of Babel," New Advent, http://newadvent.org/cathen/15005b.htm.

5. LDS Bible Dictionary, "Nimrod."

6. *Collective Works of Hugh Nibley*, vol. 6, 135.

7. George Potter and Richard Wellington, "Discovering the Lehi/Nephi Trail," 2000, unpublished.

8. With the discovery of oil in Saudi Arabia, permanent camps (at great cost) have been established in the Empty Quarter.

9. George Potter, *Ten More Amazing Discoveries* (Springville, Utah: Cedar Fort, 2005), 25–41.

10. Ibid.

11. Taylor, *Traveling the Sands*, 97.

12. Ibid., 100.

13. Ibid., 19.

14. Ibid.

15. Ministry of National Heritage and Culture, *Oman, A Seafaring Nation*, 20–22.

16. Ibid., 14.

17. Potter and Wellington, "Discovering the Lehi/Nephi Trail."

18. Ibid.

19. "Diamonds of the Sultans," http://www.adventurearabia.com/diamondsnf/htm.

20. Potter and Wellington, "Discovering the Lehi/Nephi Trail."

21. http://gcubad.magnet.fsu.edu/publicationfinal/articles/BGT/1999GC000002/a1999GC000002.html, http://www.amf.com.au/amf/porph98d.html, accessed June 2010.

22. "Oman Exports Quartz," http://www.tradeport.org/ts/countries/Oman/tradcx.html.

23. www.campublic.co.uk/science/publications/jconfabs/4/376.htm

24. http://www.utech.co.uk/world/middleeast/oman/facts/html.

25. http://billybee.com/infocenter.html, accessed June 2010.

26. Ibid.

27. Ibid.

28. Ibid

29. http://billybee.com/infocenter.html, accessed June 2010 and Ministry of National Heritage and Culture, *Oman, A Seafaring Nation*, 14–15.

30. http://book.nap.edu/books/03094295X.html/364.

31. "Honeybees of the Genus apis," http://www.fao.org/docrep/x0083e/x0083E02.htm.

32. *Evening and Morning Star*, Aug. 1832, 2.

33. Ibid.

34. Nicolas Clapp, *The Road to Ubar* (Boston: Houghton Mifflin, 1998).

35. Potter, *Ten More Amazing Discoveries*, 25–62.

36. Taylor, *Traveling the Sands*, 30.

37. David O. McKay, *Ancient Apostles* (Salt Lake City: Deseret Book, 1964), 146.

38. John Sorenson, *An Ancient American Setting for the Book of Mormon* (Provo, UT: FARMS, 1996), 279–80; cited by Jeff Lindsay at http://www.jefflindsay.com/LDSFAQ/FQ_metals.shtml#ores

39. "Excavations and Restoration of the Complex of Khor Rori, Interim Report," 4, 12–15.

40. Rev. Charles Forster, B.D., *The Historical Geography of Arabia* (London: Darf Publishers Limited, 1984), 77–133.

41. Ibid., 115.

42. Ibid., 12.

43. "Jaredites in the Bible," http://www.exmormon.org.uk/tol_arch/whyprophets/prophets/ophir.htm.

44. Genesis 10:25–29: Ophir's uncle is Peleg who lived when the earth was divided. Ophir's brother is Jerah (Jared). Genesis 10:26–30: Jerah, Ophir, and other brothers move to Mesha at Sephar, with a mountain on the east. Many scholars believe Sephar is Zopher or Dhofar in Oman, whose harbor was called Mosha (Mesha) by the Greeks. The tallest mountain in all southern Oman is Mt.

Desert in Arabia

Samban on the east end of Dhofar. During the brothers lifetimes, the Lord confounds their languages and the people are scattered (Genesis 11:9).

45. Bruce R. McConkie, *Mormon Doctrine* (Salt Lake City: Bookcraft, 1966), 463.

46. McConkie, *Mormon Doctrine*, 463, italics is in that text, which is referenced to *Juvenile Instructor*, vol. 27, 282, and *Improvement Era*, vol. 8, 704–705.

47. Forster, *Historical Geography of Arabia*, 106.

48. Al-Shahri, *Language of Aad*, 30–35.

49. Ibid.

50. Thomas, *The Arabs*, 262. Nigel Groom also notes the similarity between the names of Zufar (Dhofar) and Ophir: "Zufar is sometimes proposed as a likely word etymologically close to Ophir, while the nineteenth-century traveler Vod Wrede observed that the Mahra of south Arabia, who lived adjacent to Zufar and whose language has very ancient origins, used the word 'ofir' to mean 'red' and called themselves the tribe of 'Ofir', meaning the 'red country' " (Nigel Groom, *Frankincense and Myrrh*, 49–50.)

51. hht://www.squ.edu.om/tabid/4957/language/en-US/Default.aspx.

52. The name Camar, Qamar, or Comor are all Latin spellings for the Arabic word for *moon*. The argument would be stronger if the term were of the language of the Jaredites and not the much later Arabic language.

53. *Collected Works of Hugh Nibley*, vol. 6, 330.

54. LDS Bible Dictionary, *Cush*.

THE JAREDITE BARGES

HAVE YOU EVER wondered what the Paleo-Indians of the Americas must have thought when they saw the Jaredite ships approaching their shoreline? It would be analogous to seeing a UFO in our day. Novelist and ancient ship expert Clive Cussler provides a fictional account of similar magnitude:

> The monster emerged from the morning mists in the pearly light of dawn. The massive head, with its long snout and flaring nostrils, advanced toward the shore where the hunter knelt, bowstring taut to his cheek, eyes focused on a deer grazing in the marsh. A rippling sound caught the hunter's ear and he glanced out at the water. He uttered a fearful moan, threw the bow aside, and leaped to his feet. The startle deer disappeared into the woods with the terrified hunter close on its tail.
>
> The tendrils of fog parted to reveal a giant sailing ship.[1]

The sight of eight Jaredite ships approaching land likely put fear into the hearts of ancient Native Americans. The sailing ship had been invented in Sumer, and before the Jaredites left Sumer and its tower of Babel, they appear to have been shipbuilders (Ether 2:16). The question that needs to be answered is, "What kind of ships did they build?"

The translation of the Book of Ether uses the words "vessels" (Ether 2:22) and "barges" (Ether 2:16) to describe the Jaredite ships. What did this mean to the Prophet Joseph Smith as he translated the golden plates? According to Webster's *American Dictionary of the English Language*, First Edition 1828, we learn:

> *VESSEL* 4. Any building used in navigation, which carries a mast and sails, from the largest ship of war down to a fishing sloop.[2]
>
> *BARGE*, [D. *bargie*; It.[atlan] and Spanish; *barca*; Ir *barc. Barge*, and *bark* or *barque*, a ship, are radically one word.[3]

We learn from Webster that in 1828 the word *barge* meant a ship. Webster traced the word to *barca* or *barcoin*, which means "small boat" or "ship."[4] When the Book of Mormon uses the word *vessel* for the Jaredite ships, it was likely describing a sailing ship. This is supported in the Book of Mormon in its description of the Jaredite ships being blown by a furious wind upon the face of the waters, "and thus they were tossed upon the waves of the sea before the wind" (Ether 6:5). Even the phrase "before the wind" (Ether 6:5) is a common sailing term. Sailors refer to sailing "before the wind"[5] when the wind is blowing astern or from the back of the ship. In the Jaredites' case, this meant they must have been aboard sailing ships with the wind blowing from the rear of the ships and pushing them "toward the promised land" (Ether 6:5). Undoubtedly, Joseph Smith knew little about sailing, yet here is another example of the exactness of his translation.

Another indication the Book of Mormon text refers to Jaredite sailing ships that "were driven forth before the wind" (Ether 6:8) and which "were driven forth, three hundred and forty and four days upon the waters" (Ether 6:11) is found in Webster's 1828 dictionary. This first American-usage dictionary defines the term "driven" in Joseph Smith's time, which was well before our usage today in reference to automobiles, as being "urged forward by force,"[6] as in wind filling sails and pressing a ship forward.

The Jaredites likely were master shipbuilders. We think the Jaredites had built other Mesopotamian barges before they built the ships they sailed in to the promised land. They were commanded by the Lord to construct ships somewhat similar to those they had previously built. In so doing, it is important to remember that the Lord gave them specific instructions on how to modify their ships rather than a complete design for a vessel. In other words, it appears that the Lord showed them how to make their vessels seaworthy enough to

Mural depicting ancient Persian Gulf port, Bahrain National Museum.

cross the great oceans (Ether 2:16). Thus, it is reasonable to think that the design of Jaredite barges was not too different from what is known about ocean-going vessels from that part of the world in the earliest centuries of civilization.

An analysis of the ancient Magan (ancient Omani) ships that sailed the seas of the Near East circa 2500 BC gives a model of what the Jaredite ships may have looked like. Accordingly, we visited the Maritime Hall at the Museum of the Frankincense Land in Salalah, Oman. On display is the latest scholarly thought about these early seagoing ships. The display states:

> This is a hypothetical reconstruction of a trading vessel of the mid 3rd millennium BC, which was based on iconography and direct evidence discovered at Ras Al Jinz in eastern Oman. The vessel comprises reed bundles lashed together, with reed matting "quilted" onto the reed–built hull. The vessel is then coated inside and out with bitumen, and the outside smeared with mud. The port side of the model shows the four layers that comprise the hull. Some wooden elements, such as beams, steering gear supports and quarter rudders, as well as a bipod mast and yard, also are featured in the construction.[7]

Thor Heyerdahl was one of the earliest to identify that the reed ships of Mesopotamia match with considerable exactness the reed ships of Lake Titicaca in Peru and Bolivia. These Mesopotamian ships were amazing for their day. The Mesopotamian ships had hulls that were formed by using a light-weight composite of multiple layers of material. These unique vessels seem to match well the description of the Jaredite ships provided in the Book of Mormon. The text says the Lord commanded the Jaredites to construct ships that were "small," and "light upon the water, even like unto the lightness of a fowl upon the water" (Ether 2:16). While reeds are a light-weight material, if the entire hull were of solid reeds the heavy ship would rest deep in the water. Thus, ancient seagoing Omani ships used tight bundles of reeds to form only the outer shell of the ship. The reed shell was then water proofed by quilting a smooth layer of reed matting on both sides of the reed bundles. Then, both the inner and outer matting received a coating of bitumen (pitch or petroleum sealer). In this way, the hollow hulls of the Omani ships could hold within them the Jaredites and their provisions, and still float lightly upon the water like a bird.

Model of third millennium BC vessel in the Museum of the Frankincense Land at Salalah (near Khor Rori). Shows 4 layers of the hull.

Another informative clue that the Jaredite ships were patterned after Omani ships is that they were "tight like a dish." In fact, the Jaredite ships were airtight, completely sealed from light and air (Ether 2:19). The bottom, sides, and top of the Jaredite barges were, thus, tight like a dish (Ether 2:17). So what does that mean? Dishes in the Middle East in the third millennium BC were simple earthen-ware pottery made from a mixture of clay and sand that was dried until it was hardened by sunlight. When fully dried, the sand inside the clay sealed the pot to make it waterproof. We read that Omani ships had a final layer of pottery clay applied to the outer side of the

George discovers a 4,000-year-old earthen-ware pot in Arabia.

hull. In other words, the ships were sealed tight and had the exact outer appearance of an ancient dish and pottery.

Like Omani ships, the Jaredite ships appear to have been made of a composite sealer, two layers of sealing or tightness. The Jaredite ships were "tight like unto a dish, and also they were tight like unto the ark of Noah" (Ether 6:7) As we have noted, Omani ships had a final pottery clay shell as did their dishes. However, before receiving the mud coating the ships were coated inside and out with bitumen. What other ancient ship do we know that was coated with bitumen? It was Noah's Ark (Genesis 6:14).

Two other characteristics of Omani ships also comply with the description of Jaredite ships. First, they were peaked at both ends, with no flat sterns. Second, they were about the length of a tree. The similarities of the Jaredite ships to the newest theories on the nature of ancient Omani ships are incredible.

The Jaredite ships, however, required at least one important modification. It was a change inspired by the Lord in order for the Jaredite vessels to be strong enough to cross the Pacific. A vessel's ability to cross the Pacific is a function of both speed and strength. To cross the Pacific fast enough for its sailors to avoid dying of thirst or starvation, a sailing ship requires strong and constant winds and must sail as far south as the Roaring Forties. Such winds drive the ship; but in turn, those winds subject the vessel to pressures that would be too severe for a reed hull to withstand during long months at sea. Thus, the Lord said: "For the mountain waves shall dash upon you. . . . And behold, I prepare you against these things; for ye cannot cross this great deep save I prepare you against the waves of the sea, and the winds" (Ether 2:24–25).

For this reason, we think the Jaredites constructed ships similar to those they had previously built and that they replaced the reed-bundle shell, or at least lined it, with wooden planks and used a wooden keel and wooden beams to add significant strength for the hull. It is even possible that the Jaredites previously had built large wooden ships. Graham Faiella, author of *The Technology of Mesopotamia*, writes that the "largest boats and ferries [of Mesopotamia] were made of wood that were 20 to 30 feet (6 to 9 m) long."[8]

The Book of Mormon seems to indicate that the Jaredites used a single log to form the keels of their ship because the Jaredites described their vessels as being "the length of a tree" (Ether 2:17). If the

Jaredites formed in part the hull of their ships using wood beams and wood planks and then coated their hulls with bitumen and mud, then their ships would have been built in a process remarkably similar to how Arabian dhows (ships) are still constructed to this day. There are still shipyards along the Persian Gulf and Arabian Sea where we have observed large dhows being fabricated. Using traditional tools, shipwrights spend up to six months forming the wooden hull of the dhow. Once completed, the inside and outside of the hull is coated in fiberglass (today's bitumen). When dried, the outside of the hull receives a final coat of marine sealing-paint (today's clay and sand).

Before the Jaredites started building their ships for sailing to the promised land, they lived at the shoreline of the "great sea" for more than four years. It is likely the Jaredites had built other Omani-type ships during the four years they lived there before the Lord pointedly said "go to work and build" (Ether 2:16). It is likely they would have used these ships to learn the art of sailing in open waters. However, such ships would not have been capable of surviving a crossing of the Indian and Pacific Oceans. The Lord said "Ye cannot cross this great deep save I prepare you against the waves of the sea, and the winds which have gone forth, and the floods which shall come" (Ether 2:25). The Lord described their experience as being like a "whale in the midst of the sea; for the *mountain waves shall dash upon you*" (Ether 2:24, emphasis added). The Jaredite ships were not submarines as some may have thought but were like other sailing ships that would be subject during storms to severe high winds and great waves crashing over the ships, submerging them for a some seconds. This is confirmed in the same verse where the Lord explained the source of the waves that would cover the Jaredite ships, "for the winds have gone forth out of my mouth" (Ether 2:24). It also would have given their mud-sealed domed decks the appearance of a whale's back as the waves crashed over them. "For behold, ye shall be as a whale," said the Lord (Ether 2:24).

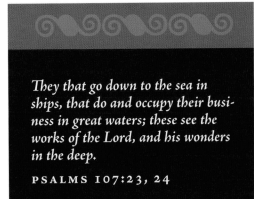

They that go down to the sea in ships, that do and occupy their business in great waters; these see the works of the Lord, and his wonders in the deep.

PSALMS 107:23, 24

As discussed earlier, the Jaredite barges would have had sails. They were "driven forth before the wind" (Ether 6:8). Without sails, a power source, the Jaredites would have had no means of steering and the eight barges could not have stayed together. It is possible that the sixteen stones not only provided light below deck, but that they also may have functioned to emanate light above deck and outward to allow a man to steer at night and keep an eye on the position of the other ships by seeing their lights at night.

Notes

1. Cussler, *The Navigator* (New York: Berkley Books, 2008), 1.

2. Webster, *American Dictionary of the English Language,* "Vessel."

3. Ibid., "Barge."

4. Webster's Classic Reference Library, English Spanish Dictionary (Ashland, Ohio: Landoll, 2000), 16.

5. See "before the wind," Sea Talk Nautical Dictionary, http://www.seatalk.info/, accessed January 19, 2009.

6. Websters, *American Dictionary of the English Language,* "Driven."

7. *The Museum of the Frankincense Land—The Maritime Hall* (Muscat: Office of the Advisor to His Majesty the Sultan for Cultural Affairs, 2007), 25.

8. Graham Faiella, *The Technology of the Ancient World, The Technology of Mesopotamia,* Google Books, accessed 8 July 2008, 21, http://books.google.com.

Give me a spirit that on this life's rough sea
Loves t'have his sails filled with a lusty wind,
Even till his sail-yards tremble, his masts crack,

And his rapt ship run on her side so low
That she drinks water, and her keel plows air.
GEORGE CHAPMAN, TRAGEDY OF
CHARLES, DUKE OF BYRON

THE VOYAGE OF THE JAREDITES TO NEW OPHIR

CHAPTER NINE

THE JAREDITES are believed to have been a "very large race of men."[1] Father Bernadé Cobo (1582–1657) was convinced that giants had lived along the Peruvian coast a short period before the first Inca and he provided several testimonials of Spaniards who had seen the skeletons of giants.[2] The Indians, Cobo explains, "say that giants had come there from the south in large rafts."[3] After the first race of humanity was destroyed by a flood, Peruvian mythology holds that the white god created a second race of humanity and "he also gave each nation the language they were to speak, the songs they were to sing."[4]

Gary Urton of Harvard University notes that the Peruvian creator god was a "trinity" of gods,[5] and provides this summary of their creation lore:

> Most versions of this origin myth start by asserting that, in the beginning of time, all was in darkness, as the sun, moon and stars had not yet been created. Into this primeval darkness there emerged the creator Viracocha; . . . [Andeans' bearded white god]. In various versions the creator is called Con Tici Viracocha, Thunupa Viracocha, and Viracocha Pachayachachic . . . certain coastal myths that identify the creator as ('maker of earth/time').
>
> In this time and space of darkness, Viracocha, who is described by Betanzos as a lord who emerged from Lake Titicaca, came forth and created the first race of humanity. These first beings, whom some chroniclers identify as a race of giants, lived in the darkness for a period of time but then, for some unspecified reason, they angered Viracocha. Because of his anger and his

Peruvian pot depicting reed fishing boat.

disappointment with them, the creator brought the first age to an end by a flood.[6]

Father Martín de Murúa, who learned to speak Quechua and Aymara, recorded that "the old Indians state that [after the Flood] the brothers saw a rainbow in the sky. Manco Capac told his brothers that the rainbow was a good sign and the world would not be destroyed again by water."[7] Urton notes:

In the version of the origin myth recounted by Cristobal de Molina, we read a slightly different account of the nature of events at the beginning of time. Molina begins when the world was already populated. Then there came a great flood, the waters of which covered even the highest mountains. The only survivors of this deluge were a man and a woman who, as the waters subsided, were thrown up onto the land of Tiahuanaco. Viracocha appeared and commanded the couple to remain there as *mitimaes* [migrants], the name given to groups of people who were moved by the Inca from their home territory to some other place in the empire.

Molina then says that after the flood subsided, the creator set about repopulating the land, fashioning the ancestors of the different nations of

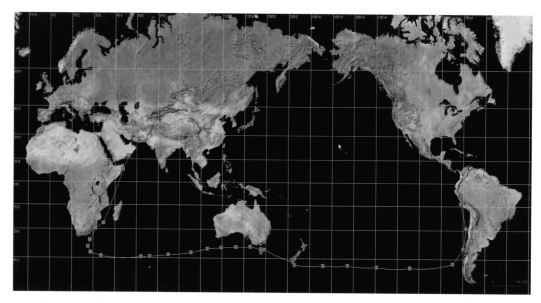

Simulated 27 legs of the Jaredite passage from southern Arabia to northern Peru.

Tahuantinsuyu out of clay, and painting them in the manner of the dress they were to wear.[8]

Then Urton quotes Molina directly:

. . . they [Incas] had an ample account of the deluge. They say that in it perished all races of men and created things insomuch that the waters rose above the highest mountain peaks in the world. No living thing survived except a man and a woman who remained in a box and, when the waters subsided, the wind carried them . . . to Tiahuanaco [where] the creator began to raise up the people and the nations that are in that region.[9]

Though the Andean creator mythology recalls events that occurred at the dawn of history, it was obvious to the Spanish that the early Peruvians had a basic knowledge of the creation and the great Flood. The Peruvians also appear to have had a communal memory that a large-sized people arrived on their shoreline and brought with them the blessings of their first civilization. The most remarkable Peruvian account of the Flood was recorded by Sarmiento (comments in brackets are by the authors):

It is related that everything was destroyed in the flood called *una pachacuti*. It must now be known that Viracocha Pachayachachi [bearded white god], when he destroyed the land as has been already recounted, preserved three men, one of them named Taguapaca, that they might serve and help him in the creation of new people who had to be made in the second age [dispensation], which was done in this manner. The flood being passed and the land dry, Viracocha determined to people it a second time, and, to make it more perfect, he decided upon creating luminaries to give it light [sixteen stones of the Jaredites]. With this object he went, with his servants, to a great lake in the Collao [in the Jaredite barges], in which there is an island called Titicaca [South America?].[10]

The latest archaeological discoveries in the Americas confirm the birth of a New World civilization that began in northern Peru at the time of the Jaredites. Charles Mann writes:

A few decades ago, many researchers would have included jump-starting Andean civilization on the honor roll of Mesoamerican accomplishments. The Olmec, it was proposed, visited Peru, and the locals, dutiful students, copied their example. Today we know that technologically sophisticated societies arose in Peru first—the starting date, to archaeologists' surprise, keeps getting pushed back. Between 3200 and 2500 BC, large-scale public buildings, the temple at Huaricanga among them, rose up in at least seven settlements on the Peruvian coast—an extraordinary efflorescence for that time and place. When the people of Norte Chico were building these cities, there was only one other urban complex on earth: Sumer.[11]

Thus, during the period of the early Book of Mormon Jaredites, a major civilization rose in Peru, with massive public buildings and temples. In contrast, in 2500 BC the Olmecs of Central America were not even on the scene, and it would be another thousand years before the first Olmec cities were built. Even the famed pyramid construction that was once thought to have originated in Mesoamerica is now known to have emerged centuries earlier from Peru.[12]

In 1941, Harvard archaeologists Gordon R. Willey and John M. Corbett worked at the mouth of one of Norte Chico's rivers, the Supe. They observed a half-dozen mounds or knolls and reported that they were "natural eminences of sand."[13] They had been fooled by the deceiving desert landscape. Fifty-three years later, Ruth Shady Solies from the National University of San Marcos in Lima discovered in the same area the remains of a 150-acre city that included six large platform mounds, sunken ceremonial plazas, six other complexes of mounds with platforms, and large stone buildings with residential apartments. The city has been named Caral.

It became quickly apparent that Caral was a very ancient city. Jonathan Hass, an archaeologist for the Chicago's Field Museum of Natural History, and his wife Winifred Creamer, an archaeologist at Northern Illinois University, in 2000 established by radiocarbon-dating that Caral was founded about 2600 BC.[14] That was just the beginning for more discoveries in the area. In the sixty-mile-long area that constitutes Norte Chico, the ruins of twenty-four other ancient cities have been discovered. From what we currently know, Norte Chico is the site of the New World's first urban complex. Charles Mann writes: "Taken individually, none of the twenty-five Norte Chico cities rivaled Sumer's cities in size, but their totality was bigger than Mesopotamia's Sumer . . . Egypt's pyramids were larger, but they were built centuries later."[15]

An urban center larger than Sumer in Peru! With a pyramid mound sixty feet tall and five hundred feet long on all sides. Of special interest to students of the Book of Mormon is that the only other city-state civilization existing at that time was Sumer of Tower of Babel and our Jaredite fame. How exciting! A sister civilization in antiquity that matched that of Mesopotamia in achievements! We remember that Sumer in Mesopotamia was the original home of the Jaredites. The discovery of Caral is of paramount importance in the study of Book of Mormon historicity. Indeed, for the first time archaeologists have discovered a civilization in the Americas that dates to the era of the early Jaredites. Further, the pyramids of Caral present a striking resemblance to the ziggurat pyramids of Mesopotamia, being composed of sunbaked bricks, terraced with successive receding levels and a ramp on one side. The Supe River runs past Caral to the nearby Pacific. Given the archaeological footprint of the Americas, we suggest the Jaredites landed in or near Norte Chico's Puerto Supe (Port Supe), a natural harbor that protects ships from the southeast Pacific swells. The harbor is located 100 miles north of Lima.

New Ophir—Another Amazing Insight from the Book of Mormon

The Book of Mormon account of the brother of Jared, who we believe was Ophir, solves a puzzle historians have failed to resolve. Why did the pre-Columbian Peruvians believe they were descendants of Ophir? And why did they originally call Peru "Ophir?" George thinks the answers to those questions are that some of the Peruvians are descendants of the Jaredites and of the brother of Jared (Ophir), and that just as they had named the Arabian harbor where they built their barges after him (Ophir/Moriancumer), they also named their new homeland after their same great founding prophet, the man who saw and talked with the Lord.

Spanish chroniclers wrote that the Incas believed the first people who arrived in their land called it *Pirua* (corrupted by the Spanish into *Peru*). Earlier, other Spanish chroniclers were told by the Indians that the name *Pirua* was derived from the name "Ophir," the same name as the Biblical brother of Jerah (who we claim is the Book of Mormon Jared) (Genesis 10:29; 1 Kings 10:11, 22).

Like later European colonizers in the Americas, Book of Mormon peoples followed the custom of naming lands they migrated to after places they had left behind, such as Bountiful (Alma 22:29), Midian (Alma 24:5), Ishmael (Alma 17:19), and Jerusalem (Alma 21:1–2). Book of Mormon scholar Janne M. Sjodahl cites, "Fernando Montesinos . . . records the theory that Ophir, a 'grandson of Noah' settled 'Hamerica,' as he spells the name, 340 years after the deluge, and that 'Peru,' the name, is derived from 'Ophir.'"[16] Montesinos believed that God led Ophir's party to Peru, gave them commandments, but that they became greedy and a war broke out over land and material possession."[17] In fact, James Adair wrote: "Postellus, Philippe de Mornay, Arias Montanus, and Goropius, are of the opinion that Peru is the ancient Ophir."[18]

Cobo conjectured that there were four reasons why many Spaniards even believed that in discovering Peru (Piru) they had located Biblical Ophir:

> First, the authority of Admiral Christopher Columbus . . . [who believed] he had discovered the land of Ophir; second, the similarity and relationship between these two names Ophir and Peru. . . .

The third conjecture that moves them to adopt this opinion is the abundance of gold, precious and exquisite woods, and many apes, peacocks, and other unusual and very valuable things that Solomon's ships brought from Ophir. . . .

The fourth and last reason is the long period of time that those ships [Solomon's] took on the trip, which was three years . . . [19]

In 1989, US explorer Gene Savoy, who is credited with discovering forty-three "lost cities" in the Andes, said that he found a King Solomon–era icon for the land Ophir on three stone tablets in Peru. According to an article posted on the website of the Neil A. Maxwell Institute (FARMS) at BYU: "At the Grand Vilaya, he [Gene Savoy] discovered carved stone Stella inscribed with what may prove to be the only known example of pre-Columbian linear writing found *in situ* in South America."[20] Of additional interest, it should also be remembered that Nephi knew the name Ophir, for he engraved it on the golden plates (2 Nephi 23:12).

The Ophir-Jaredite link in the Book of Mormon is one of the most impressive of all the available knowledge pools of material and information that collectively confirm that the Book of Mormon is a true historical account. David Calderwood provides a digest of the Flood-Ophir traditions in Peru:

Ziggurat-like pyramids, Caral, Peru.

Because many of the native American kingdoms believed in some kind of flood, many trace their origins to a post-diluvial period. One of the most interesting of the early chroniclers who supported the theory of a post-diluvial migration was a Catholic priest, Miguel Cabello Valboa, a great-nephew of Vasco Nuñez de Balboa [first European to view the Pacific]. In his book *Misceláneo Antártica: Una Historia del Peru Antiguo*, initially written in 1586, but not published until 1951, Cabello Valboa wrote that he came to the Americas with the "obsession of discovering the origin of the Americans."

Cabello Valboa believed that the fathers of these Indians separated themselves from the grandchildren and great-grandchildren of Noah at the time of the Tower of Babel when God punished the tower-builders by confounding their language. Cabello Valboa not only identified the time of this migration to America, but claimed that Ophir, the son of Joktan and the grandson of Heber, and a great-great-grandson of Shem, who was the son of Noah, was the leader of the group. In formulating his theory, Cabello Valboa cited writings from Josephus, Ptolemy, and I Kings 10:11, which record that King Solomon sent Hiram, King of Tyre, to Ophir to obtain gold. He also cited the writing of Saint Jerome, who upon discussing the whereabouts of the sons of Joktan, wrote that he had no further information about them as they disappeared at the time of the confounding of tongues.

. . . According to Cabello Valboa, Ophir and his followers were led to the Americas by God, who gave them commandments, directed them to build temples, and taught them about agriculture. He argued that these descendants of Heber kept the commandments of God, continued to worship Him, and did not have their language confounded.

He also identified numerous words employed by the Indians that appear to be a form of Hebrew. He believed the name Peru to be a derivation of the name Ophir in which Ophir became Opiri, then Piru and eventually Peru. He also believed the name of the Yucatán Peninsula in Mesoamerica was named after Father Joktan.

Cabello Valboa was not the only chronicler to provide considerable detail concerning a post-flood migration to the Americas. As mentioned previously, one of the more controversial of the early Conquistador writers was Fernando de Montesinos. By 1628, Montesinos had received the "sacred orders" within the Catholic Church and had transferred to the New World. After 1640, Montesinos finished his book *Memorias Antiguas Historials y Políticas del Perú*, in 1642, while living in Ecuador. As happened with most of the manuscripts written by the early chroniclers, Montesinos's manuscript was lost for several hundred years and was not published until 1909.

Montesinos also maintained that God led Ophir, grandson of Heber, and his descendants to the New World and gave them strict commandments to live by. These descendants lived for a few years in peace and harmony, obeying the commandments of God, but later war broke out over greed for land and material possessions. Montesinos asserted that the people became very greedy. Montesinos did not specify the route Ophir and his group followed in leaving the Old World, but indicated that, after arriving in the New World, they mainly populated Peru and Chile.

Another chronicler who stipulated that the native Americans came to the New World shortly after the universal flood was Indian chronicler Felipe Guaman Poma de Ayala. He provided supporting information to Cabello Valboa and Montesinos's theses, in his book, *Nueva Corónica y Buen Gobierno.*[21]

It is apparent that, we are left with the distinct likelihood that Peru is actually named after the great Book of Mormon leader known to us as the "brother of Jared." The amazing parallels between the Jaredite account in the Book of Mormon and the oral traditions of Peru are extremely compelling.

Reed Ship of the Peruvians

The reed sailing ships were first invented in Mesopotamia where they are still used to this day. Likewise, *Totora* reeds are still utilized to build boats in Peru by Pacific fishermen and by the *Uros* Indians on Lake Titicaca (Peru/Bolivia), the highest navigable sea in the world. The Lake Titicaca

basin was settled around 1200 BC, perhaps by remnants of the Jaredites. Thor Heyerdahl compared the reed boats of Peru to the reed boats of Mesopotamia. When he built a replica of a Mesopotamian ship, he called it the *Tigris*. However, he used Bolivians from Lake Titicaca, not Iraqis, to construct the *Tigris*.[22] The similarities between the reed boats of Mesopotamia and Peru are amazing, including the reed animal-head placed on the bow of their boats.

Mesopotamian reed ship.

The Jaredite Voyage

If passengers aboard Nephi's ship at times had a horrific passage to the promised land, think of the long and possibly miserable experience the Jaredites might have had. No wonder the legend of ancient mariners coming to Peru is still ingrained in the combined memories of their descendants' oral traditions. It would have been an event they would have never let their descendants forget. Recall, if you will, the rotten-egg smell below deck of Severin's replica ship. Then consider what the experience must have been like in airtight barges of the Jaredites. Severin wrote of sealing the hatches during a storm: "We prepared the ship for possible squalls, cleared up the clutter on the deck, and hurried to finish sewing the canvas hatch covers. *Sohar's* main hatch measured 12 feet by 6 feet, and was normally covered by an open grating to allow air to get into the fetid hold. I did not relish the prospect of covering up the hatch in a gale and trapping the gas in the bilges, but in bad weather we would have no choice."[23]

Add to that stench the smell from vomit of those seasick and stored human wastes that could not be dispensed overboard during the "many times" the Jaredites were buried in the depths of the sea (Ether 6:6). Their ships were light upon the water, and all on board must have been tossed to and fro during "tempests which were caused by the fieriness of the wind" (Ether 6:6). Undoubtedly, at times people were injured, cooking food made impossible, and items spilled. It was rough sailing, and as our computer simulator predicts, the Jaredites probable course would have been through or near the "Roaring Forties" during their entire eastward voyage. The Book of Mormon describes with exactness

229

Lake Titicaca reed ship, Peru. Photograph by Mylene d'Auriol Stoessel.

the conditions found along the simulator's "best passage" prediction. The Book of Mormon text reads, "God caused that there should be a furious wind blow upon the face of the waters" (Ether 6:5) and "that the wind did never cease to blow toward the promised land while they were upon the waters; and thus they were driven forth before the wind" (Ether 6:8).

Perhaps we can add to the Jaredites' and Nephites' physical sufferings the mental trauma of fears known and fears unknown. Having been shipbuilders in ancient Sumer, the Jaredites would have heard reports of great whales damaging primitive ships of their day. The Book of Mormon accurately describes what would have been seafaring lore that was prevalent from Ophir to the Indian Ocean as well as along the rest of the passage to the promised land: "and no monster of the sea could break them, neither could whale that could mar them" (Ether 6:10).

Severin says of the whales in the waters south of Oman:

> A baby sperm whale appeared. It was 16–18 feet long, and all alone: John guessed that it must have become separated from its parents, and was lost. Perhaps the baby thought *Sohar* could foster it, because the animal showed great curiosity. It swam up astern until only 30 yards always, and then turned and wallowed along on the quarter, inspecting the ship for some time. . . . John commented that in the 1860s there had been enough whales in the Laccadive Sea [in the Indian Ocean] to attract whaling ships. Now, so it seemed, the whale population was almost gone. The whole of the Indian Ocean had recently been declared a

whale sanctuary, but perhaps it was too late.

Saleh, who was at the tiller, now told us how "Haut," the great whale, was capable of rubbing up against a ship's side and overturning it. To frighten the "Haut" away, he said, one should bang two pieces of metal together and make a loud noise. His ideas were interesting, for his story was almost a word-for-word repetition of the early Arab tales, and I note how once again the whale has dominated so many tales of the sea.[24]

Tall tales of the sea become very real once one sails upon the vast waters and next to the giant sea mammals. George was quite relieved one day when canoeing in the San Juan Islands of the Puget Sound that a pod of beautiful Orcas (Killer Whales), no more than 200 yards from his tiny canoe, decided to pass by without paying their respects.

Spending almost a year on a passage to an unknown destiny surely tried even the patience of the most faithful followers of the prophet, the brother of Jared. Perhaps there were even some fights among the family, bouts of depression, and attempted mutinies. Maybe not, but if we were to learn of them it would be understandable.

For all the same reasons discussed earlier in this book when we studied the Nephites' journey, the Jaredites would have spent short periods on land during their 344-day journey. They had to stop for provisions and, as expected, the narrative in the Book of Mormon says there were times that the wind never ceased "while they were upon the waters" (Ether 6:8), possibly inferring that there were times they were not "upon the waters." However, being on shore had its own dangers. Besides possibly unfriendly natives, there was a real danger of coming into contact with a silent killer, a disease that they had not experienced in their homelands and for which they had no immunity. Once an infected member of a family would come aboard ship, a sickness could quickly hit an entire crew or a sickness could spread in the opposite direction to a native population who might have been unprepared for what the foreigners brought. Indeed, many a ghost ship has been burned at sea, the discoverers realizing that a lethal disease had killed everyone aboard.

But since the Jaredite barges made it to the New World, we can hope that their stops along the voyage were as uneventful and perhaps as delightful as the *Banyan's* landing on a particular South Pacific Island.

Date: Sun, 14 Jun 2009 11:04:42 -0600

We moved to another island, the small one next to Hiva Oa. The water is beautiful and there is so much fruit everywhere. We swam to shore and walked along a dirt road. We ended up getting papayas, 30 lbs of mangoes and two big bunches of bananas. We then became friends with a local kid who rowed by in his outrigger canoe. He came over the next morning with a huge bag of breadfruit and these grapefruit type fruits. He also brought a crazy necklace he made him self out of wild boar teeth and shark vertebrae. All he wanted for it was a CD with music on it. Pretty amazing. I gave him a T-shirt and some fish hooks that we won't use. He was really grateful. So now we are in a little anchorage about 2 miles from where the rest of the sailboats are. We went ashore here and found about 6 giant lime/lemon trees. We stocked up on those and also some coconuts. We have been eating off of the land for 3 days; it's incredible. The breadfruit is really delicious. You just cut it up like french fries and cook it in a pan with a bit of oil and it is perfect. 1/2 of one fills all three of us.

Our plan is to leave here later today or tomorrow and head to the Tuamotus, Rangiroa. It will take about 5 days I figure. Then from there we will maybe stop at another atoll or so and then straight to Tahiti . It should take 10 days or so...

I'll email you again when we are a day or so out!

Jody

231

Tracking the Jaredite Voyage

It took Tim Severin six months to sail his replica ship from Arabia to China. Severin stopped for repairs and provisions, but he likely had a more sophisticated sailing vessel than the Jaredites. Given the ancient design of the Jaredite barges and the distance they traveled and the furious winds that constantly pushed them toward

> *I find the great thing in this world*
> *is not so much where we stand,*
> *as in what direction we are moving:*
> *To reach the port of heaven,*
> *we must sail sometimes with the*
> *wind and sometimes against it—*
> *but we must sail, and not drift,*
> *nor lie at anchor.*
>
> OLIVER WENDELL HOLMES

the promised land, a 344-day voyage from Arabia to the New World seems an appropriate time interval (Ether 6:5, 8, 11). Using this information about the length of their trip, we reverse-engineered the passage of the Jaredites based on 344 days and the description of weather and sea conditions. Allowing for stops, the simulator described a very feasible 344-day passage from Oman to Peru. It is a route for ships taking the fall monsoons from Arabia, going along the eastern shore of Africa before joining the Roaring Forties, and then sailing east to Peru. We find it remarkable that the simulator would so closely mimic what the Book of Mormon describes in passage length and conditions experienced.

Passage Summary Report
Khor Rori to New Ophir (Peru)

For space consideration in order to not make this book too bulky, detailed information on each leg of the Jaredite voyage is in the DVD "The Voyages of the Book of Mormon Simulation Output DVD." The DVD is available on the website www. nephiteproject.com.

General Information	Data
Calculated Great Circle Distance	16846.4 NM
Calculated Rhumbline Distance	16874.0 NM
Actual Distance Traveled due to Beating	16876.7 NM
Elapsed Time to Complete Passage	343.4 Days
Fuel Consumption	0.0 Units
Average Boat Speed	2.0 Knots
Boat Speed Made Good	2.0 Knots

Waypoint #	Latitude	Longitude	Date
1	N16°55.27'	E54°34.49'	[DEPART] 1 December
2	N8°20.41'	E50°49.28'	10 December
3	S26°22.24'	E36°59.24'	24 January
4	S29°33.16'	E31°32.46'	29 January
5	S36°2.51'	E27°45.22'	8 February
6	S39°36.00'	E26°25.54'	15 February
7	S42°30.57'	E28°12.77'	19 February
8	S44°5.27'	E35°24.43'	24 February
9	S44°27.80'	E63°16.54	16 March
10	S44°20.31'	E69°27.62'	21 March
11	S43°25.89'	E82°25.84'	3 April
12	S42°26.00'	E98°25.91'	12 April
13	S40°26.51'	E109°45.94'	21 April
14	S39°57.68'	E119°32.44'	29 April

Waypoint #	Latitude	Longitude	Date
15	S39°35.11'	E129°41.31'	7 April
16	S39°28.64'	E139°21.36'	20 April
17	S40°32.62'	E146°40.12'	26 April
18	S40°48.23'	E149°8.79'	28 April
19	S46°47.12'	E168°45.05'	14 June
20	S48°3.44'	E169°42.24'	16 June
21	S48°19.12'	W171°2.18'	3 July
22	S48°14.02'	W154°7.90'	14 July
23	S48°54.10'	W134°9.47'	6 August
24	S49°9.66'	W111°10.41'	2 September
25	S47°16.08'	W81°59.61'	29 September
26	S39°59.70'	W74°41.54'	12 October
27	S28°53.64'	W72°53.00'	24 October
28	S13°27.32'	W76°35.21'	[ARRIVE] 19 November

THE VOYAGE OF THE JAREDITES TO NEW OPHIR

Leg #	Beating (Apparent wind 0° to 45°)	Tight Reaching (Apparent wind 45° to 112.5°)	Broad Reaching (Apparent wind 112.6° to 157.5°)	Running (Apparent wind 157.6 to 180)
1	0% at 0 Knots	0% at 0 Knots	0% at 0 Knots	100% at 11.4 Knots
2	0% at 0 Knots	34% at 9.1 Knots	52% at 10.3 Knots	14% at 12.6 Knots
3	0% at 0 Knots	10% at 9.1 Knots	90% at 11.1 Knots	0% at 0 Knots
4	1% at 13.5 Knots	78% at 12.7 Knots	22% at 13.1 Knots	0% at 0 Knots
5	20% at 13.5 Knots	71% at 15.3 Knots	8% at 15.6 Knots	0% at 0 Knots
6	0% at 0 Knots	26% at 12.5 Knots	63% at 17.2 Knots	12% at 15.6 Knots
7	0% at 0 Knots	0% at 0 Knots	24% at 17.3 Knots	76% at 20.0 Knots
8	0% at 0 Knots	13% at 19.8 Knots	18% at 17.8 Knots	69% at 19.6 Knots
9	0% at 0 Knots	0% at 0 Knots	11% at 16.1 Knots	89% at 17.5 Knots
10	0% at 0 Knots	0% at 0 Knots	25% at 16.7 Knots	75% at 18.0 Knots
11	0% at 0 Knots	13% at 13.5 Knots	8% at 21.3 Knots	79% at 19.9 Knots
12	0% at 0 Knots	0% at 0 Knots	22% at 20.6 Knots	78% at 18.1 Knots
13	0% at 0 Knots	0% at 0 Knots	14% at 16.2 Knots	86% at 16.7 Knots
14	0% at 0 Knots	0% at 0 Knots	37% at 16.2 Knots	63% at 23.1 Knots
15	30% at 9.6 Knots	30% at 16.3 Knots	6% at 15.2 Knots	35% at 19.4 Knots
16	0% at 0 Knots	0% at 0 Knots	51% at 14.1 Knots	49% at 21.3 Knots
17	0% at 0 Knots	0% at 0 Knots	78% at 11.1 Knots	22% at 20.5 Knots
18	0% at 0 Knots	39% at 20.6 Knots	54% at 14.5 Knots	7% at 22.2 Knots
19	0% at 0 Knots	71% at 5.0 Knots	15% at 44.0 Knots	13% at 22.5 Knots
20	20% at 16.5 Knots	12% at 14.8 Knots	25% at 23.2 Knots	43% at 22.0 Knots
21	0% at 0 Knots	13% at 9.0 Knots	50% at 15.7 Knots	37% at 17.7 Knots
22	20% at 6.3 Knots	45% at 22.4 Knots	10% at 22.2 Knots	25% at 22.4 Knots
23	0% at 0 Knots	54% at 24.3 Knots	22% at 24.7 Knots	24% at 33.0 Knots
24	7% at 17.4 Knots	26% at 21.1 Knots	24% at 23.0 Knots	42% at 30.5 Knots
25	0% at 0 Knots	54% at 17.9 Knots	42% at 19.3 Knots	4% at 12.0 Knots
26	0% at 0 Knots	12% at 8.6 Knots	39% at 10.1 Knots	48% at 14.3 Knots
27	0% at 0 Knots	0% at 0 Knots	5% at 11.5 Knots	95% at 10.6 Knots

Notes

1. "The Book of Ether," *Evening and Morning Star*, Aug. 1832, 22.

2. Cobo, 94–95.

3. Bernabe Cobo, *History of the Inca Empire*, trans. Roland Hamilton (Austin: University of Texas Press, 1996) 95.

4. Urton, *The Legendary Past*, 36.

5. Ibid., 37.

6. Ibid., 34, 35.

7. Martín de Murúa, *Historia General del Perú de los Orígenes al Útimo Inca*, originally written in 1611 (published by Información y Revista, S.A., Hermanos García Noblejas, 41–28037 Madrid. Historia, 1986), 49–50.

8. Urton, *The Legendary Past*, 36.

9. Molina, Fr., "Relacion de las fabulas y ritos de los Yngas," in H. Osborne, *South American Mythology*, 61.

10. Pedro de Gamboa Sarmiento, *History of the Incas*, written circa AD 1570, trans. by Clements Markham (Cambridge: The Haklugy Society, 1907), 28–58, available at http://www.sacred-text.com/nam/inca/inca01.htm.

11. Mann, *1491*, 197.

12. Calderwood, *Voices from the Dust*, 410.

13. Mann, *1491*, 203.

14. Laurent Beisie, "Civilization Lost?," *The Christian Science Monitor*, 3 January 2002, http://www.csmonitor.com/2002/0103/p11s1-woam.html, 2.

15. Mann, *1491*, 205.

16. Janne M. Sjodahl, quoted online at http://search.ldslibrary.com/article/view/976113, 8 January 2008.

17. Calderwood, *Voices from the Dust*, 287.

18. James Adair, *Adair's History of the American Indians*, 2d ed, ed. Samuel Cole Williams (New York: Promontory Press, 1986), 229.

19. Cobo, 65–66.

20. Maxwell Institute, "Insights: An Ancient Window," *The Newsletter of the Foundation for Ancient Research and Mormon Studies*, no. 3, (Provo, Utah: Brigham Young University, 1990), 3. "Savoy's discoveries seem to open new areas of potential research, according to Dr. Ray Matheny, his host in Provo. While much remains to be done to verify his findings and determine their significance, he deserves credit for efforts in a geographic area that others shun because of the physical difficulty of doing research there."

21. Calderwood, *Voices from the Dust*, 48–50.

22. P.J. Capelotti, "Easter Island and the *Ra* and *Viracocha* Expeditions," http://www.personal.psu.edu/faculty/p/j/pjc12/Easter%20Island%20and%20the%20Ra.

23. Severin, *Sindbad Voyage*, 104.

24. Severin, *Sindbad Voyage*, 120–21.

Reed fishing boats on Peruvian shoreline near Caral. Photograph by Mylene d'Auriol Stoessel.

W E STARTED our journey in this book by saying that its purpose was to give the reader a better appreciation for our Book of Mormon maritime pioneers and an understanding of the immense challenges they had to overcome to reach their destinies. However, there is much more to learn from the Book of Mormon's accounts and references of four great voyages. Life's lessons can become apparent. In fact, the entire Book of Mormon is packed with invaluable lessons on how to deal with life's challenges. In writing this book, we have been inspired by the faith of Book of Mormon prophets and reminded that all things are possible when we act upon the word of the Lord. Here are just a two oft-referenced examples:

Nephi lived true to the words he spoke in his youth, "I will go and do the things which the Lord hath commanded, for I know that the Lord giveth no commandments unto the children of men, save he shall prepare a way for them that they may accomplish the thing which he commandeth them" (1 Nephi 3:7). When the Lord told Nephi he would be led to a promised land, Nephi seems to have never doubted the promise of the Lord. At the time, he was a refugee living in a desert valley in northwest Arabia. Later, at Bountiful when told to build a ship, Nephi undoubtedly had no experience in shipbuilding, few resources, and knew nothing about how to sail a large ship. Rather than doubting the Lord, again Nephi forged ahead and found the resources and knowledge he needed to build and captain a ship. Using a combination of inspiration, intellect, and hard work, he finished the ship and then courageously launched it with his entire family aboard on a voyage to the New World. When we are challenged to do what might seem impossible, it is helpful to remember the example of Nephi. I love his example.

When the brother of Jared realized that the interior of his barges would be dark, did he complain about the Lord's instructions on how to build his ships? No. Instead, he trusted that the Lord would provide. Proactively, he took sixteen stones

EPILOGUE

and presented them to the Lord. Not only did he receive light, his faith opened the veil and he stood before the Lord and was taught face to face. When we feel that living the gospel has caused a challenge in our life, if we follow the brother of Jared's example of finding a solution and then taking it to the Lord, miracles can happen for us. I love the brother of Jared's example also.

In life's troubled waters, if we follow the examples of the Book of Mormon voyagers in how they kept their faith in the Lord, we also will reach our final desired destiny. Miracles will happen along our way. From the Book of Mormon's sacred pages we read:

> And now, my son, I have somewhat to say concerning the thing which our fathers call a ball, or director—or our fathers called it Liahona, which is, being interpreted, a compass; and the Lord prepared it.
>
> And behold, there cannot any man work after the manner of so curious a workmanship. And

behold, it was prepared to show unto our fathers the course which they should travel in the wilderness.

> And it did work for them according to their faith in God; therefore, if they had faith to believe that God could cause that those spindles should point the way they should go, behold, it was done; therefore they had this miracle, and also many other miracles wrought by the power of God, day by day . . . .
>
> For behold, it is as easy to give heed to the word of Christ, which will point to you a straight course to eternal bliss, as it was for our fathers to give heed to this compass, which would point unto them a straight course to the promise land.
>
> And now I say, is there not a type in this thing? For just as surely as this director did bring our fathers, by following its course, to the promised land, shall the words of Christ, if we follow their course, carry us beyond this vale of sorrow into a far better land of promise (Alma 37:38–40, 44–55).

AFT
at, near, or toward the stern.

AGROUND
stranded, keel or vessel hull
resting on the bottom.

AHEAD
toward the bow, in front of the bow.

ALEE
to the leeward side; away from the wind.

ANCHOR
a hook which digs into the
bottom to prevent drifting.

ANTIFOULING PAINT
poisonous bottom paint to retard underwater
growth or it can be an environmentally friendly
ablative and self-polishing copolymer that wears at
a measured rate.

APORT
to the left side or port side of
a vessel when looking forward.

APPARENT WIND
wind direction felt on sailing vessel underway.

ASTERN
direction of stern or bearing behind a vessel.

ATOL
a small circular coral island
enclosing a lagoon.

BACK WIND
a sail back winds another with the

wind funneling on the wrong side.

BALLAST
heavy material stowed inside a
sailing vessel to provide stability.

BEARING
direction of object as to vessel's
heading or compass course.

BEATING
sail to windward while tacking.

BEFORE THE WIND
sailing with the wind from the aft.

BILGE
curve of hull between keel and gunwale.

BLOCKS
frames to support pulleys to increase
rope pull or change line pull.

BOARD
a one-leg sail when tacking.

BOOM
horizontal spar along the foot of the sail.

BOW
the forward part of a vessel.

BULWARKS
deck railing to prevent men
and gear from going overboard.

BUTTOCK
rounding part of stern from
waterline to transom.

CATAMARAN
twin-hulled sailboat.

COMPASS POINT
is 1/32 part of a full circle
or 11 ¼ degrees.

COMPASS ROSE
graduated circle on the card
showing points of the compass.

CORDAGE
term used for all diameter line.

DEAD RECKONING
calculation for the log of a vessel's course
and distance.

DEGREE
is 1/360 of a circumference.

DEPARTURE
vessel leaving.

DHOW
a European, East African, and Indian term
for Arab lateen "boats."

DISPLACEMENT
weight of water displaced by a vessel.

DOLDRUMS
updraft barrier with little
wind at equator.

DRAFT
water depth required to float a vessel.

DRAG
anchor failing to hold a vessel.

DRIFT
a vessel's leeway-driving to leeward.

EGYPTIAN COTTON
high quality cotton fabric used
for the traditional sail.

EVEN KEEL
vessel is floating level on its lines.

FINISHING
all work accomplished in the
sewing of the sail.

FIX
finding vessel's position by land or celestial
observations.

FLYING JIB
another jib where there are several sails
forward of the mast.

FORE AND AFT RIG
uses vertical masts instead of horizontal
yards sailing.

FOREMAST
forward-most mast.

FORE PEAK
extreme bow space forward.

FORE SAIL
a head sail.

FORWARD
in front of the bow.

FOUL
jammed, stuck, sea growth on bottom.

FREEBOARD
vertical distance amid ship of a
vessel from waterline to the deck.

GALE
wind force 9.

GEAR
a general term for various
kinds of spars and sails.

GROSS TONNAGE
measurement of all spaces in terms
of weight below upper deck.

GROUND TACKLE
general term for anchor and anchor gear.

HAND
a crew member.

HATCH
opening in deck with a sliding
or hinged cover.

HEAD OF SAIL
the top edge of the sail.

HEADSTAY
forestay, forward support stay for mast.

HEAD WIND
is from dead ahead of intended course.

HEAVE
the rise and fall of a vessel in a seaway.

HEEL
to incline on one side. Tilt sideways. The
bottom of the mast.

HELM
the tiller or wheel.

HULL
body of a vessel without mast or gear.

HURRICANE
long duration storm over 65 knots wind speed.

IN SAIL
order to take in sail.

JIB
most commonly a single headsail.

JIGGER
a mizzen sail or an extra sail aft.

KEEL
fore and aft backbone of a vessel.

KNOT
one minute of latitude, one nautical mile per hour, or 6076' to 6080'.

LATEEN SAIL
a triangular sail with a very long head supported by a spar, associated with Arab dhows.

LEADING EDGE
forward part of sail.

LEE
sheltered side away from the wind.

LINE
rope becomes line when used on a sailing vessel.

LONGITUDE
distance in degrees east and west of Greenwich, England.

MAIN DECK
principal structural deck running full length of the hull.

MAIN MAST
the taller of the masts.

MAIN SAIL
the fore and aft sail set on the after side of the main mast. The largest sail.

MARCONI SAIL
a jib-headed mainsail.

MARLINE SPIKE
a wood or metal spike for securing lines or used for splicing.

MAST
vertical spar to support rigging and sails.

MASTER
captain of the vessel.

MATE
officer ranking next to the captain.

MIZZEN MAST AND SAIL
the after sail in a two-masted rig.

MONSOON
seasonal winds blowing NE or SW in the Arabian Sea and Indian Ocean.

NAVIGABLE
an area with sufficient water depth to permit passage of vessels.

NAVIGATION
the art of conducting a vessel from port to port out of sight of land.

NET TONNAGE
vessel measurement of cargo-carrying capacity only.

OFFSHORE WIND
wind blowing from the shore.

OFF THE WIND
sailing downwind. Reaching.

ON THE WIND
sailing close hauled.

PITCH
fore and aft plunging and rising of a vessel. Pine tree sap.

PORT
to the left side looking forward.

REEF
to reduce sail.

RHUMB LINE
while it may be a straight line on a Mercator chart for shortest distance, it instead becomes a curve on the earth which is a sphere.

RIG
the general arrangement of sails and spars

241

on a sailing vessel. The action of setting up all of the sails and gear.

RIGGING
the lines/ropes necessary to support the masts, to hoist and control sail trim.

RUDDER
a flat plate hinged to the after end of a keel and connected to a rudder post on the forward end with tiller at the upper end of the stock.

RUNNING
sailing before the wind.

SAILS
flexible vertical airfoils on fore and aft rigged sailing vessels.

SCARF
joining timbers by beveling each other to look as one timber.

SCHOONER
a vessel with two or more masts with the main mast aft with the largest sail.

SEAM
space between planks. The sewn joint between sailcloth.

SEAWORTHY
a vessel in good condition.

SHORTEN SAIL
to reduce the amount of sail either by reefing or changing to smaller sails or removing sails.

SQUALL
often a sudden violent wind in a small area.

SQUARE SAIL
a four-sided sail that hangs from a yard and sets across the vessel.

STABILITY
a vessel which wants to return to an upright position after heeling over.

STANDING RIGGING
the supports for the mast or masts.

STARBOARD
the right side of a vessel when looking forward.

SWELLS
storm waves caused by a storm elsewhere.

SWEEPS
long oars.

TACK
lower forward corner of a sail.

TACKING
to sail to windward close hauled in each direction.

TEREDO
sea worm that enjoys eating into unprotected wood bottom planks.

TIDE
the alternate rise and fall of ocean water.

TIGHT
a wooden vessel that doesn't leak.

TILLER
a bar secured to the rudder post to steer a vessel.

TIMBERS
large pieces of wood.

TO TACK
to turn the vessel by the sails and rudder against the wind.

TOP SAIL
the sail above the gaff rig mainsail.

TRADE WINDS
steady wind areas from 30 degrees south to 30 degrees north of the equator.

TRIM
fore and aft balance of a vessel.

TYPHOON
comparable to hurricanes for the China seas and western areas of the north Pacific.

WATERLINE
the boot top indicates the load waterline, indicating trim of vessel not underway.

WINDWARD
the direction toward the wind.

YARD
a spar to support the head of the sail, perpendicular to the mast.

INDEX

245

0 26575 59469 0